video art

Michael Rush

with 383 illustrations, 296 in colour

Thames & Hudson

For Joe Rush, father and writer

PAGE 2

Jane and Louise Wilson
TOP LEFT
1 *Crawl Space* (1995)

Pipilotti Rist
TOP RIGHT
2 *Ever Is Over All* (1997)

Michal Rovner
BOTTOM LEFT
3 *Overhanging* (1999)

Douglas Gordon
BOTTOM RIGHT
4 *Monument to X* (1998)

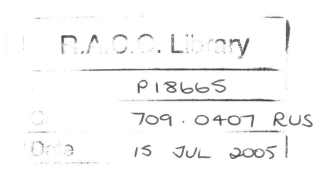
First published in the United Kingdom in 2003 by Thames & Hudson Ltd,
181A High Holborn, London WC1V 7QX

www.thamesandhudson.com

British Library Cataloguing-in-Publication Data
A catalogue record for this book is available from the British Library

ISBN 0-500-23798-0

Printed and bound in China by C+C Offset

introduction

Charles Atlas

5 *Mrs Peanut Visits New York* (1999)
Atlas brings a postmodern irony,
honed while collaborating with
'downtown' dance artists in the
1970s, to modern-day urban stories
and visually charged videos with
Performance artists like Leigh Bowery,
Lucian Freud's former model.

The Emergence of Video Art

Cinema has often been heralded as the art form of the 20th century. The moving image, so radical a departure from the still image, emerged in the late part of the 19th century with the fury of a comet: exploding all earlier modes of image making and communication and bringing a new spirit of experimentation in art. When, in the middle of the 20th century, video technology became accessible to a larger population, the art of the moving image was introduced to a new generation of visual artists. Film, bulky and expensive, albeit richly textured and lush, was suddenly not the only means of creating moving images, and television, already controlled by advertisers and multinational corporations, was not the only destination for videotapes.

In 1965, video technology in the form of the Sony Corporation's Portapak (and lesser known products made by Norelco and Concord) became available to people outside the industry, including artists and activists, and once again, a new revolution in image making occurred. No longer bound by the constrictions of Hollywood power brokers and mainstream television producers, those with a vision were able to participate in the visual communication revolution that was rapidly changing social and cultural life throughout the world. The hand-held camera and portable video tape recorder – which featured a half-inch (0.5-centimetre) tape as opposed to the heavier two-inch (five-centimetre) tape used by television professionals – brought ease, mobility, and, most of all, affordability to the art of the moving image. Though not inexpensive, these cameras, priced in the United States and Germany from $1,000 to $3,000, were markedly cheaper than the $10,000 to $20,000 television cameras. Even more than the Bolex, the portable 16-millimeter-film camera introduced in the early 1940s that opened up the possibility of making independent experimental films, the Portapak paved the way for Video art.

A Growing and Important Art Form

Video, once viewed as the poor cousin of cinema, soon became a significant medium itself in the hands of artists, documentary filmmakers, choreographers, engineers, and political activists who saw it as their ticket into the hallways of influence previously trafficked only by cameramen with 'identification badges' designating them from mainstream television stations. By 1968, exhibitions of Video art had already taken place in Argentina, Austria, Canada, Denmark, Germany, Great Britain, Japan, Spain, Switzerland, and the United States. This new medium seemed to have a message of its own, proclaiming that it was everywhere.

Video Art is intended as an overview of this remarkable medium that, in its little more than thirty-five years of existence, has moved from brief showings on tiny screens in alternative art spaces to dominance in international exhibitions, in which vast video installations occupy factory-sized buildings and video projections take

Bruce Nauman
RIGHT
6 *Wall – Floor Positions* (**1968**)

Bill Viola
FAR RIGHT
7 *Déserts* (1994)

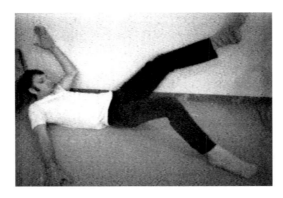

over the walls of an entire city block, as in Times Square, New York. Bordered on the south by the Panasonic screen, on the east by the NASDAQ stock exchange flickering facade, on the west by Reuter's kinetic-fronted news headquarters, Times Square is a virtual video environment.

The story of Video art embraces all the significant art ideas and forms of recent times – Abstract, Conceptual, Minimal, Performance and Pop art, photography, and digital art. The story also departs from art-historical categories into a new domain, that of the technological, which has its own referents and language.

As an 'art of time,' video has been used to extend, repeat, fast forward, slow down, speed up and stop time. In the hands of such artists as Vito Acconci, Bill Viola, Gary Hill, and Marina Abramovic, it has explored the body of the artist, the poetry of the soul, the complexity of the mind, and the inequalities fostered by gender and political prejudice.

Casting a net from eastern and western Europe, to North and South America, with brief stops in the Near and Far East, as well as Africa, *Video Art* will celebrate the breadth of this medium right up to the present revolution of digital technology, which enables artists to make use of whatever means of moving-image technology is available, frequently a combination of technologies, for their artistic expression. Since the medium has always been dependent on the availability of the technology involved (cameras, projection devices, feedback systems), it has been limited to the places that had the technology, namely, the United States, Germany, Austria, and, somewhat later, Great Britain. As video equipment became more available in other parts of the world in the late 1970s, the practice of the art grew.

An All-Embracing Art Form

Video Art will suggest multiple ways of constructing a history of the medium and offer as broad an overview as possible into the ways video artists (and artists who employ video as a part of their work) have used the video camera to make an art form now ubiquitous in the world of art. The story of Video art thus far concerns three generations of artists, who spontaneously adopted a massive communications medium for their own purposes, turning an implement of commerce (the video camera) into a material for art.

In discussing this broadly practiced, if young, art form, two immediate difficulties face a writer. First, the language used for Video art is borrowed from film; the traditional designation for speaking or writing about Video art is 'to film' rather than 'to video'. Second, no handy 'themes' or 'schools' of artists present themselves as organizing tools. Video, in the hands of some of its early practitioners like Bruce Nauman, Vito Acconci, William Anastasi, and others was merely another material put to use in the service of an idea: not an identifying material or medium that defined the artist. 'I wasn't interested in video, per se,' Anastasi said in an interview in 2001.[1] 'I used whatever was at my disposal (photography, video, drawing, sculpture) to express what I was interested in.' This attitude prevails amongst artists today. While some may identify themselves as 'video artists,' most see video as one material amongst many to be used in their art.

Thus a fluid approach to the topic has been adopted, while, for the sake of clarity and organization, three major themes, which correspond to three of the chapters in this book, have been identified as a way of approaching the subject of Video art.

First, artists have used the video camera as an extension of their own bodies and as participants in performances, linking the physical and the conceptual right from the beginning (Chapter 2). Second, Video art has expanded the possibilities of narrative, producing linear and non-linear autobiographies and futuristic fantasies, defining the political and redefining the sexual, and exploring personal and cultural identity (Chapter 3). Third, the hybridization of technology, in which video is combined and recombined, often in interactive installations, with a vast array of other materials – digital video, film, DVD, computer art, CD-roms, graphics, animation, and virtual reality – to form new artistic expressions, such as 'Filmic art', not quite film or video (Chapter 4). Because of the vast numbers of artists throughout the world who have turned to video as a medium of choice, this book will focus on a few representative artists whose body of work illustrates the topic at hand.

Blurring the Boundaries

Video art emerged when the boundaries separating traditional art practices like sculpture, painting and dance were becoming blurred. Painting, Performance, dance, film, music, writing, sculpture could be combined in single works of art, as they were during Robert Rauschenberg's and Billy Klüver's event *Nine Evenings: Theater and Engineering* in 1966. Writer Dick Higgins termed this phenomenon 'inter-media.'

Some early video artists, either emerging from, or reacting to, post-Abstract Expressionism used the video camera as an extension of their bodies. The camera became a component of the 'well-equipped' studio and artists began taping many of the actions they performed there, even in privacy. The physical and the conceptual were linked right from the start in Video art and they remain linked today. A major thesis of this book is that Performance has been highly influential in the unfolding story of Video art. Performance has emerged as the principal material in this medium, from the early videos of Vito Acconci, Richard Serra and Joan Jonas to the recent installations of Gary Hill, Sam Taylor-Wood, and Doug Aitken, amongst others.

This is not to say that other concerns were absent. Several of video's early practitioners were very engaged in technological advances such as synthesizers, image processing, computer scanning and so forth. Amongst the many innovators were Woody and Steina Vasulka, Ed Emshwiller, Dan Sandin, Keith Sonnier, Nam June Paik and Shuya Abe, Robert Zagone, Eric Siegel, and Swedish artists Ture Sjölander, Lars Weck, and Bengt Modin, to name a few. As Chapter 1 reveals, this thread in the history of Video art was one direction the form might have taken, but it did not. By

Ed Emshwiller

TOP

8 One of the leading figures in the
development of video technology, Ed
Emshwiller (1925–90, United States)
was one of the first to experiment with
synthesizers and computers in his quest
to 'sculpt with technology.' *Sunstone*
(1979) is a prime example of his artful
use of technology to create stunning
images. A timeless face, carved from
stone as a 'third eye', appears radiating
color and forms that are computer
generated.

ABOVE

9 Emshwiller's *Hungers* (1988) is an
electronic performance with music
by Morton Subotnick, sung by Joan
La Barbara, that explores basic human
cravings for food, love, sex, power,
and security.

and large, those interested in the more technological aspects of the medium did not
remain as artists, *per se*, but, like the early video activists, went in other directions,
toward television engineering, directing, or documentary-making. The Vasulkas and
Paik are notable exceptions, having remained influential video and media artists.

New Ways of Telling a Story

Video artists have invented new ways to tell a story from the start. At each turn in
the history of video, artists have taken an interest in 'time' as a medium in video. In
the early days, it was 'real time' that interested artists: video, unprocessed and unedited, could capture time as it was being experienced, right here and now, indoors or
outdoors. Today's artists are interested in manipulating time, breaking the barriers
between past, present, and future. Large-scale installations can be the venue for multiple layers of time, time as it really is experienced in our waking and sleeping states.

Interactivity

Another enduring component of video practice has been 'interactivity,' which, in
today's digital art, has become a medium in itself. Some of the most important
experiments in early Video art involved interactivity, including Frank Gillette's
and Ira Schneider's *Wipe Cycle* (1969), which will be discussed in Chapter 1, and
Juan Downey's *Plato Now* (1973), in which wired participants, sitting in meditation,
'interacted' with prerecorded quotations from the writings of Plato. Today, participants (gallery or museum-goers are now much more than 'visitors' or 'viewers') can
create their own cinematic narratives via touch screens in the elaborate installations
of Grahame Weinbren, discussed in Chapter 4.

Interaction barely describes the immersion viewers experience within such
installations as Gary Hill's *Tall Ships* (1992), in which ghostlike figures appear and
recede in a long dark space as people walk through it, or Doug Aitken's *electric earth*
(1999), a labyrinth of cloth screens on which are projected the night-time wanderings
of a youth on the streets of Los Angeles and a large digital clock with its numbers
racing through time.

A Narcissistic Art?

In her 1976 essay, 'Video and Narcissism,' the American critic Rosalind Krauss postu-
lated that video artists, in turning the camera on themselves, were engaging in
blatant narcissism. She cites Vito Acconci's *Centers* (1971), in which the artist films
himself pointing his fingers at his own image on a video monitor. '*Centers* typifies
the structural characteristics of the video medium,' Krauss writes. 'For *Centers* was
made by Acconci using the video monitor as a mirror.... In that image of self-regard
is configured a narcissism so endemic to the works of video that I find myself wanting to generalize it as *the* condition [Krauss's emphasis] of the entire genre.'[2] This is
both a misreading of the psychology of narcissism as well as a misunderstanding of
Acconci's intentions (to say nothing of the sweeping generalization about Video art,
which, especially at that time, was largely preoccupied with being a critique of television). Does photographing the self constitute pathological narcissism, the condition
of someone who (as described by Freud and quoted by Krauss) has 'abandoned the
investment of objects with libido and transformed object-libido into ego-libido?'

Nam June Paik
BELOW LEFT

10 Nam June Paik's work has become associated with fast-moving images that race across multiple screens before they can ever be digested. His interest lies in commenting on the saturation of the image in media culture. *MAJORCA-fantasia* (1989), in the midst of a furious collage of images, has outtakes from a recording of a performance by Joseph Beuys and one by Paik, in which he destroys a piano in an early Fluxist act.

Steina Vasulka
BELOW RIGHT

11 *Lilith* (1987) is an exercise in image manipulation in which the face of a woman is transformed into various shapes and sizes within a natural and manipulated landscape. The imaging techniques (focal plane shift and 'grabbing') are used by Steina Vasulka to create a mythic character.

Many early video artists used actual mirrors in their performances and videos (especially Dan Graham and Peter Campus), but, as with Acconci, their aim was to maximize the perceptual potentials of the medium as well as to engage in cultural critiques. Acconci, in fact, was expressly interested in drawing the viewer into the art process (bringing art out of the narcissistic, hermetic studio). He said of *Centers*: 'The result [the TV image] turns the activity around: *a pointing away from myself* [my emphasis], at an outside viewer – I end up widening my focus on to passing viewers (I'm looking straight out by looking straight in).'[3]

Hybridization

In these early years of the 21st-century artists are using video in combination with film, computer art, graphics, animation, virtual reality, and all manner of digital applications. Video is sometimes, but rarely, the 'pure' medium of a work. More often it is a hybrid, a mixture, for example, of film and video, television and video, computer graphics and video. New artistic expressions are emerging from this hybridization. For some, the digital era heralds the end of Video art. Is the next stop for Video art obsolescence? As installations become more elaborate in the hands of Lynn Hershman, Granular Synthesis, Iñigo Manglano-Ovalle, Jeffrey Shaw, and, certainly, Matthew Barney, will Video art cease to be the intimate medium it once was? In fact, it already has.

Krauss returns to the subject of Video art in her important essay, *A Voyage on the North Sea: Art in the Age of the Post-Medium Condition* (1999): 'For, even if video had a distinct technical support – its own apparatus, so to speak – it occupied a kind of discursive chaos, a heterogeneity of activities that could not be theorized as coherent or conceived of as having something like an essence or unifying core. Like the eagle principle [referring to her ideas around Marcel Broodthaer's installations, the main focus of her essay], it [video] proclaimed the end of medium-specificity. In the age of television, it broadcast, we inhabit a post-medium condition.'[4] Krauss points to the multifaceted bases of video practices as central to understanding the current condition of artistic discourse: namely, we live in a time when ideas – and not specific media – are central to artists. To suggest that video 'proclaimed' this shift is to express, boldly, its importance to contemporary art.

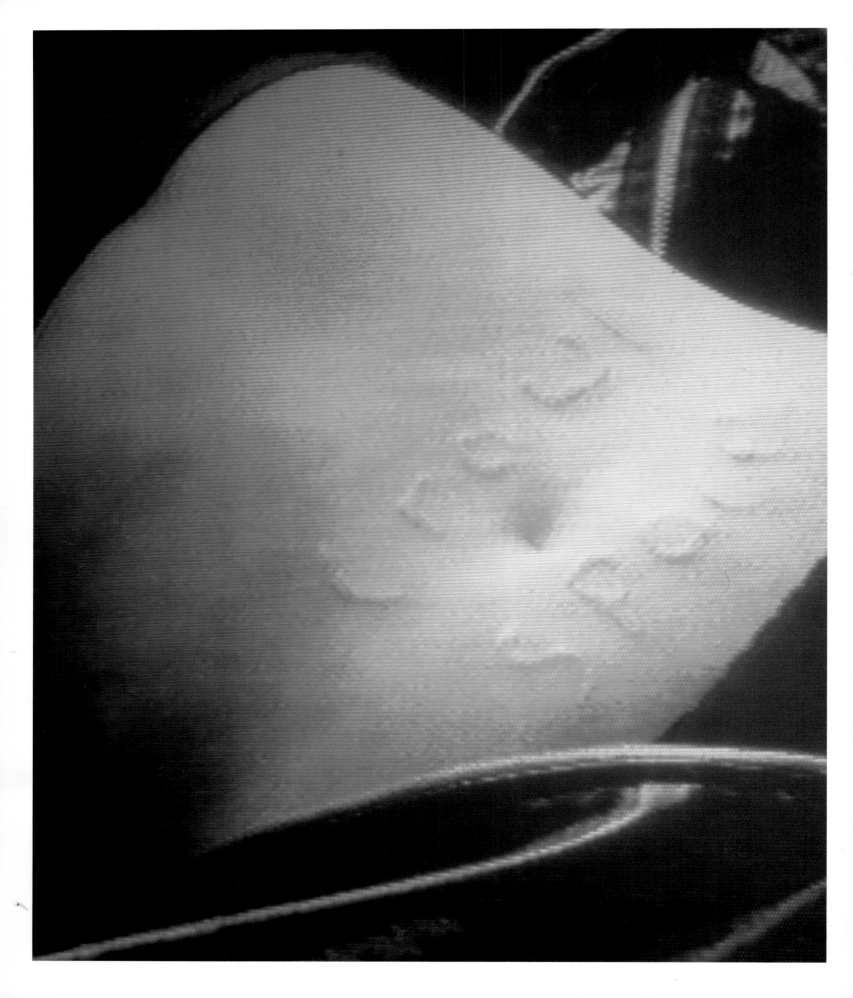

chapter 1

Shaping a History

Jane and Louise Wilson
12 *Crawl Space* (1995)

Attempting a history of Video art is a complicated venture. The origins of the form were too multifaceted to be identified with one or two individuals, no matter how influential they may have been. In general terms Video art emerged in a complex international cultural environment characterized by anti-war protests and sexual liberation movements, all of which were increasingly visible on home televisions. This scene, combined with a moment in art history that, exhausted by the muscular trappings of Abstract Expressionism, was embracing new forms influenced by dance, theater, performance, film, and nascent multicultural awareness, made video the natural choice for art that was both a critique and a bold new experiment. In retrospect, the words of American artist Hermine Freed written in 1976 seem prescient:

> The Portapak would seem to have been invented specifically for use by artists. Just when pure formalism had run its course; just when it became politically embarrassing to make objects, but ludicrous to make nothing; just when many artists were doing performance works but had nowhere to perform, or felt the need to keep a record of their performances; just when it began to seem silly to ask the same old Berkleean question, 'If you build a sculpture in the desert where no one can see it, does it exist?'; just when it became clear that TV communicates more information to more people than large walls do; just when we understood that in order to define space it is necessary to encompass time; just when many established ideas in other disciplines were being questioned and new models were proposed – just then the Portapak became available.[1]

Freed's essay is notable for another reason: early on (certainly by the early 1970s) video had become historicized with the language of art history. Freed spoke of 'formalism,' 'objects,' 'sculpture,' 'space,' all words associated with the study of art. If the appearance of the Portapak in 1965 was a defining moment in the creation of this new medium, within minutes, or so it seemed, Video art found a place in galleries and museums, in the United States and Germany; festivals with Video art were springing up in Paris and New York; public television stations were offering residencies to video artists; and cities like Buenos Aires (hardly ever mentioned in histories of Video art) were home to Video-art distribution centers. Such synergy could only have resulted from multiple influences brewing simultaneously in different parts of the world. Martha Gever and Martha Rosler's caveat against mythologizing video history in the person of one or two progenitors is worthy of attention, not so much because of their feminist perspective (however convincing), but because, in the threads of its history, Video art embraces an extraordinary diversity and richness that deserve investigation.

First, the earliest practitioners of Video art represented a cross-section of politically motivated artists who saw in the new medium an opportunity to participate in media culture in a way previously impossible to single artists and to counter the power of commercial television. Second, artist/documentary filmmakers who found in video an accessible means of recording political changes, social upheavals and art movements. Third, visual artists who either emerged from Fluxus or were already participating in the Conceptual art movement who discovered in video a companion in their explorations of artistic process and ideas. A fourth category, comprising a much smaller number of people than those already mentioned, included experimental film artists who used video occasionally as an extension of their film work.

Television: Friend and Foe

Video technology has a complex and checkered history like any innovation that eventually involves large sums of money, in this case television. In the late 19th century, scientists, including Alexander Graham Bell, had developed ways to transmit pictures by wire through mechanical scanning devices that used rotating discs. These instruments converted images to electrical impulses, which in turn could be received as images at another location. All of this was dependent on radio wave technology, which became more efficient by the 1920s.

In the early years of the 20th-century, scientists, including the British engineer A. A. Campbell Swinton, focused on the cathode ray as the most efficient way to scan images electronically for transmission. It was not until 1927 that the actual means of accomplishing this was developed by American inventor Philo Farnsworth, who is credited with making the first workable television set. At virtually the same time a Russian scientist, Vladimir Zworykin, who later emigrated to the United States, patented the 'iconoscope,' an electronic means of transmitting images.

By 1939, the cathode ray tube, an outgrowth of the cathode tube developed commercially by the Braun Corporation in the 1920s, became the basic component of the television set. In Germany, this technology was already in place in some form by the 1936 Olympics. Picture and sound were synchronized in the transmission of live action from these Games.

It was radio executives like David Sarnoff, chief of the Radio Corporation of America (RCA), who saw the mass potential in this technology, which led to the development of the history-changing phenomenon known as television.[2]

Even before Sarnoff, another sort of visionary had intuited the potential of television. In 1931 Futurist artist and polemicist Filippo Tommaso Marinetti published a manifesto entitled 'Il teatro futurista aeroradiotelevisivo.' According to German critic Friedemann Malsch in his essay *Video and Art* (1995), Marinetti, echoing an even earlier manifesto written in 1919 by Fedele Azari, proclaimed the notion of a 'total theater' ('teatro totale') that would include large television screens. Malsch reports that Marinetti had heard about the huge television screen ($23^5/_8 \times 70^7/_8$ in.; 60×180 cm) introduced by John Logie Baird at the 1930 Berlin Fair. Such progress was irresistible to Marinetti, who envisioned this projection surface as part of his world theater. In his 1933 manifesto 'La Radia', Marinetti prophesied that the radio-based technology (television) would replace film and 'abolish time and space.'[3]

Michael Smith

13 In the late 1970s artist Michael Smith invented 'Mike,' an alter-ego who absorbs the media like a sponge. He is extremely gullible and innocent. In numerous tapes, including *Secret Horror* (1980), Mike finds himself in a world totally fashioned by media. Here he is in his own apartment, which looks like a poor version of a set from *The Partridge Family TV* show, except that the ceiling seems excessively low.

Video Art

Michael Smith
14 *OYMA (Outstanding Young Men of America)* (1996)

What was so exciting about this new technology was that it captured real events instantaneously. Time, in a sense, was being manipulated by a human invention. Of course, still photography and film had already done this, but now everything was speeded up, for it was no longer necessary to wait for chemical processing to view the recorded image.

Though many early video artists vigorously countered the commercial excesses of television in their work, television was not the wasteland some critics make out. In his 1986 exhibition at the Museum of Broadcasting in New York devoted to the televised video works of American comedian Ernie Kovacs, curator John Minkowsky made a strong case for Kovacs's original use of video as a new form of direct and spontaneous communication with an audience. In these programs dating from 1957, Kovacs forged a vocabulary for television that only came of age (albeit in simplified form) with the late-night talk shows of Steve Allen, Jack Paar, and Johnny Carson. This critical/comic sensibility has endured in the Video art tapes of Michael Smith (b. 1951, United States) and the early tapes of Tony Oursler (b. 1957, United States).

15 One of the central tenets of early Video art was that video could serve as an alternative to commercial television. Groups like TVTV (Top Value Television), Ant Farm, Paper Tiger TV, and Raindance formed in the United States to offer news reports, documentaries, and other countercultural forms of input. *Four More Years* (1972) was filmed at the Republican National Convention when Richard Nixon was nominated. Using hand-held, one-half inch video equipment, the TVTV team, including Skip Blumberg (see p. 57), Ira Schneider, Chip Lord, Michael Shamberg, infiltrated the convention floor, interviewed network newscasters in an 'off-the-record' manner and captured candid shots of Nixon supporters, including The Young Republicans and The Nixonettes.

In her book *Video et Après* (1992), French curator Christine van Assche links Kovacs and French artist Jean-Christophe Averty (b. 1928) as two video pioneers inspired by Surrealism. The case for Averty in this regard is probably stronger. In the late 1950s, while working for French television, he created what he called video 'fakeries' or 'tricks,' experiments in images inspired by his contact with the French Surrealist group, whose meetings he attended in the late 1940s. His tapes from the 1960s and 1970s, such as *Ubu Roi* (1965) and *Les Mariés de la Tour Eiffel* (1973), reveal Averty's fondness for collage techniques similar to those of Max Ernst.

Even earlier than Kovacs, television news programs were using the immediate feedback of video technology. One particularly memorable moment occurred on Edward R. Murrow's program on CBS News when he and future producer Fred Friendly were seen live on a split screen with one man in San Francisco and the other in New York. This was not an 'installation,' but a consumer-oriented news event making use of new technology.

This direct audience contact gains its appeal from what American critic Bruce Kurtz called 'an obsession with the present tense.' In fact, according to Kurtz, television created this obsession. 'Newness, intimacy, immediacy, involvement, and a sense of the present tense, are all characteristics of the television medium.'[4] These attributes were responsible for diverting the attention of several artists away from their easels when portable video technology became available in the late 1960s.

The theorist who most fully understood both the potential benefits and the potential risks of this new technology was Marshall McLuhan (1911–80, Canada). As early as 1951 this scholar, who began as a literary critic, wrote in his seminal book, *The Mechanical Bride: The Folklore of Industrial Man*:

Ours is the first age in which many thousands of the best trained individual minds have made it a full-time business to get inside the collective public mind. To get inside in order to manipulate, exploit, control is the object now. And to generate heat not light is the intention. To keep everybody in the helpless state engendered by prolonged mental rutting is the effect of many ads and much entertainment alike.[5]

The emphasis placed here on the American role in early video is simply a matter of television statistics. By 1953 sixty-six percent of American households had television sets; by 1960 ninety percent had. McLuhan's passionate words became rallying points for intellectuals, students, and others who had concerns over the encroaching power of this new medium. In numerous essays and books, particularly *The Gutenberg Galaxy: The Making of Typographic Man* (1962) and *The Medium is the Message: An Inventory of Effects* (1967), McLuhan examined the radical transformative influences of the major media with catchy phrases such as 'hot' and 'cool' media and 'the medium is the message.' The 'hot' media – radio, photography and cinema – contain substantial information and therefore allow less involvement from the user, while 'cool' media – television, telephones and cartoons – have less information and permit greater sensory participation by the user. For McLuhan, the most cogent force against the manipulative nature of the media was the user. He encouraged users, or viewers, to enter into the communication process, to become, in a sense, co-producers of the communication product. Several early video collectives and

video artists, including Les Levine (b. 1935, Ireland), Frank Gillette (b. 1941, United States), Ira Schneider (b. 1939, United States), Ant Farm (founded 1968), Raindance (founded 1970), Videofreex (founded 1969), TVTV (Top Value Television, founded 1972) took McLuhan's populist notions to heart.

Though TVTV disbanded in 1979, many new groups have emerged since then to continue the spirit of 'guerilla television.' Many of these collectives have formed around political protests of large meetings of multinational institutions, such as the International Monetary Fund/World Bank. TVTV-inspired groups include Big Noise Productions, Headwaters Action Video Collective, Video Active, and Whispered Media.

Frank Gillette

The American artist Frank Gillette, after studying philosophy at Columbia University and painting at Pratt Institute in New York, became, in his own words, 'obsessed with Marshall McLuhan,' the media guru and author. 'Painting and the anti-war movement weren't reconcilable to me in the late 1960s,' he says.[6] Through his friend Paul Ryan, who was an assistant to McLuhan at the Center for Media Understanding at Fordham University in the Bronx, New York, Gillette gained access to four Sony Portapak video cameras. The president of the Sony Corporation was on McLuhan's Board of Trustees at the Center and gave it the Portapaks which Gillette and Ryan (amongst others) used to make alternative television.[7] For Gillette, personal use of the cameras was his way to 'enter the communication process,' and cease being a passive recipient of commercialized media. 'I was, and am still, interested in intercepting the systems (in this case electronic) and turning them toward artistic use,' he says; 'I wanted to decentralize the power base of broadcast television.'

In 1968 he created *Keep*, a four-monitor installation featuring tapes he made at home with his friends. Though primitive looking by current standards, Gillette's installation was a very advanced way of exhibiting tapes for the time. He denies, however, that he was interested in the sculptural qualities of the work. 'I was never sculptural,' he insists. 'My idea was never to make a sculptural statement, but to break down the single focus of a viewer on to one television set.'

In 1970 Gillette and his friends in the Video art collective Raindance sat on a beach in Point Reyes, California, turned their portable video camera on and passed it around 'like a joint,' as Gillette remembers. He, Paul Ryan, and Michael Shamberg taped their youthful musings on life, television, and the imposing transmitter jutting up to the sky just across the road. 'We were naively idealistic,' Gillette says. 'We thought we were going to revolutionize television, put it in the hands of artists and radicalize the medium.' The resultant tape, 'The Rays,' was given its name because the nearby transmitter caused 'rays' to distort the video image, a fact that pleased Gillette very much.

Appealing to these artists was the real time immediacy of video tape. Unlike film, whose lush texture required chemical processing, video was instantaneously

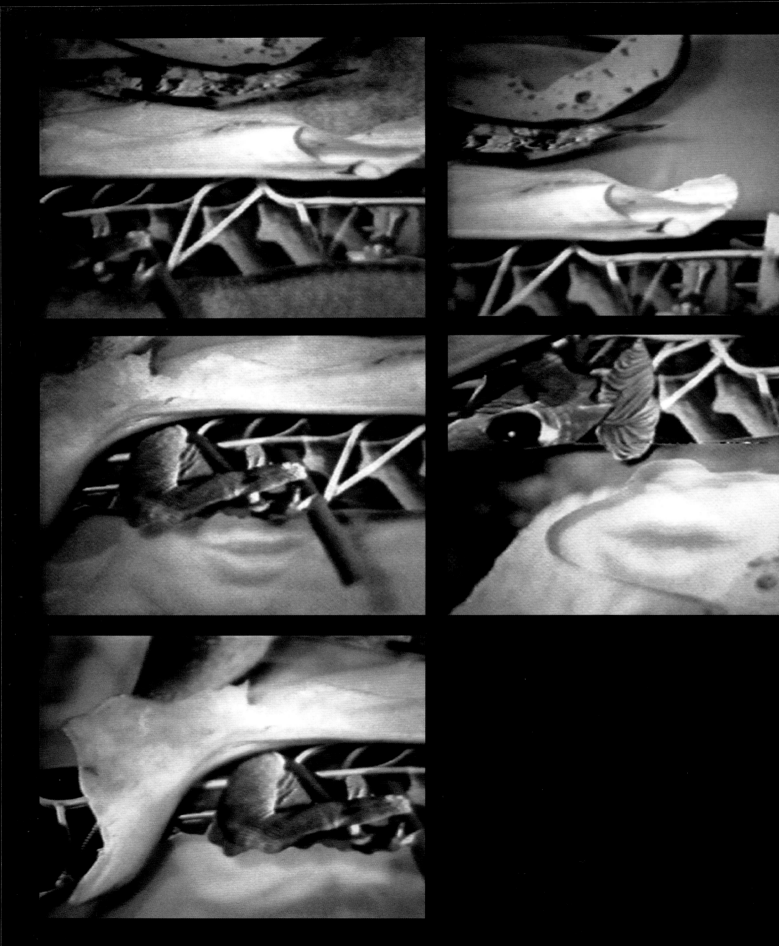

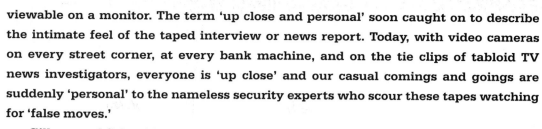

Frank Gillette

LEFT

16–20 *Rituals For a Still Life* (1974–75) is a work for collage and video. Expressive of Frank Gillette's roots as an abstract painter, this video features an assemblage of collages arranged in front of a video monitor that is showing Gillette's videotapes. Moving and still images merge into a landscape that is both aesthetically appealing and technologically innovative.

viewable on a monitor. The term 'up close and personal' soon caught on to describe the intimate feel of the taped interview or news report. Today, with video cameras on every street corner, at every bank machine, and on the tie clips of tabloid TV news investigators, everyone is 'up close' and our casual comings and goings are suddenly 'personal' to the nameless security experts who scour these tapes watching for 'false moves.'

Gillette and Schneider made one of the first installations of Video art, *Wipe Cycle* (1969) – an exceptionally influential work that anticipated the video installations of the 1980s – for the Howard Wise Gallery in New York. The exhibition 'TV As a Creative Medium' was the first show in the United States devoted to Video art.[8] *Wipe Cycle* featured nine video monitors, four of which showed pre-taped material (some taken from television shows) and five of which played live and delayed images

Frank Gillette

ABOVE

21–24 Frank Gillette has always been interested in taking technological systems and 'turning them toward artistic uses.' In *Wipe Cycle* (1969) he wanted to make a break with television by subverting the usual single viewing screen with the use of multifocal, multiple screens. He also experiments with the time-based qualities of video projection that allow for feedback and time delay. Commercial television is only now catching up with this work in so-called 'Reality TV', in which participants are taped live in a variety of everyday situations.

of viewers as they entered the gallery. 'Viewers were mystified,' Gillette says. 'They were seeing themselves on television mixed in with all these other images from TV shows and they were shocked as well as delighted.' Recalling Andy Warhol's visit to the gallery, he says, 'Andy, of course, loved seeing himself on television, but even he was a little confused by the multiple images and time delays. He kept shifting his briefcase from hand to hand to see if he was really being filmed live or not.'

The American curator Ben Portis described the impact of the exhibition in this way: 'Although "TV As a Creative Medium" is renowned as the seminal video art exhibition in the United States, its subject was truly television, and, by "TV" was meant television at its most pervasive. As with other revolutionary exhibitions... "TV As a Creative Medium" was both the grand finale of an idea – the kinetic art movement of the 1960s – and an unresolved indication of the future – the impact of video and television in the hands of artists. It was transitional as well as formative.'[9]

In keeping with the spirit of the times, in which countercultural activities were often accompanied by manifestos, pamphlets, books, and other publications, Raindance published a periodical, *Radical Software*. From 1970 to 1974 *Radical Software* was the theoretical voice of the video movement, reaching an audience of 5,000 readers. In their second issue, editors Phyllis Gershuny and Beryl Korot wrote:

In issue one of *Radical Software* (Summer, 1970) we introduced the hypothesis that people must assert control over the information tools and processes that shape their lives in order to free themselves from the mass manipulation perpetrated by commercial media in this country and state controlled television abroad. By accessing low-cost half-inch portable videotape equipment to produce or create or partake in the information gathering process, we suggested that people would contribute greatly to restructuring their own information environments: YOU ARE

Ant Farm

NEAR RIGHT

25 The American video collective
Ant Farm (Chip Lord, Doug Michels,
Curtis Schreier) was known for filming
simulated enactments of major
media events. Their most famous
one, *The Eternal Frame* (1975), made
with another video group, T. R. Uthco,
re-enacts one chilling scene from
the Zapruder video of the Kennedy
assassination. The eternal frame of
the title suggests the lasting effect
of these videotaped images on the
world's psyche.

**Bruce and Norman
Yonemoto**

ABOVE RIGHT

26 Reality and fantasy, the stuff of
Hollywood sagas, are, in *Made in
Hollywood* (1990), rendered to the
extreme in a comic scenario of
different hopeful types who come
to Hollywood to seek their fortune
on the big screen. Featuring such
seasoned Performance artists as Ron
Vawter and Rachel Rosenthal, the
video artist brothers turn clichés into
poignant comments on the endless
allure of the Hollywood dream.

THE INFORMATION.... In particular we focused on the increasing number of experiments conducted by people using this half-inch video tool: experiments in producing
locally originated programming for closed-circuit and cable TV and for public access
cablevision....[10]

As Gillette notes, the cable television movement was an important, if little noted,
element of early Video art. Cable television had been introduced in the late 1940s
as a service to people living in remote areas of the United States who were unable
to have normal signal reception. By the late 1960s cable companies, in an agreement
with the federal government, were required to make video equipment and taping
facilities available to the community so that individuals and groups from the locality
could make their own tapes for broadcast on local cable channels. Though this
opportunity was never fully exploited, many artists and groups, in the United States,
Canada and Great Britain, did receive their first access to video equipment through
cable companies.[11]

A Critique of the Media

Much of the first decade of Video art was preoccupied with critiques of television
and other media. As Video art and artists were fashioning a new identity with this
medium, many reacted to the pop identities promulgated by television and advertising. Classic examples include Nam June Paik's *Global Groove* (1973), an hallucinatory
barrage of images appropriated from television and magazines that mimics media
saturation and *The Eternal Frame* (1975), a biting commentary on the 1963 Zapruder
film of the Kennedy assassination in Dallas, created by the video collectives T. R.
Uthco and Ant Farm. The Zapruder film had been played endlessly on televisions
throughout the world. In *The Eternal Frame* the artists re-enact the event in a mock-
documentary, which questions the veracity of the memory of the tragic event even
as it calls into question the media spectacle it became.

Muntadas (b. 1942, Spain) has been a thorn in the side of mainstream media for
nearly thirty years. An artist with a passionate skepticism of television, newsmedia
(including newspapers and magazines), and some government institutions, he
creates video and media installations as platforms to expose the hypocrisy of the
media. From *Media Eyes* (1982) to *On Subjectivity (About TV)* of 1978 and *Video Is
Television?* (1989), he, like the early Nam June Paik, and, later Stan Douglas and
Fabrice Hybert, has used video to question the very fabric of what he calls the

BETWEEN THE LINES

LITERALLY WHEN WE SAY
WE ARE READING BETWEEN
THE LINES. WE ARE COM-
PLETING INFORMATION
FROM THE TEXT WITH OUR
OWN PROCESS OF THINK-
ING. KNOWLEDGE. INFOR-

MATION. SUBTLETY. WE
ARE LOOKING DEEPER
THAN THE PRINTED WORDS
WE DO THE SAME THING
WITH DRAWINGS. PHOTO-
GRAPHS. ETC. WITH TELE
VISION IMAGE AND WORDS
TOGETHER. TELEVISION
WATCHERS USE THE SAME
PROCESS LESS CONCIOUS-

LY ONE DIFFERENCE BE-
TWEEN TEXT AND TELE-
VISION IS SPEED: WITH
TEXT IT IS EASY TO
STOP AND THINK. WITH
TELEVISION THERE IS NO
TIME TO STOP AND THINK
WHILE WE ABSORB THE
INFORMATION FROM A
MOVING IMAGE.

January 30, 1979

Mayor Kevin H. White
meeting with the
Action for Boston
Community Development
seminar

Sharon Stevens report-
ing for WGBH News

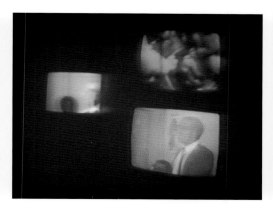

This tape focuses on
the role and responsi-
bility of the reporter
as the transmitter be-
tween the facts and
the TV audience.

The Ten O'clock News

CONTEXT

Muntadas

ABOVE
27–35 Muntadas made *Between the Lines* in 1979. In it he examines 'the invisible mechanisms' that lie behind the news on commercial television every night.

LEFT
36 Muntadas has made a career of criticizing the media through biting and skilful videos and installations. In *Video Is Television?* (1989) a television set, which has displayed a dizzying array of fragmented images from films, popular television shows and newscasts, disintegrates before the viewers' eyes, as if exhausted from all its showy broadcasting.

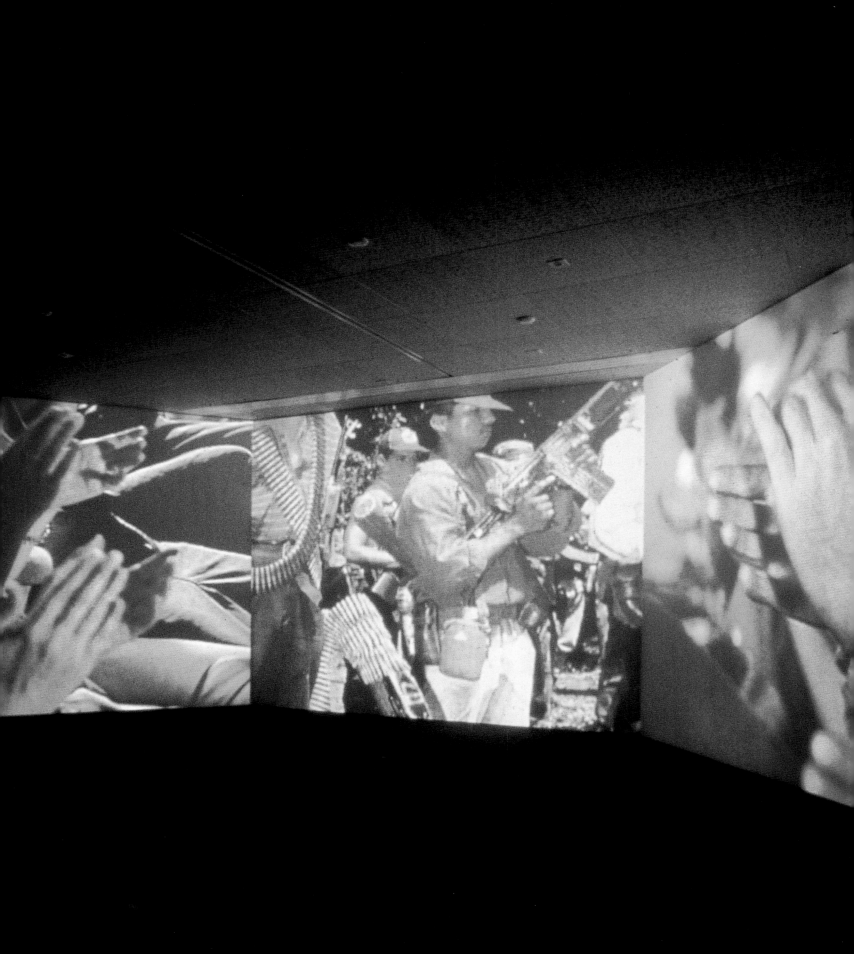

Muntadas

LEFT

37 In the triptych *On Translation: El Aplauso* (1999), the central screen shows an audience sitting quietly, then suddenly erupting in applause. The two adjoining screens have close-ups of their hands as they clap, sometimes mechanically, sometimes enthusiastically. In these short sequences, Muntadas manages to evoke political gatherings in Nazi Germany, Fascist Italy, or Spain, as well as the imprisonment of perceived enemies of the state in stadiums in Argentina or China. As an artist, Muntadas understands how to use the image to serve his own critical ends, in this case to create strong anti-Fascist statements.

Muntadas

BELOW

38 In *La Siesta/Dutje/The Nap* (1995) Muntadas expresses his appreciation for the enduring power of the image to frame memory. He incorporates footage from the war films of Dutch filmmaker Joris Ivens in an installation of Proustian ambitions. A single armchair draped in white fabric sits in a corner. Projected on to it and the walls beyond are a stream of images of people racing down streets (perhaps during an air raid) or conversing in darkened corners. These black-and-white shots are interrupted by a color still of a hand extended as if draped over the chair during a nap (it also has a strange resonance with David's *The Death of Marat* of 1793). If the imagined occupants of this chair were dreaming these images, their sleep would not be restful.

Klaus vom Bruch

39–45 In *Azimut* (1985) by Klaus vom Bruch, the artist's body collides with technology and advanced communication systems. A satellite dish is superimposed on to the face and body of the artist as he tries to protect himself from danger by covering his head with his hands. Vom Bruch often engages with deadly fears brought on by modern systems of war and commercial production.

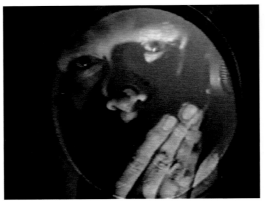 

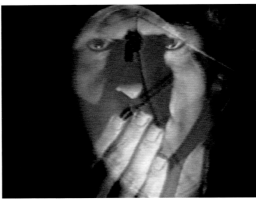 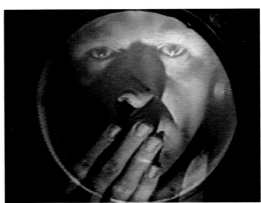

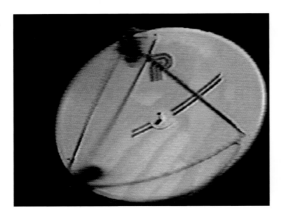 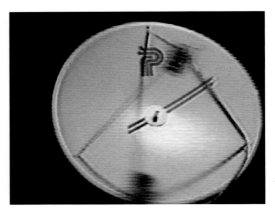

Klaus vom Bruch
46 *Hood* (1981–98)

Dara Birnbaum

47 *Kiss The Girls: Make them Cry*
(1978–79)

vast 'media landscape' created by television. In recent years, he has taken to creating installations that extend, in both size and political breadth, far beyond the television set. His work penetrates deep into social structures, cultural memory, and architecture.

Another artist to take a critical approach to television is Dara Birnbaum (b. 1946, United States). She made the highly influential tapes *Technology/Transformation: Wonder Woman* (1978–79) and *Kiss the Girls: Make them Cry* (1978–79) to counter the banal and sensational images of women presented in popular television shows. In both cases she used actual footage from television to subvert the intended meanings of the programs.

In another vein, Klaus vom Bruch (b. 1952, Germany) challenged media manipulations of history, using archival footage from war films in *Propeller Tape* (1979). In this tape he also introduced his own image within the appropriated material, thus embarking on an examination of the self within cultural history that endures to this day. Klaus vom Bruch has created numerous fast-paced videotapes since the late 1970s that reflect his interests in philosophy, disintegration of society, mass media, and the individual. He is also no stranger to irony. *Das Softiband (The Softi Tape)* of 1980 is a self-portrait as commercial and collage. Using images from a facial tissue commercial (Softi brand), cross-cut with World War II footage and shots of himself clowning in front of the camera, vom Bruch suggests two of the most important influences on the construction of the modern personality: war and advertising.

Turning the Tables: Surveillance Techniques and the Viewer as Participant

This desire on the part of artists to take on television directly was also evident in what has become known as 'surveillance' tapes, a rather broad heading embracing practices that turned the camera on viewers whether they knew it or not. Clearly derived from the uses of video in military technology, surveillance, which still occupies some artists' attention, highlights the ever-intrusive eye of the government in both repressive regimes and supposedly democratic societies. At this particular time, when the world has become preoccupied with security amid fears of international

Dara Birnbaum

BELOW LEFT

48 Birnbaum appropriated images from popular television shows to expose how emotion is achieved through technique (cross-cuts, reverse shots) and how manipulative this popular TV imagery can be. In *Pop-Pop Video* (1980) she engages in some manipulation herself as she provides visual models for violence resulting from corporate culture.

BELOW RIGHT

49 *Technology/Transformation: Wonder Woman* (1978–79)

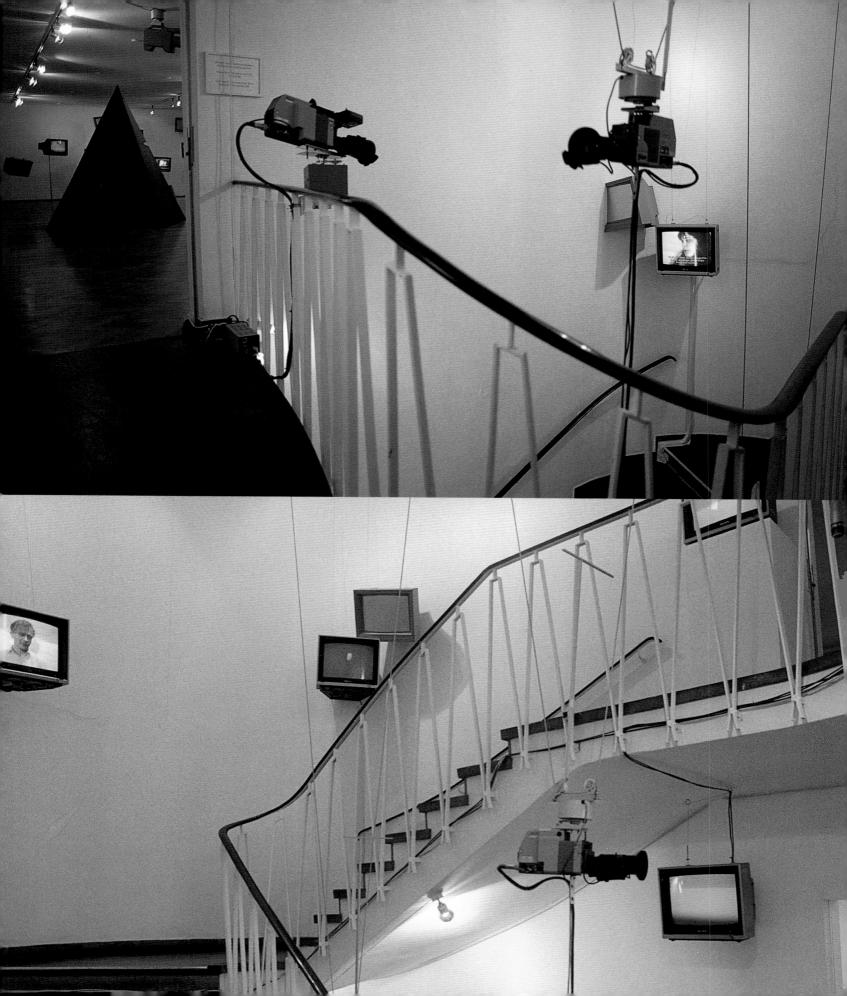

Dieter Froese

PREVIOUS SPREAD AND ABOVE
50–54 *Not a Model for Big Brother's Spy-Cycle* (1987)

terrorism, it is ironic that surveillance video is used by both law enforcers and artists.

Curiously, popular television shows in the early part of the 21st-century – such as the successful *Survivor*, which was conceived in Europe in the late 1990s and imitated in the United States – have adopted surveillance techniques as forms of entertainment. Yet thirty years before, millions of viewers worldwide fretted over the fates of the *Survivor* participants (supposedly 'ordinary people,' despite some of their highly toned bodies, who were placed in extreme conditions on deserted islands or on the plains of Africa), Frank Gillette and a host of others had already placed cameras discreetly amongst their friends and taped private conversations.

New York video artist and editor Dieter Froese (b. 1937, Germany, lives in the United States) made video performances and surveillance tapes in the early 1970s by videotaping visitors in a downtown New York gallery, then projecting their movements on to a monitor as an 'immediate work of art.' To these displays he invited critics who would write 'instant reviews' of the performance videos. In his *Not a Model for Big Brother's Spy-Cycle* (1987), Froese combined closed-circuit television with a two-channel pre-taped video. Visitors to the gallery were taped and shown on monitors as they watched others (pre-taped) on monitors being interviewed about their political activities.

If critics of the current Reality TV shows lament the collapse of distinctions between public and private in these programs, artists like Vito Acconci (b. 1940) blasted private domains thirty years ago in live performances and videotapes. The difference is that when he did it, he was pointing to the futility of suggesting that TV or even art could offer real intimacy or real personal revelation. In *Theme Song* (1973), Acconci is seen lying on the floor in front of a striped couch, cigarette in hand, his face only inches away from the camera. Chain smoking and listening to songs by The Doors, Van Morrison, Bob Dylan and others, he implores the viewer to 'Come in close to me…come on.…I'm all alone…wrap your legs around me…. I'll be honest with you…really…come on.' His blatant manipulations exposed the covert enticements of advertisement-funded television (If you wear these jeans you, too, will be thin, blonde, and desirable.)

Vito Acconci

OPPOSITE

55–60 Vito Acconci always questioned inherent falsities in communication systems. In *Theme Song* (1973) he pretends to be getting intimate with his viewers (the way television programs do), when he is actually being reduced to a pathetic seducer incapable of making any real contact with another person.

Another element of their art often shared amongst early video artists – in contrast to current Reality TV practitioners – was a sense of humor. Acconci's stream-of-consciousness monologues for the camera are nothing short of hilarious. In *Face Off* (1973), he is seen bent over a reel-to-reel audio tape recorder that is spewing forth intimate details of his life. When the tape becomes a little too personal the artist starts screaming at it so that the viewer cannot hear what it has to say.

In addition to Gillette, Froese, Acconci, and Dan Graham, several other early video artists created installations in which the ordinary viewer became the camera's subject. Bruce Nauman (b. 1941) and Peter Campus (b. 1937, United States) are two examples of artists using the camera to 'spy,' in a sense, upon themselves and a willing public. With 'surveillance,' Video art mingled with law enforcement

Bruce Nauman

techniques that had come to define the realization of George Orwell's concept of Big Brother. Video technology had allowed the law to watch us all the time. Some artists liked being watched. In fact, the video camera allowed them to watch themselves and others.

Bruce Nauman's *Performance Corridor* (1968–70) was a claustrophobic enclosure consisting of two floor-to-ceiling parallel walls that formed a tunnel. At one end, two monitors were stacked on top of one another, beckoning viewers to see what was on them. After the wary participants inched their way down the opening, they were confronted with their own image taped from a surveillance camera. American critic Margaret Morse wrote at the time, 'To me it was as if my body had come unglued from my own image, as if the ground of my orientation in space were pulled out from under me,' while New York critic Peter Schjeldahl called it 'ruthless' and 'somber.' Nauman's work took inspiration from the confined worlds created by playwright Samuel Beckett (1906–89), who, in many works from *Endgame* and *Not I* to *Worstward Ho*, placed anonymous characters in desolate surroundings.

Amongst other artists who used viewers as collaborators, willingly or not, in their

Video Art

installations was Peter Campus, whose video installations from the early 1970s, including *Interface* and *mem*, made viewers the artwork. In both cases, visitors to an exhibition found their own image projected on to large screens as they were being taped by a camera. Placement of the projectors or discreetly planted sheets of glass resulted in the image appearing enlarged or skewed. In what may seem an ironic twist from our present position, Campus was trying to shake viewers out of their passive role as spectators. Thirty years later, passivity rules as television viewers, like the Romans in the Forum, watch the Reality TV participants trying to survive the psychological barbs of their supposed teammates.

To this day video artists like Jordan Crandall are taping ordinary people, not in an attempt to make them celebrities, but in order to enlist them as participants in art as well as to warn them about the seductions of camera culture. New York artist Julia Scher (b. 1954, United States) has been unmasking the power games inherent in surveillance video for the past fifteen years. 'I grew up in LA in the 1950s,' she told the author in a 2000 interview. 'Hollywood is a cult of surveillance and I was happily a

Peter Campus

ABOVE LEFT
62 *Interface* (1972)

ABOVE RIGHT
63 *mem* (1975)

part of it. If you were surveyed, it was a compliment. Reality was always mixed with TV and surveillance. Of course it only worked for people with nice bodies.'[12]

Julia Scher turns the industry of surveillance on its head by exaggerating it, manipulating it, aestheticizing it. She was the first woman member of the Metropolitan Burglar and Firearm Association in New York and a 'certified alarm installer.' In numerous installations since the 1980s she has created surveillance environments (called *Security by Julia*) in museums and galleries. In 1991 she wrote: 'We are moving towards the maximum security society comprised of data, where bodies without organs of thought are turned into images. The form, the skeleton upon which surveillance images hang, is even more brilliant than its TV counterpart. Its luminance has become interchangeable with information. The image has become knowledge.'[13]

Security by Julia, an installation shown in several venues in the United States and Europe, makes use of standard security industry equipment. When visitors enter the space, they are greeted by a woman wearing a 'Security by Julia' uniform and seated in front of a bank of seven black-and-white monitors. They are invited to make printed copies of their own image as it is then appearing on the monitors

Julia Scher

or to make prints of anyone else's image from half a dozen other monitors scattered throughout the space. Visitors can look at themselves, spy on others, and become paranoid about who else might be watching them from some unseen venue in the gallery, all at the same time.

Scher's work resonates with many contemporary critical issues such as 'the gaze,' image manipulation, interactivity, information as art. In a world increasingly defined by terror, however, the paranoia she packages may be the most prescient aspect of her work. Scher, who suggested a surveillance show to the cable MTV channel in 1995, says 'Reality TV is our attempt to come to grips with the constant intrusions in everyday life. These shows play out our fears.'

They also offer a mix of reality and fantasy. Unlike early Video art, which was rarely edited, these shows are heavily edited to maximize the quick cuts to which audiences have become accustomed. If the show's limited action becomes boring, as it often does, the scene cuts to a new game of endurance or a hastily arranged 'visit' by one of the show's producers/overseers who function as a kind of Orwellian Big Brother.

At the birth of Video art, artists turned the camera on themselves (another crucial distinction from television) or on others to investigate new meanings of time and identity or to create new definitions of space and perception in a gallery setting. Naturally, there was an innocence in all of this, but there also was a quest for ideas, a hunger for experimentation. Audiences were part of the action, a necessary component of the experiment. In turn, they were offered a role in developing an alternative to television, an interactive art that really did need them and really did place them center stage.

Television is a medium of desire: it creates dreams, answers dreams, sells dreams. It promises to reflect viewers back to themselves, but it ends up bouncing back what they long to see. Reality TV is a part of this mechanism of desire, more akin to the lottery than to everyday life. Perhaps this is as it should be. The images of themselves that viewers might have seen in an installation by Frank Gillette or Bruce Nauman can now be viewed in department-store windows or on multiple screens in electronics stores. They can 'star' in a video display on the Champs Elysées or on

Douglas Davis
69–71 *Ménage à Trois* (1986)
anticipated the 'real-time' narratives
now being seen in theaters and on
television. Douglas Davis created
a murder mystery that was followed
on radio and video via satellite in
three locations: Venice (during the
Biennale); the Guggenheim Museum
in New York; and the Stedelijk
Museum in Amsterdam. Davis plays
the accused murderer and pleads
with viewers to call in and clear his
name. The video camera becomes
an active participant in the drama,
as the viewers do worldwide.

Fifth Avenue or in the Ginza anytime they want. All they have to do is walk in front of the camera.

However, what set the artists apart was their different motivation for turning on their portable cameras. They did not know if anyone would ever watch their primitive videos or venture into their newfangled techno-installations. Nor did they think someone would actually pay them to make these tapes or broadcast them on television. They had a camera. They knew it had far-reaching possibilities and they wanted to find out what they were.

Video Art in Europe

In Europe, the use of video technology by artists began slightly later than in the United States for two reasons: availability of equipment (most importantly) and the very different nature and structure of television. In Europe, television, until recently, had been highly centralized, usually under the auspices of government sponsorship. In the late 1960s and early 1970s, as British critic Edward Lucie-Smith has noted, 'The absence of local television has not been to the advantage of radical or minority groups who want to make their own video and control its content. They may succeed in making it, according to their own ideas, but they seldom or never succeed in getting air-time for it.'[14]

Germany, Netherlands and Austria

In Germany, where the earliest examples of art video are often traced to Wolf Vostell and Nam June Paik, gallerist Gerry Schum is credited with introducing video production on a broad basis to an art community that was accustomed only to art film. According to German critic Wolfgang Becker, 'Schum followed the lead of such New York galleries as Ileana Sonnabend or Howard Wise, who, since 1970, have shown video work or offered video prints in limited editions. By tirelessly demonstrating his material in museums, exhibitions, and at such international events as the Venice Biennale, he convinced museums of contemporary art to acquire video facilities.'[15] Schum's own galleries, the TV-Gallery in Berlin, and the Videogalerie in Düsseldorf, both founded in 1969, were the first spaces devoted to the new medium in Europe.

In that same year Schum produced two extraordinary series of films, the first on earthworks with such artists as Dennis Oppenheim, Robert Smithson, Walter de Maria and others; the second on conceptual works made with various artists, including Joseph Beuys and Gilbert and George. Only a few were actually video-tapes; most were 16-millimeter films.[16]

Beuys's 1966 *Felt-TV* (a group of monitors covered in his signature fabric) was filmed and transferred to videotape in 1970 for Schum's exhibition 'Identifications,' which also included works by Mario Merz (b. 1925, Italy), Alighiero e Boetti (1940–94, Italy), Lawrence Weiner (b. 1942, United States).

In other countries, like the Netherlands, the video exhibition of the Rotterdam Art Foundation in 1973 featured very few 'fine art' video artists compared to social video makers and experimental cable television directors. The extensive development of Video art in Austria, which was closely linked to movements in Performance art, will be discussed in the following chapter.

Video Art

Great Britain

The emergence of Video art in Great Britain took a similar course to that of the United States: individual artists and politically charged co-operatives turning to video in response to the intrusion of television as well as to social issues. In 1969, John Hopkins founded the co-op, TVX, a workshop and research center devoted to electronic media. Hopkins's aim was to make television accessible to the public at large to be used as a political and educational tool, in much the same way as his contemporaries in the American collectives Videofreex and Raindance did. At the same time another center in London, Arts Lab, headed by David Curtis, received some video equipment from the Beatles, no less, and offered it for use to artists. In 1975, Hopkins and Sue Hall founded the Fantasy Factory, a community-based post-production facility that survived until the end of the century.[17]

The most influential figure in formalist Video art was David Hall (b. 1937), whose earliest work from the 1970s, like that of Nam June Paik, reflected the sculptural qualities of the television set, for example *7 TV Pieces* (1971). Hall cannot be described solely as a formalist, however. He was especially interested in the interactive qualities of video installations, describing the viewer as a 'collaborator rather than a spectator.'[18]

Hall was the centerpiece of two significant exhibitions in Britain in the early 1970s, 'A Survey of the Avant-garde' at the Gallery House, London, in 1972 and the 'Video Show' at the Serpentine Gallery, London, in 1975. Hall, Stewart Marshall, and Tamara Krikorian participated in a video exhibition at the Tate Gallery, London, in 1976.

The London of today, of course, is home to several video artists of international renown, including Sam Taylor-Wood, Steve McQueen, Maria Marshall, Jane and Louise Wilson, Chris Cunningham, Gillian Wearing, to name a few.

Marshall, an Iraqi Jew born in Bombay in 1966 and educated in England, is on intimate terms with paranoia and displacement. In a work called *I did like being born,*

John Adams

72 In common with other international video artists of the late 1970s and 1980s, John Adams (b. 1953, Great Britain) created narratives that incorporated cultural and media critiques, often using appropriated footage from television and other media. Adams often shot on 16mm film, thus anticipating the current trend among media artists to make use of whatever filmic material best suits their artistic ends. *Intellectual Properties* (1985) was shot on 16mm and deals with political and art-world culture through a collaged narrative featuring John Wayne films, commercials, and a fictional lecture on copyright law.

Maria Marshall

73 Dreams and nightmares have
long provided material for artists and
storytellers. Montaigne thought that
it required an artist to sort dreams out
and understand them. For the British
artist Maria Marshall fears and
nightmares take shape in raw,
unexplained mini-tales about her
children, whom she imagines in
dangerous, even life-threatening
situations. In *When I grow up I want
to be a cooker* (1998) she filmed her
then two-year-old son taking a long,
slow drag on a cigarette.

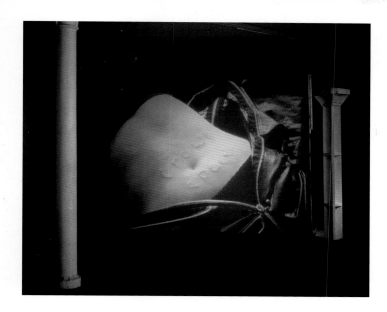

Jane and Louise Wilson
74 *Crawl Space* (1995)

I falled out of the air, I put my wings open, then I flied (1999) – Marshall creates her titles from phrases spoken by her children – a boy is seen floating on his back in what looks like a black-and-white home movie of a first swimming lesson. The loud sound of water crashing and the extended length of the child's head under water soon suggest something far more menacing. Shot on 8mm film and transferred to laserdisk for projection, this piece is marked by an intense claustrophobia.

Don't let the T-Rex get the children (1999) opens with a close-up of an angelic-faced boy, shot from above using 35mm film. In one long, slowed down reverse zoom shot, the camera pulls up to reveal the shaved headed youth tied in a straitjacket, seated in the middle of a padded cell.

Once up on (1999), shot in super 16mm, is a super speeded-up shot of schoolyard activity filmed over a six-hour period and compressed into one minute, forty-five seconds. The frantic editing makes the children look like an embattered ant colony, with bullies and pranksters rushing to and fro. The sound track is a child reciting a made-up fairy tale about a 'big, bad pig who huffed and puffed' and, when he couldn't blow the little wolves' house down, exploded it with TNT instead.

Marshall is herself a trickster. Digital technology is what makes her children look as though they are smoking, drowning, or abandoned in a cell. She knows how to use the technology for the image she desires. In this sense she is making movies: little ones, scary ones, personal ones that give us a glimpse into her very adult concerns.

France

In France, several groups similar to Raindance and Videofreex in the United States used video as a social tool. They included Vidéo OO, Slon vidéo, Immedia, Vidéo Out, and Les Cents Fleurs. It must be remembered that in 1968 great political upheavals spread across Europe and the United States, often originating in universities. In France the theories of Guy Debord (1931–94) were espoused by the Situationist International movement, a loose collective of intellectuals and artists who believed theory can, and should be, the locus for 'aesthetic actions.'

Prominent at this time was one of the most influential video and filmmakers of the 20th century who, because he is identified so strongly with the French cinematic avant-garde, is often left out of video histories. Yet his use of video has only increased in recent years as he pursues his quest for the perfect combination of thought, image, and sound.

Jean-Luc Godard

He sits in front of a blank screen, back to the camera, cigar in hand. Images start to appear dimly on the white surface of the screen, the filmmaker's canvas. 'You see the world first, then you write,' he says. 'It has to be seen to see if it exists.' Words, sounds, more images take shape, and thus, like a tract on Creation itself, does Godard

Finding the right words isn't easy

There... and back

To find it, of course...

To be able...

begin his video *Scénario du Film Passion* (1982). Ostensibly a commentary on the development of his film, *Passion* (1982), *Scénario* is an invitation into the secrets of the creative process by this constant experimentalist. 'Faced with the invisible,' he goes on to say, 'with Mallarmé's blank page, I find myself seeking the corner of memory.' Godard's constant seeking, through the mechanism of the filmed or taped image, provides living proof of the endurance of the avant-garde despite repeated reports of its demise.

Godard (b. 1930) started making films in 1954. By 1968, when he purchased a portable video unit, he had made some of his most important films, including *A Bout De Souffle* (*Breathless*) (1959); *Une Femme Est Une Femme* (*A Woman is a Woman*) (1961); *Vivre Sa Vie* (*My Life to Live*) (1962); and *Le Mépris* (*Contempt*) (1963). Always politically radical, at least in thought, Godard placed, in 1968, video cameras in factories in Flins and Rhodiaceta and encouraged workers to film themselves at their jobs. This served the dual purpose of legitimizing and elevating worker activity through the 'exclusive' language of filming (or recording) action the way 'movies' do, while, at the same time, creating a document of the monotony of labor experienced by millions of nameless workers.

Anticipating Dogma 95, a current movement amongst some European filmmakers, most notably Lars Von Trier, who use digital video cameras and no props, sets, or artificial light to make their films, Godard, in 1967, made *Le Gai Savoir* (*Joyful Wisdom*) in the studios of The French National Television and Radio Services. Though filmed on 35 millimeter, Godard's methods of eliminating a plot line completely subverted the traditional intentions of both cinema and television and proved highly influential for generations of video artists and experimental filmmakers who followed.

As American film historian Wheeler Winston Dixon notes, *Le Gai Savoir* superficially masquerades as a feature film, while actually attacking the commodity/exchange system of the theatrical cine-construct full force.'[19] In the film, popular French actor Jean-Pierre Leaud played Emile Rousseau to Juliet Berto's Patricia Lumumba (a take-off on the powerful African political leader of the day, Patrice Lumumba). For ninety-one minutes they engage in a splintery philosophical dialogue that takes references from Rousseau to Marx, Nietzsche to Mao Zedong.

With his work with video as well as film Godard was attempting at this time to erase his image as a celebrated 'director' and remove evidence of his hand as the 'author' of his work. He wanted to be seen as a worker whose job was the making of films. According to Dixon, 'Godard here signals that he is onto something altogether new, a film that does not even need an audience, a film existing primarily as a personal statement, as an abrogation of narrative, and the traditional filmmaker/viewer, social/economic contract.'

Since 1976, when he began collaborating with filmmaker Anne-Marie Miéville, Godard has made numerous videos, most of them for television and all of them experimental in nature. Included amongst them is the six-part *Six Fois Deux/Sur et sous la communication* (Six Times Two/On and Beneath Communication) (1976), one of Godard and Miéville's earliest 'essays'. It criticizes and comments upon commercial television images through a mixture of interviews with workers as well as a montage of abstract images and sounds, which, in effect, offer a new type of television.

Jean-Luc Godard
82 Six Fois Deux/Sur et sous la communication (1976)

His eight-part series *Histoire(s) du cinéma* is nothing less than an attempt to comment on the entire history of cinema through an onslaught of single shots from thousands of films. It appears as though Godard is trying to say everything he can about cinema all at once through this series that is densely packed with texts, quotes, and references to philosophy and literary theory. With strobe-light intensity, words and pictures flash on to the screen in what looks like a frenzied attempt to control time and at the same time mimic the numbing repetition of the Hollywood image machine.

Godard constantly reminds us of his own resistance to the commercialization of ideas, even as he dazzles with his command of the filmic environment of sound, image, gesture, and word. It is Godard's uncompromising and personal vision that invigorates the avant-garde and keeps us keen to discover it when it emerges, however rarely, in unexpected places, such as in the animated films and videos of South African artist William Kentridge, discussed in Chapter 4. Godard's cerebral, philosophically dense videos and films may echo the historical experiments of Surrealism and neo-Dada, but he has clearly forged a new filmic language charged with poetics and politics.

Critics will argue that the avant-garde is dead, or at least meaningless, in this age of instant appropriation, but in the artistry of Godard an essential practice of the advanced guard, namely, the re-direction of perception (and, thus, meaning) away from the recognizable toward a new, and perhaps disturbing, understanding of reality, is refreshed. The enduring avant-garde, as represented by Godard, is a constantly evolving self– (as well as cultural) examination that unearths essential tools of the moving photographic medium (words, images, sounds, movements), scrutinizes them anew, manipulates them, and presents them, not to shock, like a Dada prank, but to question deeply the role of art and artist in the world.

The disquieting montages in *Scénario du Film Passion* and *Histoire(s) du cinéma* do jolt us in the manner of the historical avant-garde, but they accomplish much more. As the *tableaux vivants* based on Tintoretto and Goya in *Passion* or the quick cuts from myriad films in the *Histoires* battle for our attention, Godard both shares his own artistic affinities and holds up to us a mirror that reveals our reactions to inhabiting a world full of distracting images. He simultaneously questions the validity of reproducing images like his, and, like a character out of Beckett, goes on doing it, even to the point of obsessive frequency, as in *Scénario*. Standing in his editing suite, he projects scenes from *Passion* on to himself and on to a blank screen beyond, while at the same time replicating all of these on monitors placed throughout the studio. Layers within layers, superimposed images and words appearing as from a mist, reveal the inner processes of the artist's mind; colors and shapes in fluid motion sparked by the nerve charges of the creator at work. For Godard, experimentation is autobiography; montage, instead of masking meanings, is revelatory.

Godard's later films and videos are a record of his battle with himself to find a valid voice for the simultaneous love/hate/obsession/repugnance he feels for cinema.

Video Art

Jean-Luc Godard
83 *Le Gai Savoir* (1967)

Peter Callas
OPPOSITE
86 Peter Callas (b. 1952, Australia) works wonders with computer graphics to produce pictorial narratives that reflect his interest in individual and cultural identity in a technological world. *For Lost in Translation (Part 1: Plus Ultra)* of 1999, Callas developed his own 2D and 3D animation techniques to tell his version of colonial and post-colonial Brazil. Using images from history books, maps, and other sources, Callas creates a history that is at once a critique and a challenge to those involved with technology to be responsible for their images and their narratives.

Freeze-frames, deafening bursts of music, staged gestures, overlapping texts ('I make waves,' he says in *Scénario*) serve his unflappable will to express 'the possibility of the world,' even though this world keeps its meaning invisible.

Other French artists

In the spirit of the 'sound and image' preoccupations of artists like Godard, Robert Cahen creates sophisticated meditations on time and memory in works such as *Juste le Temps* (1983). In this tape a woman is seen in a train traveling through the French countryside. As she sleeps, images and sounds, electronically processed and manipulated, appear and disappear in an abstract narrative that parallels the reality of dreams. Cahen's work often involves travel, which, for the artist, is a metaphor for time and the passage of time. In a series called *Cartes postales vidéo* (**Video Postcards**) of 1984–86, he created thirty-second video postcards of cities around the world, including Lisbon, New York, Rome, Cairo, Quebec, and others. Another paean to a city and its sounds is *Hong Kong Song* (1989).

Thierry Kuntzel (b. 1948, France), a film theorist, who studied linguistics and semiotics, turned to making films and videos in the late 1970s. He brought his interests in psychoanalysis and semiotic theory to dream-inspired videotapes such as *Nostos 1* (1979), *Time Smoking a Picture* (1980), and *La Peinture Cubiste* (1981).

Video Art in North America

Canada

It is important to mention that across the Atlantic in Canada a vigorous video community burgeoned in the 1970s and earlier. Once again community-oriented groups established public media centers that nourished early Video art here as well. Groups such as Intermedia, Metro Media, Intermedia Press and Pacific Cinémathèque, the Western Front, Satellite, Trinity Square Video, Video Exchange, Women in Focus, Centre Véhicule Art, amongst others, were founded in the early 1970s to support videomakers. Canadian video pioneers included David Askevold, Colin Campbell, and Eric Cameron.

Marker
BELOW LEFT
84 *Prime Time in the Camps* (1993)

BELOW RIGHT
85 *Bestiare* (1985–90)

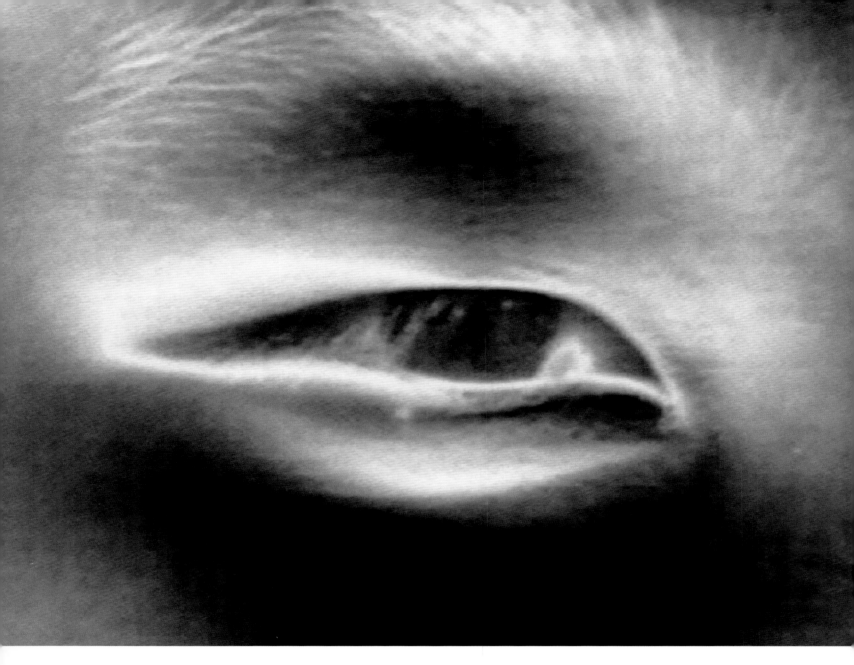

Robert Cahen

87 *Sept Visions Fugitives* (1985)

Robert Cahen

88 Robert Cahen is keenly aware
of the power of time and enjoys
capturing it, manipulating it,
reversing it, essentially attempting to
control it in his images. Sophisticated
sound elements also highlight a
certain romanticism in his travels
in time, such as in *Juste le Temps*
(1983).

Andy Warhol
89 *Outer and Inner Space* (1965)

Thierry Kuntzel

90 In *La Peinture Cubiste* (1981),
a tape that combines video, film, and
painting, Thierry Kuntzel portrays
everyday life as if it were a Cubist
painting. It is an abstract narrative of
a man who perceives the world in the
fractured and multilayered manner of
a Cubist canvas. Kuntzel employs the
many possibilities of time shifts and
image manipulation that video allows.

Canada's strong history of video art was documented in part in the exhibition, 'Magnetic North' (2000). In it, thirty years of Canadian video were represented by more than three dozen videos and installations. In recent years Canadian artists like Stan Douglas (b. 1960), Janet Cardiff (b. 1957), and George Bures Miller (b. 1960) have received widespread acclaim for their work.[20]

Andy Warhol

In shaping this history of video through the examples of significant practitioners, another artist of enormous significance, often omitted from video histories, emerges. There can be little doubt that Andy Warhol was an artist of singular importance.

Filmmakers in the early to mid-1960s began using video technology for its graphic art potential and to simulate the 'real time' viewing experience of television. No one used it better than Warhol, though others, like the American artist Scott Bartlett, synthesized video and film technologies to great effect in works like Bartlett's *OFFON* (1967), described by Gene Youngblood as 'the first videographic film whose existence was equally the result of cinema and video disciplines.'[21]

Warhol was amongst the first to use portable video cameras. In 1965, according to American critic and curator John Alan Farmer, Warhol was asked by *Tape Recording* magazine to experiment with the portable Norelco slant-track video recorder, a remote-control television camera with a zoom lens, and a Concord MTC 11 (brand name) hand-held video camera with a Canon zoom lens.[22] It is likely that Warhol's footage made with the portable video camera in the summer of 1965 was the first artist videotape to be shown in public.

On September 29, 1965, at a party in a large underground railroad space (it was important that the party be 'underground' for the presentation of the 'underground' tapes) beneath the Waldorf-Astoria Hotel in New York, Warhol showed videotapes of conversations with one of his favourite actress/collaborators, Edie Sedgwick. The party, organized by Richard Ekstract, editor of *Tape Recording* magazine, was also taped and then played back to guests. He also made two thirty-minute tapes of Edie Sedgwick, and incorporated them into his first double-projection film, *Outer and Inner Space* (1965).[23]

This film is also significant in that it represents one of the first examples of what has developed into video installation art, now ubiquitous in the art world. Warhol spearheaded what was a common preoccupation of early video artists: television. Unlike others, however, in alternative video documentary groups, Warhol wanted to exploit the uses of television in his work. In the Sedgwick sequences, for example, according to Farmer, 'the filmed image captures her visage in grainy tones of black and white, while the taped image is in a process of constant deformation.'[24]

Warhol's love affair with media and fame found focus in video technology. He would go on to produce several television programs that captured for him the immediacy of 'the present tense' in a way that only video can.

Introducing Warhol into this history of Video art is a way of embracing it in the context of art history in general, for Warhol is clearly an icon of the art world. It is within this art-historical context that the central figure in Video art's history (that is the history of Video art viewed as *art* as opposed to Video art as a *practice* used by people other than visual artists) presents himself: Nam June Paik.[25]

Wolf Vostell

91 *TV Dé-coll/age No. 1* (1958)

Nam June Paik

Various individuals and groups emerged in the mid to late 1960s either from Fluxus or from alternative activist collectives who were responsible for introducing video as art. Wolf Vostell (1932–98, Germany) and Nam June Paik (b. 1932, Korea, lives in the United States), having participated actively in Fluxist performances in Germany, both began experimenting with television sets as potential media sculptures at roughly the same time: Vostell in the late 1950s; Paik in the early 1960s. Television, by this time, had already invaded millions of households and was fast becoming the focus of media culture. Artists, naturally, felt drawn to this medium, both as participants (many of the early television directors were already influential as film or theater directors) and as provocateurs. Vostell's *TV Dé-coll/age No. 1* (1958) featured six television monitors arranged behind a canvas, which the artist slashed open with a knife. 'The TV set is declared to be the television of the future,' he said, mimicking a type of Futurist bravado.

Paik, for his part, put thirteen television sets every which way on the floor of the Galerie Parnass in Wuppertal, Germany, in 1963 and distorted the television image

Nam June Paik

on each of them. In both cases, television was manipulated by artists in their attempt to interrupt the signal, so to speak, of a commercial medium and transform it into a material for art, in this case as sculpture.

In 1965, as political protests of all kinds were brewing throughout the western world, the Sony Portapak, or portable video camera, became available at a cost of about US$3,000, which was a small fraction of the cost of movie cameras. Nam June Paik purchased one in New York, where he began filming casual shots of personal interest to him and showing the unedited results in places where artists gathered in the downtown part of the city. Not long after, several groups of politically active students and workers seized on the Portapak as their chance to subvert normal television news reporting by 'crashing' political conventions and interviewing candidates themselves. Groups in the United States, like Ant Farm, Videofreex, TVTV, and others, entered the video era with a vengeance, creating new types of television reporting and editing along the way.

It is not hard to recognize the artistic roots of protean video artist Nam June Paik. From the atonal compositions of Arnold Schönberg to the messy Fluxus performances of George Maciunas and the quiet compositions of John Cage, his work ranges from the raucous to the meditative, from the mystical to the political. Having been trained in music in his native Korea, Paik, always one to ingest the cultural moment and project it back into the world in the form of art, became engrossed in media technology early on, first through music and recorded sound, then through television.

Paik was already in his thirties and living in Germany when televisions became ubiquitous in western households in the early to mid-1960s. His interest in 'the tube' was that of critic, not, to be sure, sit-com producer or soap-opera director. He knew how this techno-box was changing society forever, and, rather than let it control him, he, as artist, decided to exercise control over it: first by using it as a sculptor, later as a videographer suffusing multiple screens with images displayed at dizzying speeds.

This critical attitude toward television was dominant in Video art from its inception in the mid-1960s to the mid-1980s. Like the Fluxus artists before them, video artists, following Paik's lead, took it upon themselves to comment, often in the ironic tones of postmodernism, on the cultural wars surrounding television.

What is significant about Paik, however, is that he did not stop there. From the late 1960s to the present he has pursued a path of striking originality, fashioning the medium of video into his own artistic universe, and, in the process, re-imagining the very nature of the image in art and culture. Paik's long career and tireless vision was celebrated in a retrospective at New York's Guggenheim Museum in 2000, organized by curator and media scholar John Hanhardt.

Paik's visual precocity was evident from 1965 in *Moon is the Oldest TV,* a black-and-white tape that he updated in color in 2000. In this version, thirteen monitors display a dark sky with larger and larger slices of the moon on each of them. Thanks to video's special quality of capturing images in real time, the moon seems close at

Skip Blumberg
102 Alternative television was an essential component of early Video art. In the hands of activists like Skip Blumberg, in works such as *Pick Up Your Feet: The Double Dutch Show* (1981), the portable camera began to change the way in which 'news stories' were chosen and covered forever.

NAM JUNE PAIK

Nam June Paik

TOP LEFT

103 *Moon is the Oldest TV*
(1965–76)

Photo by Peter Moore © Estate
of Peter Moore/VAGA, New York/
DACS, London 2003

BELOW LEFT

104 *Video Fish* (1975–97)

Photo by Peter Moore © Estate
of Peter Moore/VAGA, New York/
DACS, London 2003

hand, sitting not far off in a winter's night, but near enough to touch. Paik's contemplative affinities for light are also keenly present in *One Candle (Candle Projection)* from 1988, which features a lit candle being videotaped live and then projected on to multiple screens. Linked to this is *Video Buddha* (1976–78), Paik's well-known closed-circuit installation in which a camera on a tripod is focused on a bronze sculpture of the cross-legged Buddha, whose image appears live on a small TV, buried in dirt, save for its screen.

Paik has also demonstrated a playful side. *Video Fish* (1975–97) features fish swimming around in tanks that appear to have blue-screen monitors in them (they are actually behind the glass) displaying a disjointed array of images from flying planes to a dancing Merce Cunningham. His *Family of Robot* series (1986) includes a Father and Mother Robot, and Baby-Tech Robot – all made from old television sets that produce a galaxy of colorful images. *TV Chair* (1968) has an upended television where the seat should be. For Paik, every aspect of the televised image is fair game for both his critiques and his enjoyment; and, if the television is everywhere, it can also be anywhere. Paik's importance in media art cannot be overemphasized. An inventor and innovator, he realized a synthesis of art and technology that other artists are only beginning to achieve.

Shigeko Kubota

Paik's life and career have been intertwined with his wife of more than thirty years, the video artist Shigeko Kubota. Born in 1937, Kubota incorporated her keen sense of space into Video art as early as 1968, when she photographed Marcel Duchamp (1887–1968) and John Cage (1912–92) playing their famous game of chess on a board wired for sound. She videotaped these images and electronically altered them, creating the tapes *Duchampiana: Chess* (1968–75). Duchamp's wicked ironies provided inspiration for several of her works, including *Duchampiana: Nude Descending a Staircase* (1976), in which she mimicked the shape of a staircase with several video monitors showing a synthesized nude woman 'descending' from one monitor to the next; and *Bicycle Wheel* (1983), a reconceived version of Duchamp's readymade, this one with a monitor attached to one of its spokes.

Shigeko Kubota

RIGHT

105 *Marcel Duchamp and John Cage*
(1972)

Courtesy Electronic Arts Intermix,
New York

Shigeko Kubota
106 *Sexual Healing* (1998)

In 1996, Nam June Paik suffered a debilitating stroke from which he has never completely recovered. A few years later, Kubota created a multi-part installation *Sexual Healing* (named for the pop song by Marvin Gaye) that lovingly reflected on Paik's painstaking recovery process.

Free-standing handrails, like those installed in Kubota and Paik's apartment, marked out sculptural spaces within which Kubota placed all manner of video containers: video bed, video chair, video window, and video stick figures of a man and a woman looking as if they are ready to dance. Images of Paik, laughing in characteristic fashion through the obvious pain of recovery, assisted by young female physical therapists at a New York hospital, were projected throughout the gallery.

This is not the diary of a devoted housewife who, on a whim, decided to make home movies of a life-changing event in her domestic life. Shigeko Kubota, often eclipsed by the tremendous and influential output of her husband, has been a pioneering video artist almost as long as he has. She tapes Paik struggling to take his first post-stroke steps, kissing everybody who is trying to help him. We see him sleeping, his familiar round head multiplied on to three monitors fitted into the springs of a bed. In such a setting it is hard not to think of the sleep of

Video Art

death, but Kubota wisely wards off the maudlin with the sultry sounds of Marvin Gaye's song.

Kubota has been creating a video diary of her life since the early 1970s. She has chronicled everything from her travels through Europe with a Sony Portapak (1972), to Paik's return to Korea after a thirty-four year absence (1984), to the destruction of their loft (and many of their videotapes) from water damage (1985). In a sense she has had two life companions: Paik and her camera. Both reflect her life back to her, both are repositories of things she may not even know about herself. Of her life with Paik she said in a statement accompanying the installation, 'What Fluxus and video art have in common is that both are art of the moment. The process of capturing events that are invisible to others, with your own eyes, becomes art. Through Fluxus we became a couple and since then have lived in the same ex-factory building. During these years many of the artists who were involved in the movement with us have passed away. However, we want to live forever. Nam June comforts me by saying, "Shigechan, I am always with you." As long as he lives, I cannot die.'

Dominant Trends in Contemporary Art

In this art-historical view of the development of Video art it is necessary to understand what was going on in the rest of then contemporary art. Minimalism and Conceptualism were the dominant trends amongst visual artists and several early video practitioners emerged from within these movements. Critic Lucy Lippard characterized this period in art as the time when art became 'dematerialized,' that is the focus of art shifted from the 'object' (the painting, the sculpture) to the 'idea.'[26]

Artists used language, photography, film, video, slides, and performances to express their ideas. The forms may have shifted, but this attitude prevails today: materials are at the disposal of the artist. It is not the artist's job to conquer paint, or metal, or marble. The interdisciplinary nature of art work, particularly the incorporation of photography, performance and dance into the visual arts, heightened artists' awareness of time, so that time actually became a medium, especially in the form of video.

Video, in this art-historical view, emerged as artists were experimenting with all sorts of media: film – American artists Andy Warhol, Robert Whitman (b. 1935), Canadian artist Michael Snow (b. 1929); slide projections – Dutch artist Ger Van Elk (b. 1941), Irish artist James Coleman (b. 1941), German artist Lothar Baumgarten (b. 1944), American artist Robert Barry (b. 1936); and live-feed media sculptures – Japanese-born Yoko Ono (b. 1933), American artist William Anastasi (b. 1933). British-born curator Chrissie Iles suggests that 'during the 1960s and early 1970s the projected image played a critical role in creating a new language of representation as artists used film, slides, video, and holographic and photographic projection to measure, document, abstract, reflect, and transform the parameters of physical space.'[27]

This spirited time saw the museum replaced by the white box as the primary locus for new art and the white box altered to a black box for the viewing of video and film on monitors and walls. Painters did not stop painting, nor sculptors sculpting, but a new breed of artist, not wedded to a particular medium, began to dominate artistic discourse. Names like Vito Acconci, Bruce Nauman and VALIE EXPORT became synonymous with the art of this time.

chapter 2

Video and the Conceptual Body

A Cross-Disciplinary Spirit

It is a commonly held belief that Jackson Pollock's work – dripping and pouring paint on to the canvas in the mid-20th century – and Hans Namuth's photographs and films of Pollock taken in his studio in 1950 helped place the body at the center of the work of art. For Namuth, watching Pollock paint was 'like a great drama…the flame of explosion when the paint hit the canvas; the dance-like movement; the eyes tormented before knowing where to strike next; the tension, then the explosion again.'[1] It is not surprising that Namuth had originally hoped to be a theater director.

American curator Paul Schimmel, who organized the highly influential exhibition, 'Out of Actions: Between Performance and the Object, 1949–1979' for the Museum of Contemporary Art in Los Angeles, states that 'Pollock's desire to maintain "contact" [Pollock's word] with the canvas essentially transformed the artist's role from that of a bystander outside of the canvas to that of an actor whose every actions were its subject.'[2]

Artists, of course, had always used their body to make their work, but after Pollock (and the Argentine-born Italian Lucio Fontana and the Japanese Shozo Shimamoto as well) the body itself was considered to be a material in art. When video became available, artists drawn to Performance and Conceptual art saw the camera as an intimate way both to study and expose the role of gesture in their art. Just as the body became a material in art in the 1960s, Performance has become a material in Video art in our day. In a certain sense, Performance has always held a special place in the visual arts. Is it not true that Manet's *Olympia* (1863), or Zurbarán's *Hercules* (1624) are 'performing' for their artists? Surely, *Viejos Comiendo Sopa (Old Men Eating Soup)* of 1819, are jesting for Goya's pleasure. More directly, Francis Bacon's *Head VI* (the shrieking Pope Innocent X of 1949) was inspired by the screaming nurse in Sergei Eisenstein's film *Battleship Potemkin* (1925).[3]

From the early 1970s to the present day there is a strong link between video and the body. It is central to the work of numerous artists, including Vito Acconci, Bruce Nauman, Joan Jonas, Robert Rauschenberg, Carolee Schneemann, Adrian Piper, Sophie Calle, Nam June Paik, VALIE EXPORT, Marina Abramovic and Ulay, Robert Wilson, Martha Rosler, Jürgen Klauke, Steve McQueen, Lucy Gunning, Tony Oursler, Paul McCarthy, Gary Hill, Klaus Rinke, Nayland Blake and Pipilotti Rist.

In the early days of Video art, three types of artist/ practitioners emerged: those who used video to create

Pipilotti Rist
OPPOSITE
107 *Ever Is Over All* (1997)

Sophie Calle
BELOW
108 *Double Blind* (1992)

Lucy Gunning
109 *Climbing Around My Room*
(1993)

alternatives to television; activists drawn to the community and mass appeal of video technology; and artists who saw video as an extension of their artistic practice. In Darwinian terms the last group remained dominant and historically must be recognized as the precursors to contemporary Video art. The first two groups (with some exceptions of individual artists like Frank Gillette) found a home in cable community television, documentary video and film, leaving the art form in the hands of those whose interests and methods had been shaped by the history and profession of art. So instead of the 'public' possibilities of video dominating its growth as an art, what might be called intra-art issues began to dominate early on. They included ideas important to all artists of the mid-1960s and beyond: the dematerialized art object; time as a medium in art; use of industrial materials and technology in making art; the abandonment of traditional boundaries between painting and sculpture; the introduction of everyday objects into the work of art; the intermingling of several artistic disciplines, including painting, dance, sculpture, music, theater, photography, and video.

Even prior to Minimalism and Conceptualism, the dominant art 'isms' at the birth of Video art, the artists who best represented this new cross-disciplinary spirit were Robert Rauschenberg, whose influence (often unsung) on early Video art was

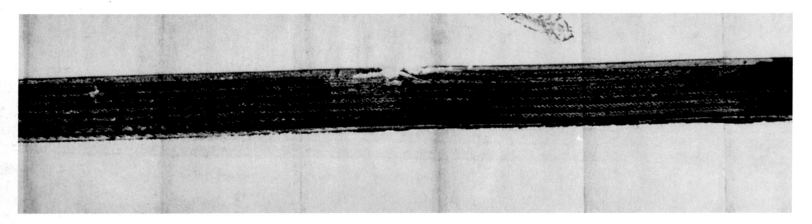

Robert Rauschenberg and John Cage
ABOVE
110 *Automobile Tire Print* (1953; detail)

Nam June Paik
OPPOSITE
111 Paik's earliest collaborator was Fluxist artist Charlotte Moorman. Together they created numerous performances with video and music that were seen as scandalous when Moorman appeared topless. This tape, *'Topless Cellist' Charlotte Moorman* (1995), was made in memory of Moorman, who died of cancer in 1991.

enormous, and musician John Cage. In 1953, Rauschenberg and Cage pasted twenty long strips of paper together and after Rauschenberg poured black paint into the grooves of the tires on Cage's Model A Ford, Cage drove his car over the paper. They mounted the 'print' on canvas, lengthened like a Japanese scroll, and called it *Automobile Tire Print*. In this bold work, the everyday, represented by tires and a car, intruded upon painting in a Performance act. The resulting work of art hung on a wall defying anyone to deny its place as a work of art. During the next decade Rauschenberg created numerous dance/theater projects with leading experimental choreographers, including Trisha Brown, Steve Paxton, Deborah Hay, Yvonne Rainer, Lucinda Childs and others. Though Rauschenberg made no single-channel videos, he, along with engineer Billy Klüver, mounted *Nine Evenings: Theater and Engineering* (1966) at the Sixty-Ninth Regiment Armory building in New York. It featured several electronically manipulated art objects as well as a video projection of infra-red images of volunteers in Rauschenberg's own performance during those evenings. Technology of all kinds was introduced with a bang, so to speak, into the creation and presentation of art.

Nam June Paik

ABOVE
112 *Zen for Head* (1962)

BELOW RIGHT
113 *Zen for Film* (1964)
Photo by Peter Moore © Estate
of Peter Moore/VAGA, New York/
DACS, London 2003

One year earlier than the Rauschenberg and Cage *Automobile Tire Print*, **Cage composed** *4'33"* a musical 'composition' consisting solely of instructions for the piano player to sit in front of the keyboard, and after opening the piano cover, remain seated for the duration of the piece (four minutes, thirty-three seconds) doing nothing. Listeners hear only what is in their environment (such as coughs, breathing, street noise), thus incorporating, in a radical manner, the everyday into a work of art. The everyday actually becomes the work of art according to the intention, or concept, of the artist (Cage).

In 1956, as a twenty-four-year-old Korean music student, Nam June Paik went to Germany to study with experimental composers, ending up working with Karlheinz Stockhausen in 1957 and John Cage in 1958 at the International Summer Courses for New Music in Darmstadt. Shortly afterwards Paik participated in the anti-art, anti-establishment performances of the international Fluxus movement. The group also introduced him to their experiments with film. Amongst his performances of this period was *Zen for Head* (1962), in which he dipped his head, hands and tie into black paint and crawled backwards down a lengthy strip of white paper, applying the paint as he went (echoing what Rauschenberg and Cage had done with their car tire). Paik called it his own interpretation of composer La Monte Young's *Composition 1960 #10 (to Bob Morris)*.

In 1964, Paik made *Zen for Film* (referred to as Fluxfilm No. 1), which consisted of nothing but clear film leader running through a projector. This film action, as it

 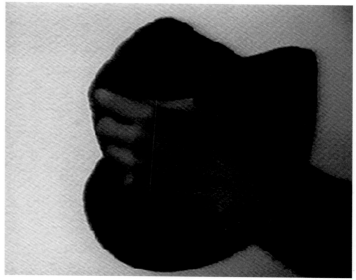

John Baldessari

ABOVE LEFT

114 Even when body art and
process art were in full swing,
John Baldessari, with his studied
awkwardness, brought his conceptual
humor to the pretenses he found
lurking in some 1970s art practices,
as in *I Am Making Art* (1971).

ABOVE RIGHT

115 *Folding Hat* (1970–71)

might be called, was made in the anti-art, anti-commercial atmosphere of Fluxus performances. Paik eliminated the film image completely, partly in jest, but mostly as an act of defiance against the highly aestheticized filmed image of even such experimental filmmakers as Stan Brakhage and Kenneth Anger. About forty Fluxfilms are on record, ranging from Dick Higgins's *Invocation of Canyons and Boulders for Stan Brakhage* (**Fluxfilm No. 2, 1963**) to Wolf Vostell's *Sun in Your Head* (**Fluxfilm No. 23, 1963**) to Paul Sharits's *Word Movie* (**Fluxfilm No. 30, 1966**). The Vostell film has particular significance for the history of Video art in that he used his 8-millimeter film camera to shoot videotaped material from television programs, thus displacing both the 'revered' film image (by focusing his camera on already videotaped material) and the 'direct' video image (by re-recording it with film). This type of subversion of social and artistic structures was a hallmark of Fluxus.[4]

It is clear, then, that prior to the arrival of the Sony Portapak in 1965 artists like Paik, Vostell and Yoko Ono had for several years been involved with European performative art associated with artists like George Maciunas, Joseph Beuys, Yves Klein, theater artist Tadeusz Kantor, as well as electronic musicians and experimental sound artists, all of whom stretched the traditional parameters of their art to include technology, everyday objects and sounds, as well as Performance. It is from these multifaceted beginnings that artists like Paik began, and then expanded, the art of video. What American curator and media historian John Hanhardt says of Paik is also true of Vostell, Ono, Higgins and other artists of this period: 'It is important that we examine Paik's treatment of video as a whole as opposed to developments achieved in one area...Paik always worked in many media and in a number of directions at once: videotapes, television projects, performances, installations, objects, writing.'[5]

The same might be said of some video pioneers such as Vito Acconci, John Baldessari, Richard Serra, Dennis Oppenheim (b. 1938) and Bruce Nauman, but others, like Peter Campus, Beryl Korot and Juan Downey, focused on video as their primary art rather than as a by-product of a larger art practice. Nonetheless, all of them made tapes that may be called 'performative,' in that they were based on the artist performing some action, either as a type of body sculpture or as a gesture associated with the body as a material for art.

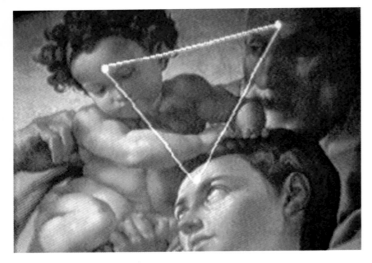

Juan Downey

LEFT

116 Juan Downey's work often involved explorations of the self in the context of culture and historical systems that could make people feel exiled even within their own land. In *Information Withheld* (1983) he juxtaposed codes from everyday life, such as traffic signals, and art-historical works to illustrate critic Leo Steinberg's statement that signs were unambiguous and fully understandable, whereas art relied on information withheld.

CENTER LEFT

117 *Hard Times and Culture: Part 1* (1990)

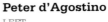

Peter d'Agostino

LEFT

118 *DOUBLE YOU (and X, Y, Z)* (1981–86) is an interactive videodisk with 48,000 frames that users can work in any sequence. Its subject is no less than the process of acquiring language, beginning with birth itself.

Peter d'Agostino

RIGHT

119 Peter d'Agostino (b. 1945, United States) has worked in video since 1971. Also a theorist and critic, he has published books and articles on semiotics and technology. He has combined his intellectual and artistic interests in numerous tapes and interactive disks that amount to a personal, rigorous examination of the effects of technology on the individual and society. *TransmissionS* (1985–90) is d'Agostino's history of 20th-century communications. Appropriated images from Edison's early films, television shows, and many others merge into a narrative about a young boy trapped in a well, surrounded by dozens of news cameras. D'Agostino deftly uses personal observation and historical references to formulate a unique and powerful story.

Bruce Nauman

Bruce Nauman

Conceptual Art

In Video art, Performance, as introduced into the art world by Allan Kaprow, Jim Dine and others, and Conceptualism, the increasingly dominant form of the late 1960s and 1970s, were united in a technology-based medium that afforded an immediacy and intimacy sought by artists of this time.

The aspect of Conceptual art that filtered most strongly into the practice of young artists was not the strict, manifesto-like notion heralded by Joseph Kosuth and Sol LeWitt that, in Kosuth's words, 'actual works of art are ideas...models (which are) a visual approximation of a particular object I have in mind.' Instead, what infiltrated art was Kosuth's idea that 'artistic practice locates itself directly in the signifying process and that the use of elements in an art proposition (be they objects, quotations, fragments, photographs, contexts, or whatever) functions not for aesthetic purposes...but rather as simply the constructive elements of a test of the cultural code.'[6] In other words, what is essential to the practice of art is the motivating idea possessed by the artist that questions existing codes or expressions, both in the world of art and in the culture at large. The centrality of 'the idea' led to a rapid increase in the use of varied materials from at least the 1980s onwards, so that anything from paint to pipe cleaners, cotton fibers to fiber optics could be used as a material for art. It is this reality that has led American art critic and philosopher Arthur Danto to proclaim the end of art as we have known it, by which he means that the story of art, of art as painting and sculpture, has come to a conclusion and a new story is being developed.[7]

Concept-based Performance appeared immediately in the work of Acconci, Serra, and Nauman, the last of whom, like Kosuth, was enamored of Ludwig Wittgenstein's linguistic philosophy. Wittgenstein, especially in his *Philosophical Investigations* (1953), liberated language from the strongholds imposed on it by the logical positivists by suggesting that all language is, in a sense, a game, by which he meant it has a context. Language, as an everyday practice, reflects various forms of life and is legitimized by these forms of life, even if one may not identify with this or that particular form. (For example, one may not believe that 'ethics,' or 'moral' behaviour has any legitimacy in philosophical discourse, but, for Wittgenstein, it does, as a language, or as a 'language game' which some people play with great seriousness.) Wittgenstein's emphasis on everyday language was very attractive to Conceptual artists.

For Nauman, video was an extension of his sculpture. He 'performed' various activities in his studio in front of a camera, calling them 'representations.' He would assume varying everyday positions (sitting, walking, bending, squatting), thus creating living sculptures with his body. In *Black Balls* (1969) the artist applied black paint to his testicles in what can be seen as a prescient representation of sex and death. During the 1960s Nauman made about twenty-five videotapes consisting of repetitive, mundane movements that showed the influences of serial music by Terry Riley, Philip Glass, and Steve Reich. Nauman's interest in language as an activity that can be both revealing and concealing has endured to the present day. In the 1990s he created a series of installations with Performance artist Rinde Eckert that explored personal identity, language and communication: *Anthro/Socio (Rinde Facing Camera)* of 1991 and *Anthro/Socio (Rinde Spinning)* of 1992.

Bruce Nauman

NEAR RIGHT

125 Nauman's performative videos are prime examples of artists' attempts to record the intimate relationship between their bodies and their work. In Nauman's case, he also used patterned movements, learned from choreographer friends, to create bodily sculptures. In *Slow Angle Walk* (1968), in a homage to the playwright Samuel Beckett, he makes patterns in his studio that reflect the inescapable and repetitive nature of daily life. In so doing, he also reflects art and life as unfolding processes.

FAR RIGHT

126 *Bouncing In the Corner No. 1* (1968)

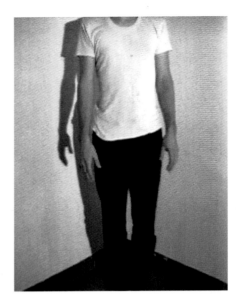

Vito Acconci

BELOW

127 *The Red Tapes* (1976) may be considered Vito Acconci's video masterwork. This three-part project is an exploration of individual and cultural identity through images of the self and the American landscape. Acconci, originally a poet, here applies poetic texts and poetic imagination to a video adventure that moves stealthily from the individual psyche (Acconci himself blindfolded) to the collective psyche acted out in a theatrical performance that included artists like David Salle.

For Nauman, the 'process' of art making was just as important as the art that was made. In a series of tapes, inspired by the linguistically and existentially complex work of 20th-century playwright Samuel Beckett, Nauman 'performed' for the camera in his studio. In *Slow Angle Walk*, subtitled *Beckett Walk* (1968), he walked around his studio in a strained manner similar to patterns Beckett had written in plays like *Footfalls* (1975) and *Quad* (1982).

This preoccupation with the artistic process and the studio as the place for process was the theme of Nauman's installation *Mapping the Studio II with color shift, flip, flop, & flip/flop (Fat Chance John Cage)*, shown in 2002. Filmed in 2001 with a small digital camera and projected on seven walls with a running time of five hours and forty-five minutes, *Mapping the Studio* looks back to the artist's earliest videos in which he also turned on the camera and taped his movements for as long as the camera ran. In this case, however, the artist's body is largely absent, apart from an occasional lower leg caught as he exits the studio. Instead, the camera focuses on the life of the studio without the artist, the inanimate objects strewn about, or the cat moving stealthily through the space. It is a curious turnaround from an artist whose body was often so central to the making of his work. For Nauman, however, the process of art is not just making, but questioning. In this case he seems to be paying homage to the ever-questioning Cage, leaving his own body out of the equation to allow room for Cage's legacy to fill the space.

Process, language, and a certain defiance of earlier art practices informed the performative videos of Vito Acconci, who began as a writer and turned to Performance as a 'means of escaping from the page.' Acconci's work was marked by keen attention to language, a sense of humor and, often, irony. Acconci has an important place in the history of Video art because he brought his performances into the gallery (at the Reese Paley Gallery in New York and at other spaces with the avant-garde enthusiast Willoughby Sharp), as did others like Dennis Oppenheim. *Corrections* (1971), *Second Hand* (1971), and *Command Performance* (1974) were all performed in galleries, thus identifying Video art and Performance early on with the 'art world' as opposed to experimental theater or avant-garde film and video.

Video Art

Dennis Oppenheim
128 *Rocked Hand* (1970)

Dan Graham

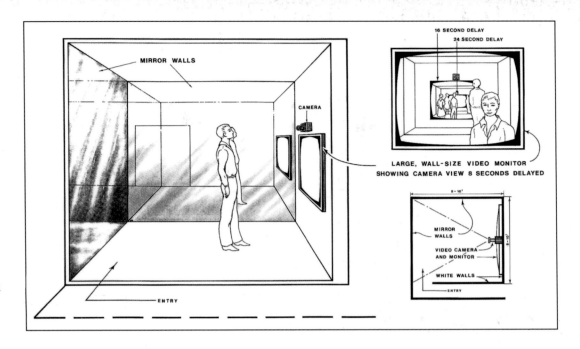

The gallery space, in contrast to the private world of the studio, also encouraged interaction with an audience. For artist Dan Graham (b. 1942, United States), involving the viewer was (and is) central to his art practice. From 1970 to 1978 Graham made several video installations that placed viewers in the midst of an architectural environment of glass and mirrors, including *Present Continuous Past(s)* (1974) and *Performance/Audience/Mirror* (1975). What may at first have appeared as a rather basic self-conscious experience became for the audience a lesson in feedback, watching, self-analysis, and objectivity. In a sense, Graham was exposing some of the most basic tenets of the filmed image to an audience already in the rapture of television.

This 'serious playfulness' regarding perception has also been central to the work of Nauman and Michael Snow. Video technology afforded these artists the opportunity to question traditional notions of perception. Nauman's 1970 multi-screen film installation, *Spinning Spheres*, for example, features a steel ball turning vigorously on a glass plate in a white room. The images reflected on the ball are intended to destabilize the viewer's perspective as it becomes impossible to detect where the real walls of the space are.

Michael Snow has been toying with viewers' perceptions for almost forty years in films and performances like *Wavelength* and *Right Reader* from the 1960s. *Two Sides to Every Story* (1974) features a suspended aluminum screen, on both sides of which are projected images of a woman, engaging in various gestures, filmed from front and back. Viewers need to keep looking at both sides of the screen in order to appreciate what is happening, a rather dizzy-making task. In a sense, viewers themselves become performers in the artwork.

This incorporation of the viewer into the work of art, at least as co-conspirator, has been central to the practice of artists since Marcel Duchamp had viewers spinning parts of his sculptures in *Bicycle Wheel* (1913) and *Rotary Glass Plates (Precision Optics)* of 1920. He also experimented with perception in film – *Anemic*

Bruce Nauman
BELOW
135 *Spinning Spheres* (1970)

Michael Snow
OPPOSITE
136 *Wavelength* (1967)

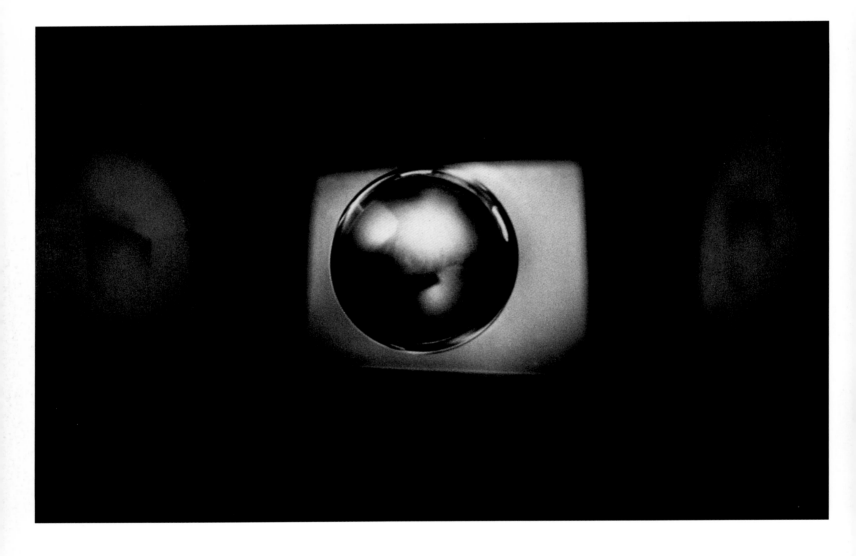

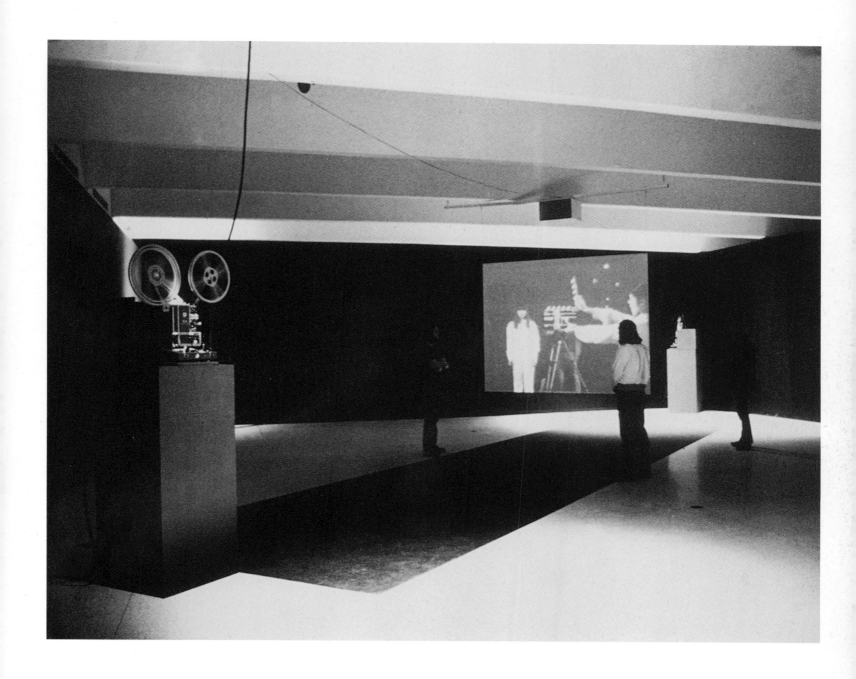

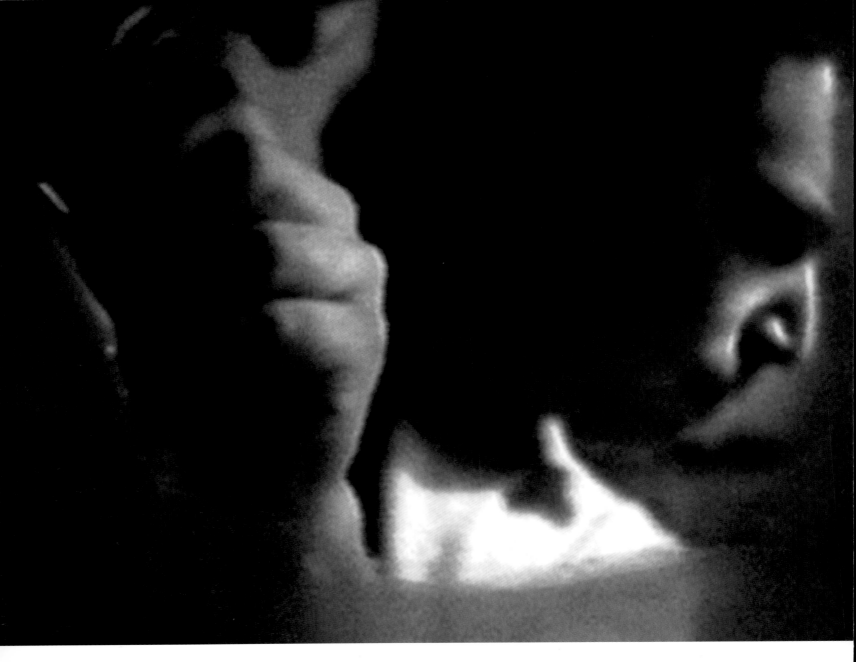

Peter Campus
140 *Dynamic Field Series* (1971)

Cinema (1925–26) – and in scores of sculptural constructions in his long career. This Duchampian interest in perception bending also surfaced in Conceptual art.

As American critic Lucy Lippard and, after her Peter Wollen, have emphasized, Conceptualism (and, by extension, Video art) emerged during a time of significant cultural upheaval characterized by Vietnam War protests, the rise of feminism and black power, and student revolts throughout western Europe and the United States. Peter Wollen writes: 'Conceptual artists too wanted to create a new kind of relationship between artist, gallery and public, a relationship that would challenge not only the commercial nature of the art world but also the idea of the viewer as passive consumer of sensations rather than thoughtful interlocutor. Text, photography and found objects were incorporated into artwork not simply because they were interesting new media...but because they offered specific ways of engaging the attention of the art public.'[8]

To this list video, especially in its performative aspects, could be added: through Performance, video artists expressly invited audiences to participate in the work of art, indeed required participation for the art to function at all. Peter Campus's closed-circuit video installations (fifteen in total made during the 1970s) involved the viewers in many ways, projecting their images on large screens and small, in shadows and upside down, as in his 1977 *aen*, in which a wall-mounted camera, flipped upside down, projected inverted heads and shoulders of visitors as they entered the gallery.

Performance assumed an essential role in the Video art of women artists, who, through the feminist movement, were now demanding a place at the art table long dominated by men, especially the men of 'heroic' and macho Abstract Expressionism. As in much of art history, women had simply been ignored.[9]

By the mid-1960s, however, women began fighting against the silence surrounding their life and work. Feminist outcries, though begun in the early part of the century and not fully felt until the 1970s, were evident in art in the 1960s, coinciding with other movements of liberation, including those of African Americans and gays and lesbians. The feminist influence upon video and Performance was substantial.

Peter Campus

BELOW LEFT
141 In *Three Transitions* (1973) Peter Campus explores identity through the technological tools available in video. In what appear to be magician's tricks, he appears and disappears, burns himself into extinction, and wipes the features off his face. Illusion and reality compete in this seminal work of Video art.

BELOW RIGHT
142 *Winter Journal* (1997)

Martha Rosler

ABOVE
143 *How Do We Know What Home Looks Like?* (1993)

BELOW LEFT
144 Steeped in knowledge of semiotics, Rosler does not burden the viewer with words, but rather uses gestures in *Semiotics of the Kitchen* (1975) to express the frustration and claustrophobia of many a kitchen-bound housewife.

BELOW CENTRE
145 *Vital Statistics of a Citizen, Simply Obtained* (1977)

BELOW RIGHT
146 *Born To Be Sold: Martha Rosler Reads the Strange Case of Baby SM* (1989), and made with Paper Tiger Television, is a send-up of a true story in which a surrogate mother tries to reclaim the baby she had. The video (in which Rosler plays all the parts, including the baby) becomes an indictment of class and gender as the surrogate mother must yield to the demands of the middle-class father.

Photographer, video artist, and installation artist Martha Rosler is representative of the new feminism in art. Born in New York, Rosler created some of her most enduring work in Performance, video, and photography during her time in California as a student and, later, as a teacher. *Bringing the War Home* (1967–72) is a series of twenty photomontages that places images of Vietnam War victims (girls with missing limbs, mothers holding their dead children, wounded soldiers) in the midst of tranquil suburban American interiors cut from the pages of *Life* magazine. As art historian Alexander Alberro says of this series, 'She was, in effect, making concrete "the war abroad, the war at home" produced by the mass media that imported images of death from Vietnam into American homes every evening.'

Domesticity also played a role in *Semiotics of the Kitchen* (1975), a video in which the artist, dressed in an apron and with a deadpan facial expression, sends up television cookery shows and a woman's place in the kitchen, engaging in mannered gestures with a variety of cooking utensils. Like so much of her early work, *Semiotics* is striking both for its innocence and its sophistication. Rosler's photos and videos display a strong grasp of technique and youthful exuberance. In her 1977 Performance and, later, video, *Vital Statistics of a Citizen, Simply Obtained*, the artist submits to having every part of her nude body measured and recorded by two white-coated men as a 'chorus' of women stand to the side silently observing. 'This a work about how to think about yourself,' Rosler says in a voice-over on the videotape. The strategies of measuring spaces and gallery walls, as practiced by Minimalist artists, as well as the 'directions' given by Fluxus artists in their interactive performances, were here combined with a strong feminist consciousness that commented on the use and abuse of the female body in advertising and media.

The spareness of her scenarios in videos like *Semiotics of the Kitchen*, combined with a biting sense of humor, took some inspiration from the films of Jean-Luc Godard, whom Rosler met while an undergraduate at the University of California, San Diego. There she also encountered filmmaker Roberto Rossellini and several influential intellectuals, such as Marxist theorist Herbert Marcuse and the literary critics Jean-François Lyotard and Fredric Jameson. In Godard, the young Rosler found a model artist who resisted the commercialization of ideas while he dazzled with his command of striking images, sounds, and texts. 'My art is a communicative act, a form of an utterance, a way to open a conversation,' Rosler says.[10]

Another highly significant woman artist whose work reflected the primacy of Performance in the development of Video art is Joan Jonas (b. 1936, United States). Jonas has created a unique vocabulary of media art that seamlessly combines her

Joan Jonas

147 Joan Jonas's own body soon became central to her work. Influenced by dance (Yvonne Rainer, Anne Halperin, Deborah Hay, each of whom had worked with Merce Cunningham and John Cage) and the process art of Richard Serra, Gordon Matta-Clark, and others, Jonas equated the body with conceptual experimentation early on in her career. While manifestly dealing with the physical properties of the mediums of film and television, *Vertical Roll* (1972) features close-ups of the artist's body in what amounts to a loud proclamation of the body's (especially the female body's) presence in the work of art.

interests in feminism, ritual, mythology and sculpture. In her highly personal works (she still performs in many of them), her enduring practices in mixed-media art (dance, video, sculpture) surface in poetic tales of human struggle and endurance.

Jonas started using video in 1970 when she bought a Portapak on a visit to Japan. She was an admirer of experimental film (Russians Dziga Vertov and Sergei Eisenstein; Frenchman Jean Vigo; American Maya Deren) and considers her earliest video work a reflection of avant-garde film techniques, such as Vertov's out of synch images and sounds.

While participating in dance workshops with members of the legendary Judson Church group in New York (Trisha Brown, Deborah Hay, Steve Paxton and others), she used video and film early on in live performances, such as *Organic Honey's Visual Telepathy* (1974) and *Mirage* (1976). Her poetic, non-narrative presentations – complete with cones, masks, chalk drawings, taped images, and sounds – to this day express the artist's close connection to the earth and mythology. More recent large-scale multimedia performances have included *Volcano Saga* (1989) and *Sweeney Astray* (1994).

Video and Performance: The Vienna Connection

In the aftermath of the World War II, two countries deeply involved with the destruction that occurred during the war became the breeding ground for radical new forms of Performance and media: Japan, which had attacked the United States at Pearl Harbor, Hawaii, and Nazi-occupied Austria. The Gutai Group in Japan consisted of painters and performers who were involved with the materials of their art in a violent way. Prominent from 1954 to 1958, though they existed until 1972, Gutai artists shot at canvases with arrows tipped with paint or crashed through canvases with their own bodies in acts of rage against established art practices as well as cultural repressions. Their work was captured on film in *Gutai on Stage* (1957) and *Gutai Painting* (1960).

Even more radical were the *Wiener Aktionisten*, the Viennese Actionists, who had a profound influence on future generations of Performance and media artists not only in Austria, but throughout the world. The principal Actionists were Hermann Nitsch (b. 1938), Otto Muehl (b. 1925), Günter Brus (b. 1938) and Rudolph Schwarzkogler (1940–69). The films of Muehl and Kurt Kren (b. 1929) inaugurated an extraordinary period of energy in the development of experimental film and then Video art.

These artists sought to outrage their viewers by engaging in performances that often involved blood and animal slaughter (Nitsch and Muehl), explicit sadistic sexual activity (Muehl) or sensational bodily performances (Brus, Schwarzkogler, and Muehl). In films like *Funèbre* (1966) and *Scheiss-Kerl* (Shit-Guy) of 1969, Muehl provided graphic descriptions of humans and animals drenched in blood and paint. Emerging in the center of Freudian psychoanalysis (Vienna) and influenced by

Joan Jonas

Joan Jonas

BELOW
150–55 Based on a 13th-century Icelandic tale, *Volcano Saga* (1989) is about a woman who marries four times. Using filmed footage of the dramatic Iceland landscape, Joan Jonas creates a dreamscape with multiple projection and performance surfaces to tell the story of this woman who lives out the prophecy of a seer.

Antonin Artaud's Theater of Cruelty and the international Fluxus movement, the Actionists took Performance and media in dangerous new directions. They exalted 'destruction' as a key element in artistic and personal freedom (together they attended the 'Destruction in Art' symposium in London in 1966). As Austrian critic and curator Robert Fleck has observed: 'The Viennese Actionists believed that the body was an essence they could use.'[11]

Kurt Kren became the filmmaker of Actionism, making an original contribution to 1960s avant-garde film by his unique camera and editing work with the films of performances by Muehl and Brus. He subjects the body images of performances by Muehl and Brus to the structural fragmentation then dominant in experimental film. In the same way that the filmmakers Stan Brakhage and Bruce Conner (both Americans) had emphasized the 'materiality' of film (the tape itself acting like a canvas), so, too, the Actionists used their bodies as 'material.' It is here that the sensational body art of Muehl and Brus connected with Kren's interests in material film. His films with Muehl and Brus – *Mama und Papa* (1964), *Leda mit dem Schwan* (1964), *Selbstverstümmelung* (1965), and *Cosinus Alpha* (1966) – are classic examples of structuralist collage film. Working in the same vein of sexual liberation, but in a much more tame fashion, were the Americans Kenneth Anger with *Scorpio Rising* (1963) and Jack Smith with *Flaming Creatures* (1963).

Though not officially a member of the Viennese Actionist group, one young woman (whose feminist interests alone might have excluded her from the often misogynist Actionists) introduced new forms of media Performance with the video camera in the Vienna of the mid-1960s.

VALIE EXPORT

At age the age of twenty-eight, VALIE EXPORT (née Waltraud Hollinger in 1940) proclaimed her presence in the Viennese art world. Eager to counter the perceived abusive tactics of the Actionists against women, she sought a new identity unlinked to her father's name (Lehner) or her former husband's name (Hollinger). She transformed herself from Waltraud into VALIE and took the bold step of appropriating the name of a popular cigarette brand, EXPORT, as her last name. From the start she used the upper-case spelling. By adopting the trade name she engaged in an act of provocation that would characterize future performances, especially *Action Pants: Genital Panic* (1969), during which she marched into an artfilm house in Munich, wearing pants with the crotch cut out. What was artistically unique about EXPORT was that, unlike the Actionists, or other early Performance artists like Allan Kaprow, Jim Dine and Robert Rauschenberg, EXPORT was not a painter first.

Her earliest art production were films and installations she referred to as 'expanded cinema' projects after the title of the influential book, *Expanded Cinema* (1970) by American critic Gene Youngblood, in which he describes cinematic art removed from the movie house: video, experimental film, installations, and mixed-media art.

Born in Linz, Austria, EXPORT arrived in Vienna at the height of 'Viennese Actionism.' It was in this environment that she developed her own brand of what she called Feminist Actionism. The male Viennese gang of four were often accused of misogynist practices, so, in a sense, EXPORT was actually responding to them as

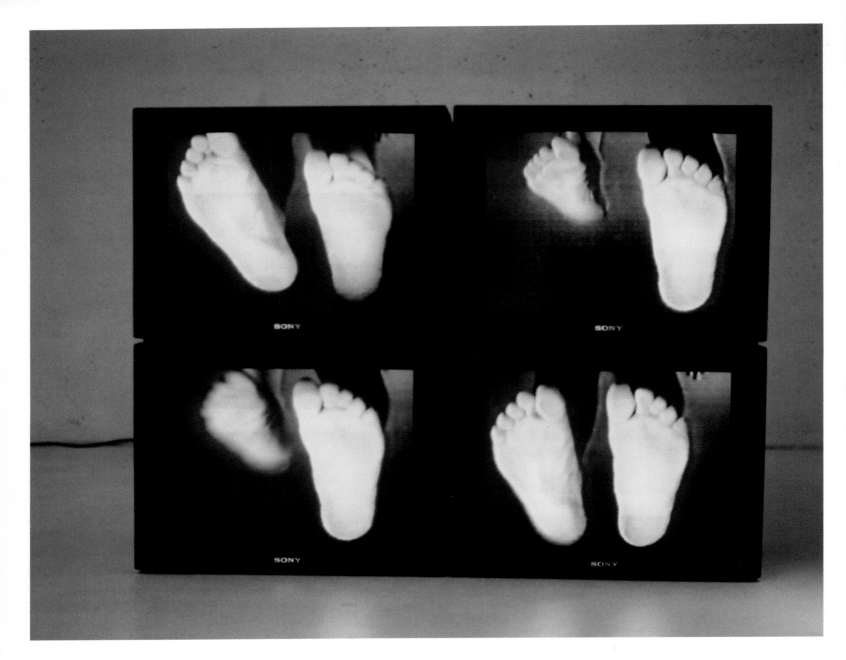

VALIE EXPORT

157 *Touching, Body Poem* (1970)

Video Art

well as to other male-dominated practices. 'All my works are self-portraits,' she says, including her first Performance, her name change. For EXPORT that work was the 'perfect expression of my desire to export my inner ideas outside into the world.'

EXPORT relates the development of her early work to the International Style of art she encountered in the mid-1960s in an exhibition in Sweden, where she saw John Cage, Fluxus artist Dick Higgins, filmmakers Michael Snow and Hollis Frampton. While it may seem curious that she mentions only male artists, there was a paucity of female models at the time. She – along with a loose international consortium, including Carolee Schneemann, Adrian Piper, and Yoko Ono (United States), Ulrike Rosenbach (Germany), Friederike Pezold (Austria), and Lygia Clark (Brazil) – became the model for future generations, including many currently heralded artists such as Janine Antoni, Pipilotti Rist, Mona Hatoum, and Gillian Wearing.

What is striking about EXPORT, in addition to her longevity in what has been an often hostile art environment, is her extraordinary diversity. Though feminism was her springboard, her artistic investigations reveal her knowledge of psychoanalysis, literature (especially Gertrude Stein, Virginia Woolf, Samuel Beckett), and the history of art, expressed in a large collection of work in many media. Both her early photographic work predicted – and later video installations explored – her keen interest in conceptual relationships between city architecture and the body. With the eye of a Berenice Abbot, she photographed trains, street corners, edges of buildings, her own body on the ledge of a staircase or curved around the corner of a street, as if to assert the female self in an anonymous urban environment. Echoing the body sculptures of Robert Morris and others from the early 1960s, EXPORT takes the vocabulary of Minimalism and makes it resonate with personal as well as social meaning.

EXPORT committed herself to unmasking the politics of the female body in what can rightly be called Feminist Actions. In a 1972 manifesto she wrote:

> The history of woman is the history of man, for man has determined the image of woman for men and women. The social and communicative media such as science and art, word and image, clothing and architecture, social intercourse and division of labor are created and controlled by men. The men have imposed their image of woman upon the media, they have shaped women according to these media patterns and women have shaped themselves the same way. If reality is a social construct and men are its engineers we are faced with a male reality.
>
> This is why I demand, give the floor to women, so they can find themselves. In order to arrive at an image of woman determined by ourselves and thus a different depiction in the social function of women, we women must participate in the construction of reality through the media.
>
> This will not be allowed to happen without resistance, therefore fighting will be necessary! If we women want to achieve our goals: social equality, self-determination, a new consciousness of women, we will have to express them in all areas of life. This struggle will have far-reaching consequences not only for ourselves, but also for men, children, the family, the churches; in a word, for the state, and will affect all aspects of life.
>
> Woman must therefore avail herself of all media as a means of social struggle and social progress in order to free culture from male values. She will do this also in

art. If men have succeeded for millennia in expressing their ideas of eroticism, sex, beauty, their mythology of power, strength and severity in sculptures, paintings, novels, films, plays, drawings, etc., thus influencing our consciousness, it is high time that we women use art as a means of expression to influence everybody's consciousness, to allow our ideas to enter the social construct of reality, in order to create a human reality. The question of what women can give to art and what art can give to women can be answered like this: transferring the specific situation of woman into the artistic context establishes signs and signals that are new artistic forms of expression that serve to change the historical understanding of women as well.[12]

If issues of identity are recognizable in all her early Performance work, EXPORT's film and video installations illustrate how she injected this concern into formal explorations of the mechanisms of cinema. Her 'expanded cinema' projects, most notably *Splitscreen: Solipsismus*, **a ninety-second, 8-millimeter film from 1968, played with viewers' perceptions in a manner shared by, amongst others, Michael Snow – in films like** *Right Reader* **(1965) and** *Wavelength* **(1967). She started using video in 1968, creating early on what she called 'Videoinstallations' that often required viewer participation. In** *Split Reality* **(1970), her image appears on a TV monitor above an LP record player. The viewer is invited to play the record as EXPORT, wearing head-phones, sings along to the record. But the sound of the spinning record is turned off so all that is heard is EXPORT singing a cappella, thus 'splitting' the reality for the viewer.** *Touching, Body Poem* **(1970) is a classic piece of Conceptual video. On four monitors stacked 2 × 2 in a grid are images of feet walking, shot from below so the**

VALIE EXPORT
159 *Body Tape* (1970)

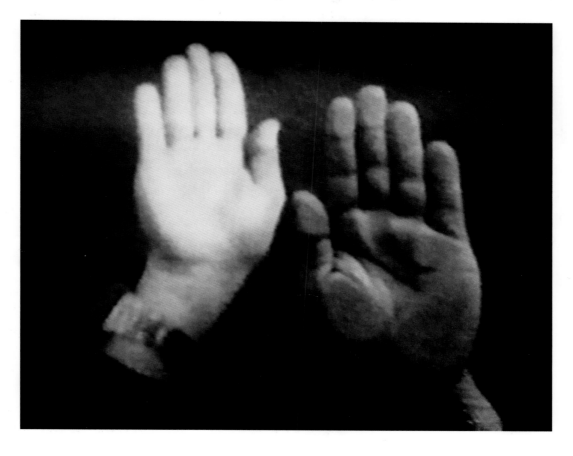

viewer sees the bottom of the feet. In a similar Conceptual vein is *Body Tape* (1970), in which EXPORT engages in various gestures, including touching, boxing, tasting, and pushing. At the same time Vito Acconci was carrying out similar work in the United States, but with a much more ironic subtext.

EXPORT's *Autohypnosis* (1969/1973) is, by any measure, an elaborate interactive video installation that anticipated the interactive installations of the late 1980s and after. Four monitors, arranged in a circle, are electronically preset to play a tape of people applauding loudly. Visitors were invited to step on a diamond-shaped 'map' imprinted with words like 'self,' 'possession,' 'development,' 'love,' etc. Only by stepping in a prescribed manner can the visitor activate the sensors that trigger the monitors to play the enthusiastic applause. In other words, by conforming to a certain norm, people are rewarded.

EXPORT has continued to create elaborate video installations, from the *I (Beat [It])* (1980), in which a photo of the artist, naked with shackles on her arms and legs, floats in a shallow pool of black oil as three German Shepherd dogs bark on different video monitors, to her 1998 *The Un-ending –ique Melody of Chords*, a 25-monitor installation, each containing a pounding sewing machine turned on its side. In both cases women are tied (literally) to the orders of others.

Along with a handful of other women artists, EXPORT has brought a new, intensely female perspective to contemporary art, thus fulfilling the promise of her 1972 manifesto: 'So far art has been largely produced by men, and it has usually been men who dealt with the subjects of life, the problems of emotional life, and contributed only their statements, their answers, their solutions. Now we must articulate our statements and create new concepts that correspond to our sensitivity and our wishes.'

Though a few years behind the United States and Germany in the development of Video art, Austria had, by 1970, witnessed the growth of a substantial video community supported by galleries and alternative presentation venues. The 'Multi Media 1' exhibition was held in 1969 at the Galerie Junge Generation in Vienna, and several other galleries, including the Modern Art Gallery, the Vienna Galerie nächst St Stephan, the Kringinger Gallery and the Taxis Palais Gallery regularly presented Performance and Video art.[13]

Other important Austrian video artists, in addition to EXPORT, are Peter Weibel (b. 1945), with whom EXPORT collaborated for some years in performances and media works, Gottfried Bechtold, Ernst Caramelle, Richard Kriesche and the noted painter Arnulf Rainer (b. 1929), who made several Conceptual body tapes in the 1970s, including *Face Farces* (1973), *Confrontation with My Video Image* (1974), *Slow Motion* (1974), and *Mouth Pieces* (1974). Weibel's work has extended over four decades. Based in Performance, his early video works were called *Teleaktionen* (Teleactions), referring to the Actionists mixed with the then new video technology.

Video and Performance: An Enduring Practice

Performative video continues to this day as a vital component of Video art, in part because artists, many of whom have been trained in art schools in the 1980s and 1990s, echo work from the 1970s. One artist who bridges Viennese Video art of the 1960s and 1970s and current practices is Paul McCarthy (b. 1945, United States).

Mike Kelley and Paul McCarthy

OPPOSITE

162–67 Combining Performance art
and Grand Guignol, Paul McCarthy
and Mike Kelley offer an alternative
to the popular, bucolic children's story.
In their version, *Heidi*, from 1992,
Heidi and other characters act out
a scenario of abuse and control that
unveils the radical dysfunction that
can underlie seemingly normal family
relationships.

Paul McCarthy

Perhaps the best introduction to the work of this iconoclastic artist is his 1992 video collaboration with American artist Mike Kelley, a retelling of the story of the beloved Swiss maiden Heidi. Never one to leave an icon unsullied, McCarthy places her in the care of an abusive, anal-fixated grandfather who engages the girl in unnatural rituals. Entitled *Heidi, Midlife Crisis Trauma Center and Negative Media-Engram Abreaction Release*, the video is a prime example of McCarthy's career-long fixation with the underbelly of popular culture. In videos, media installations, sculptures, drawings and writings the artist has persistently debunked the false idealism he regards as rampant in Hollywood films, advertising, and folklore.

In performances and videos dating back to the early 1970s McCarthy has subjected his body (and his viewers' eyes) to acts of simulated self-mutilation, defecation, dismemberment, vomiting, suffocation, to name but a few actions. With names like *Meatcake*, *Hot Dog*, and *Heinz Ketchup Sauce*, his early performances featured the artist semi-dressed or naked ingesting excessive amounts of hamburger meat, hot dogs and condiments, the 'packaged goods' with which America is identified. In his hands mayonnaise, ketchup and mustard became body fluids indelicately splattered all over himself and the surrounding Performance area.

From this description alone, McCarthy's work would seem to have much in common with the Viennese Actionists, who, as discussed above, were known for politically and sexually brazen performances and films created in reaction to Nazism. They wanted their art to be sensational, not only in response to social repression, but also as an antidote to the high modernism embraced by museums. It would seem that McCarthy's work echoes a 1963 statement from Otto Muehl: 'I can imagine nothing significant where nothing is sacrificed, destroyed, dismembered, burnt, pierced, tormented, harassed, tortured, massacred, stabbed, destroyed, or annihilated.' Though McCarthy read about the Actionists in the late 1960s and does admit to being influenced by them, he separates himself from their bloody displays in one very important respect. 'My work isn't about the blood,' he says. 'It really is about the ketchup.'

Firmly based in the traditions of 1960s Performance art (he studied with ur-Performance artist Allan Kaprow in the early 1970s) and in the climate of Hollywood (he has lived in Los Angeles most of his adult life), McCarthy uses media and Performance as platforms for artistic ruminations on the excesses of American culture. In *Pig Man*, a Performance piece from 1980, he dons a pig mask, splatters himself with ketchup and, in a simulation of grotesque self-mutilation, slices a long hot dog placed between his legs. It is all too tempting to dwell on the gross manifestations in McCarthy's work, partly because they can be so sensational as to be hilarious (intentionally). However, underneath the muck lurks the soul of a serious and impassioned artist keenly aware of the sources of his work, from experimental film (Stan Brakhage, Bruce Connor, Andy Warhol) to post-Fluxus Performance art (Allan Kaprow) and Minimalism (Donald Judd).

'In 1966 I jumped out of a window as a homage to Yves Klein,' McCarthy says, recalling his first Performance and Klein's famous photograph of himself jumping off a roof. 'It was a pathetic jump,' he says of his own feeble attempt to re-enact a photo, which he never actually saw, but only heard about. There is something symbolic in

Video Art

the fact that Klein's photo was a fake. The impresario had rephotographed collaged images of himself from other photos. In a sense, McCarthy has been reacting to the fakery of filmed images (especially of the Hollywood kind) ever since.

He was introduced to video technology while doing community service work in San Francisco before he moved to Los Angeles. Like other video artists of his generation, he became involved in community television while living in the Haight Ashbury district of San Francisco. He taught courses there in video making to community groups and started a public access television station. He also worked in a mental hospital, where he would videotape patient groups as part of a therapy process.

Since the early 1970s, McCarthy has used his own body as a place for social criticism, mutilating it, caressing it, humiliating it, exalting it, all in an atmosphere of humorous, if grotesque, mockery. As his work has proceeded from one-man shows with wigs, masks, and props to full-scale video installations like *Cultural Gothic* (1992), *Yaa Hoo Town, Saloon* (1996), and *Santa Chocolate Shop* (1997), both his materials (video, film, massive architectural constructions) and his subjects (household goods, family relationships, the unconscious) have expanded to suit his broad artistic ambitions.

It is the tension between the real world of pop culture and the intra-art world of artistic movements that has made McCarthy's work so appealing to younger artists and, at least lately, to critics and curators. For many years, until two important exhibitions organized by Paul Schimmel for the Los Angeles Museum of Contemporary Art – the 1992 'Helter Skelter: L.A. Art in the 1990s' and the 1998 'Out of Actions: Between Performance and the Object, 1949–1979' – McCarthy's work was little known outside Los Angeles in the United States. According to the American curator and Director of the New Museum of Contemporary Art in New York, Lisa Phillips, McCarthy, and other American artists, such as John Baldessari, Joseph Kosuth, Dan Graham and Bruce Nauman, were heralded in Europe decades before Americans were aware of them.

European Performance-Based Video Artists

Performative video, especially amongst female artists, has been prominent in Europe since the late 1960s. Belgrade-born artist Marina Abramovic (b. 1946) worked for years in media and Performance with her partner Ulay and to this day creates compelling video installations that combine her dual interests in Performance and politics. *Balkan Baroque* (1997) is a three-screen installation about the turbulence in late 20th-century Central Europe. In this moving scenario Abramovic films her parents as representative of the elderly population who have suffered so much during protracted wars in Yugoslavia and herself as both an academic lecturer and a frantic sensual dancer.

Other prominent European Performance-based video artists include: British artist Gillian Wearing (b. 1963), best known for her installations – *I'd Like to Teach the World to Sing* (1996) and *Drunk* (1997–99) – and

Marina Abramovic and Ulay
BELOW
169 As the body became a material in the making of art, endurance tests demonstrated how far artists were willing to go to proclaim the body as the focus of artistic struggle. For Marina Abramovic and Ulay, body and concept reached furious heights in *Performance Anthology (1975–80)* (1975–80) as the artists shouted and slapped each other while enacting the battle between the sexes with expressive gestures.

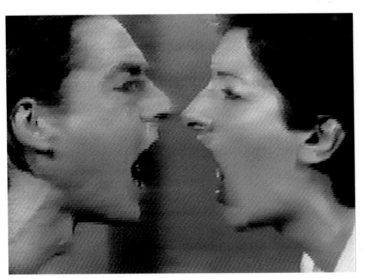

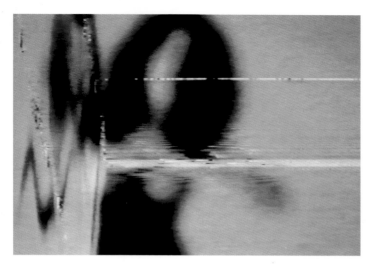

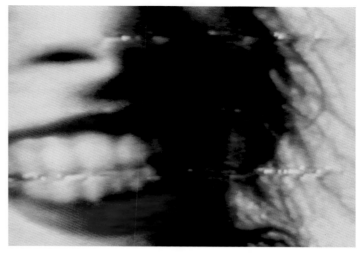

Pipilotti Rist
171–74 Like some of her female contemporaries, Rist is a clear descendant of pioneers such as Joan Jonas, VALIE EXPORT, and Marina Abramovic. *I'm Not the Girl Who Misses Much* (1986) is a speeded-up homage to Abramovic's *Freeing the Body* (1975), in which the artist danced to a drumbeat so furiously that she eventually collapsed. Rist, with her hair maniacally frizzed and wearing a dress that barely covers her, dances and sings the words of a John Lennon tune. As she moves faster and faster, helped by editing technology, she looks like a wind-up doll who has lost all sense of control as she tries to 'please' her audience.

Gillian Wearing
170 *Homage to the Woman with the Bandaged Face* (1995)

her early performative work like *Dancing in Peckham* (1994); Susan Hiller (b. 1940, United States), who has lived and worked in London for many years, and is also known for her installations, such as *Wild Talents* (1997) and *Psi Girls* (1999); and Swiss artist Pipilotti Rist (b. 1962).

Rist, also a rock singer and leader of her own band, Les Reines Prochaines (The Next Queens), is often the leading performer in her video works, such as *I'm Not the Girl Who Misses Much* (1986), in which she gyrates in front of the camera while screeching the refrain from John Lennon's 'Happiness Is a Warm Gun.' This sometime pop-star in Europe is no stranger to audience adulation, but here she seems to resist it, wanting instead to expose the abuse women can suffer trying to satisfy the male gaze.

Her *Ever Is Over All* (1997), a title that suggests some kind of a Beckett endgame, is a game all right, but not to the death. It is a life-affirming, breezy feminist tract on the girl taking the city by storm, shattering (literally) the quiet passivity of an obsessively clean street in Zurich, where Rist lives. In this richly colored two-projector

Pipilotti Rist
RIGHT AND OPPOSITE
175–76 *Ever Is Over All* (1997)

installation, Rist juxtaposes the narrative of a smartly dressed young woman walking down the street holding a peculiar looking flower-tipped stick on one screen with fluidly filmed shots of a country garden on the other. The two videos, blending into one another across the corner of two walls, are only four minutes long, but Rist puts them on a continuously running loop that suggests a seamless repetition of her compelling (and funny) central image: the woman, in her blue chiffon dress and red shoes, suddenly wielding that strange looking flower, now revealed to be a metal club, and smashing car windows as she skips (in slow motion) down the street with a delighted grin on her face. A policeman is seen coming toward her from a distance, but as he approaches, it turns out that he is a she, and she walks on by, giving a 'go-girl!' smile to our protagonist, who continues her rampage. Sweet harmonies, written and sung by Rist herself, emanate from the soundtrack, pierced with the occasional loud bursts of the metal thrust on to the car windows.

Katarzyna Kozyra

LEFT
177 *Men's Bathhouse* (1999), which was awarded a prize at the Venice Biennale, features the artist, Katarzyna Kozyra (b. 1963, Poland), disguised as a man, complete with chest hair, beard and meticulously designed prosthetic genitalia, filming herself surreptitiously among the naked patrons of a Budapest bathhouse.

BELOW LEFT
178 In *Boys* (2002), Katarzyna Kozyra reverses the surveillance techniques she used in the *Men's Bathhouse* installations by openly filming young men dressed only in thongs prancing around the lobby of the neo-classical Zacheta Gallery (now the Museum of Contemporary Art) in Warsaw.

Katarzyna Kozyra

ABOVE
179 *Untitled (New Project)* (2002)

OVERLEAF
180 *Rite of Spring* (2001)

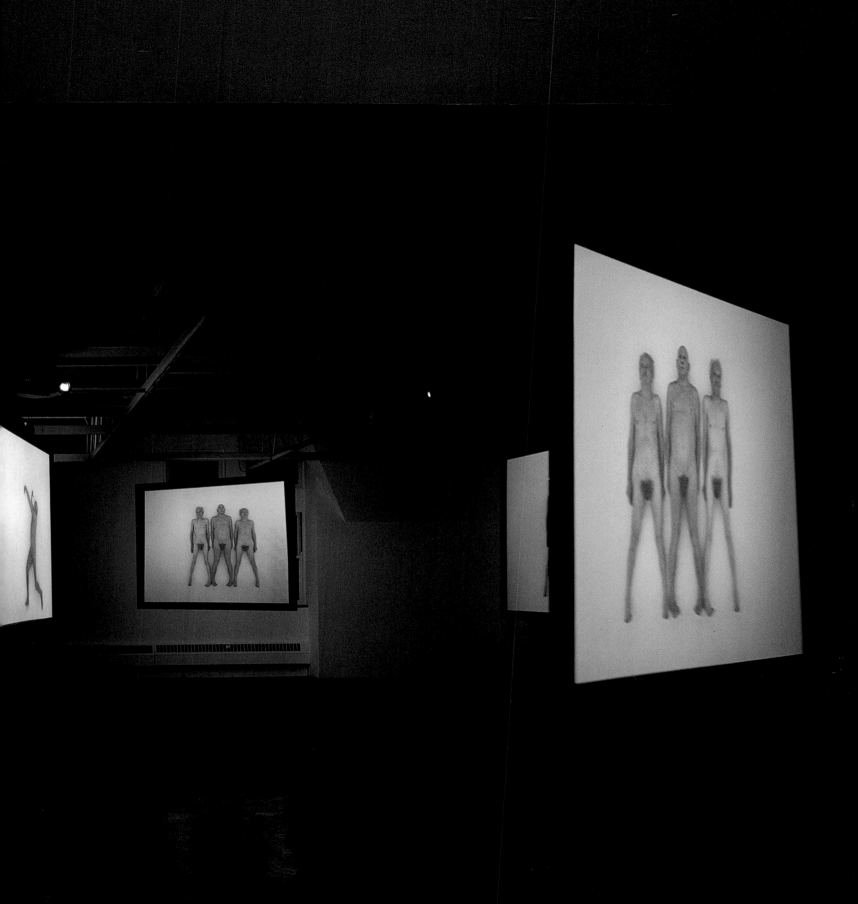

Hannah Wilke
181 *So Help Me Hannah* (1985)

Rist's strong sense of composition and sensitivity to color (blues, oranges, rich reds) are reminiscent of her fellow countryman, Jean-Luc Godard, whose affinity for painterly camera shots Rist clearly shares. Like a petty thief out of a Godard mock gangster movie, Rist's minor felon is undeniably appealing, but, unlike Godard's heroes, she's a woman. Rist possesses a subversive elegance; a well-controlled craftiness that is equally at home with humor as with biting political commentary.

Transgression is a time-honored practice in the history of art: Manet's *Olympia* (1863) and Duchamp's *Fountain* (1917), a urinal. In the history of Performance and media art, women artists especially have exercised a transgressive voice: Lynda Benglis photographing herself with a huge phallus between her legs for an *Artforum* advertisement in 1974; Carolee Schneemann pulling a scroll from her vagina in her 1975 performance, *Interior Scroll*.

Katarzyna Kozyra's work has been surrounded by controversy from the start. Her first public piece, *Pyramid of Animals* (1993), was a sculpture of four taxidermied animals (a horse, dog, cat, rooster) that had been killed for the project. In 1996 she exhibited photographs and a video portrait of herself posed like Manet's *Olympia*. Naked, bald and woefully thin, unlike Manet's voluptuous nude, and lying on a hospital gurney instead of a silk-sheeted bed, Kozyra is seen being treated with intravenous chemotherapy for Hodgkin's disease, which had been diagnosed in 1992. 'My illness was sucking me dry,' says the artist. 'I wasn't dying, but I wasn't getting better either. The most important part of the work was to record myself receiving my injection. This helped me create a distance from my illness.'

Katarzyna Kozyra likens herself to the woman in *Olympia* in other ways: she is defiant and aggressive. Her *Bathhouse* videos, though highly invasive, were intended not only to expose the differences in the behavior of men and women in vulnerable situations ('women take better care of themselves…men are constantly looking at each other') but also to make naked men the subject of the camera's gaze. 'Why not see what men are like without their protective layer…without all their status symbols, their designer suits, their cars?' she asks.

Phyllis Baldino
NEAR RIGHT
182 Phyllis Baldino creates wry, often poignant, installations that deal with everyday mishaps, failed communications, incongruities, and other failings of the human condition. Her off-beat sensibility is well expressed in *Color Without Color* (1999), which explores the condition of color blindness.

Marie André
FAR RIGHT
183 *Repetitions* (1985)

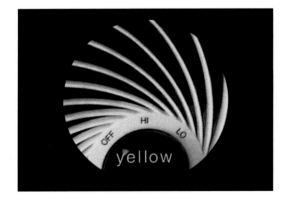

Hannah Wilke

184–88 This feminist critique, *Gestures* (1974), looks at first like a familiar television commercial for facial cream or other products. However, as Wilke's performance unfolds, her gestures become more violent as she attempts to erase her face in protest to the commercialization and abuse of the female body in the media.

Sam Taylor-Wood

OPPOSITE
193–94 *Third Party* (1999) is a film installation shot with seven cameras and shown using seven projectors on four walls. Visitors feel immersed in this moving portrait gallery of largely disaffected people at a London cocktail party. A loud soundtrack of fragmented voices and rock music accompanies this ten-minute loop. In one fragment rock singer turned actress Marianne Faithfull sits alone sipping beer and chain-smoking.

Other international women artists whose video work is clearly performative in nature include: Estonian artist Ene-Liis Semper (b. 1969) and South African artist Minette Vari (b. 1968), both of whose work echoes Viennese Actionists, as well as the filmed performances of Ana Mendieta; Chantal Michel (b. 1968, Switzerland); Tracey Rose (b. 1974, South Africa), whose *Ciao Bella* (2001) is an elaborately costumed feminist send-up of the Last Supper; and American artists Cheryl Donegan (b. 1962), Sadie Benning (b. 1973), and Phyllis Baldino (b. 1956).

Sam Taylor-Wood (b. 1967, Great Britain) has created several tapes in which alienation amongst the young, loneliness, and the battle between the sexes are recurring themes in installations such as *Travesty of a Mockery* (1995), *Atlantic* (1997) and *Sustaining the Crisis* (1997). In *Brontosaurus* (1995) a nude man dances alone to frantic jungle music. Taylor-Wood slows down the balletic movements and introduces an adagio by Samuel Barber that is expressive of the pleasure of the moment. A pink stuffed animal in the foreground highlights the privacy of this dance, even as the viewer (or voyeur) peers into the scene. Facial gestures, sometimes violent, are the focus of *Hysteria* (1997) and the silent *Mute* (2001).

Peter Sarkisian

RIGHT
192 Peter Sarkisian's kinetic video installations place Minimalist art and Performance art in a contemporary psychological context. *Hover* (1999) is a white cube that suddenly becomes illuminated with moving images of a naked mother and child. They appear to be embracing, then trying to escape the cube as their movements are speeded up through editing. Sarkisian takes the innocence of a mother/child encounter and transforms it into a disturbing comment on the speed of contemporary life and the passing of time.

Oladélé Bamgboyé
TOP LEFT AND LEFT
195–96 In this installation, *The Hair or the Man* (c. 1994), Bamgboyé (b. 1963, Nigeria, lives and works in London) questions fetishized notions of masculinity and strength associated with dreadlocks. He says of the piece, 'An ex-partner who knew me when I had the dreadlocks and without commented that her friends wondered whether she preferred the hair or the man. Nowadays the locks are a sign of fashion and their only signification of past struggles are that the wearer is able to claim some sort of ethnic right to don them. For me personally, the shedding of the locks happened during my first visit to my native Nigeria after a sixteen-year absence. I was twenty-eight, arrived as a Dada (dreadlocked man) with fading memories of my place of birth and inspiration.'

Oladélé Bamgboyé
ABOVE
197 *Blink* (2001)

Steve McQueen
198 *Bear* (1993)

However, it would be wrong to suggest that women have cornered the performative Video art market. Plenty of men are making their mark in this field as well.

British artist Steve McQueen (b. 1966), awarded the coveted Turner Prize (1999), has been represented in exhibitions worldwide – Documenta X, the Johannesburg Biennale, the Stedelijk Museum in Amsterdam, the Marian Goodman Gallery in New York, and the Museum of Modern Art in New York. His video installations (which are shot on both 16-millimeter film and video and usually projected on DVD) are presented as full floor-to-ceiling wall projections that give them a Cinemascope feeling, even though they are made economically.

A black artist, McQueen is repositioning the black male at the center of films that, to date, have always starred himself. In *Bear* (1993), two naked men are filmed in a boxing match that becomes an intimate *pas de deux*. *Deadpan* (1997) presents McQueen as the 'heroic' artist: he stands tall in his jeans and white T-shirt, booted feet planted firmly on the ground; eyes staring straight ahead, as the front wall of a cabin behind him separates from its structure, and comes crashing on top of him. His body remains erect as a glassless window opening spares him the crush of the cabin's weight. It is a fantastic image, repeated several times, from different angles. The tension is palpable, for if McQueen's figure were to move just slightly in any direction, the open window would not save him and he would be crushed. As it is, he remains unflinching, his stare inscrutable; perhaps a little sad, as if such a triumph were masking a deeper disturbance which he does not want to share with anyone.

Despite its brevity (it is only four minutes long), McQueen's film leaves the viewer reeling with associations. Is this self-assured man (McQueen) standing defiantly as 'Uncle Tom's Cabin' attempts to bury him? Has he literally captured a 'window of opportunity' and escaped the certain death his surroundings have pre-destined for him? The film, a remake of Buster Keaton's silent film, *Steamboat Bill Jr* (1928), is also an example of the widespread practice currently in use amongst young

Steve McQueen
RIGHT
199 *Deadpan* (1997)

artists of appropriating Hollywood movies as well as experimental films and videos from the 1960s and 1970s. They share this practice with other artists, such as Cindy Sherman, Sherrie Levine, and the Ur-appropriator, Andy Warhol.

McQueen and Isaac Julien (b. 1960, Britain) are interested in reshaping images of the black male. Void of all previous associations of the black man as victim (Rodney King) or as gun-toting super-hero (Shaft) or jock extraordinaire (Michael Jordan), McQueen's characters are powerful, living sculptures, enigmatic, erotic, and solitary.

Tony Oursler

There is no mistaking the video installations of American artist Tony Oursler. Part circus, part house of horrors, part evening news-type exposé, and part home movie, Oursler's videos, a unique blend of gothic humor and techno-wizardry, have made him a popular participant at new media art exhibitions internationally.

Of the 'big three' American video installation artists who came of age in the 1980s (Bill Viola, Gary Hill, and Tony Oursler), Oursler owes the least to books (whereas Viola is interested in eastern mystical writings and Hill in linguistic analysis). His sources are popular culture, especially television, and he is preoccupied by psychological isolation. His highly theatrical imagination favors stage sets, immobile puppets, sound scores of overlapping words, and filmed images of actors that he projects on to all sorts of objects in his own ontological theater, to borrow a phrase from American playwright Richard Foreman, the master of macabre word play. Oursler's intentions may be serious, but his sensibility is definitely comic, another trait distinguishing him from Viola and Hill. His early single-channel tapes expressed a youthful enthusiasm for simple objects (spoons, paper, crayons) that endures to the present. Without concealing his economical means, including low-tech videography, Oursler in these tapes created off-beat scenarios that often addressed the vicissitudes of relationships between the sexes or the hegemony of television in popular culture, such as in *The Loner* (1980), *Grand Mal* (1981), **and** *Spheres of Influence (Diamond)* (1985).

Oursler is best known for the array of projection surfaces he creates for his videos, especially his 'puppets,' for want of a better word, which are clothed stick figures with oval pillows for heads, on which Oursler projects the real talking head of

Tony Oursler

200 *EVOL* (1984) is representative of Oursler's fantastical theatrical videos that use decidedly low-tech and kitschy props, lighting and mechanistic acting. In this tape (EVOL is LOVE spelled backwards) a lonely young man, played by artist Mike Kelley, tries to understand why he cannot find, or be successful in, love. He sets up his own downfall in this dark, appealing comedy.

Video Art

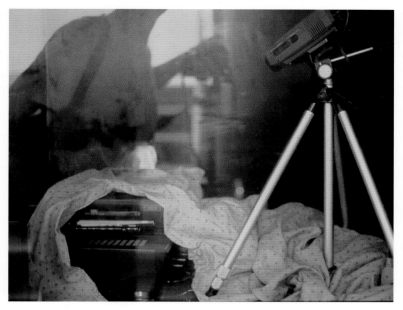

Tony Oursler

ABOVE

201–204 In *The Watching* (1992)
by Tony Oursler, a large hand-made
head is suspended from the ceiling,
spouting some banter that is hard to
decipher, but seems to have something to do with the movie industry's
preoccupation with sex and violence.

205 The pathetic little creature lying on top of a stack of pillows in *Insomnia* (1996) lies in a state of isolation. Cursed by sleeplessness, the stick figure in pajamas with a tiny pillow for a head murmurs in despair, 'Breath in, breathe out,' and 'You're dead and you don't know it.'

an actor (frequently the performer Tracy Leipold). Oursler often has his 'characters' spitting various forms of venom at viewers, particularly in *The Watching* (1992) and the large installation *Judy* (1994), whose many parts are carefully scattered on the floor. Judy, a hapless woman diagnosed with multiple personality disorder (psychologically linked with childhood sexual abuse), is found lying under a tilted couch mouthing 'Hey, fuck you,' or 'Go to hell' to anyone who passes by. Her clothes are lying on the floor or on the trailer-park furniture Oursler has assembled for her. Emanating from a stand of artificial flowers is a punishing voice, presumably Judy's mother, constantly commanding 'No! No! No!' or 'Do it!'

Oursler's video environments are stage sets that incorporate many elements associated with theater and Performance. Within them he places his motionless puppet creatures, like 'Judy,' which are handmade by him, and consigns them to lives of terror and isolation, such as the little figure in *Insomnia* (1996), who is unable to sleep. And there is the little man in *MMPI (Red)* of 1996, trapped under a fallen chair, who seems resigned to his fate as he mumbles, 'Time is irrelevant,' and 'I'm fascinated by children,' and the man whose detached head is submerged in a Plexiglas waterbox. He forever holds his breath, for such is the nature of the video loop: an endless cycle of repeated images, never varying hour after hour. Oursler has found the perfect medium for his humanoid pets. With the flick of a switch, they say only what he wants them to say, and they never contradict him. Beneath all the artifice, Oursler gives voice to the mortified, the lonely, the abandoned. In real life, characters like this walk the streets with their heads down, mumbling to themselves. In his installations they are the star of the show, and viewers feel for them, deeply.

Representative of artists for whom video is only one amongst many modes of expression is the Performance-based American artist Nayland Blake (b. 1960), who is also an accomplished painter, photographer, sculptor and installation artist. His video *Starting Over* (2000) has him in a puffy white bunny outfit trying to do a two-step. The soundtrack features the highly reverberated noise of his size thirteen tap shoes,

Nayland Blake
RIGHT
206 *Starting Over* (2000)

which can hardly be lifted from the floor because of the nearly 400 pounds (181 kilos) descending on them. In addition to Blake's own 270 pounds (123 kilos), his costume was fitted with 146 pounds (66 kilos) of navy beans, equal to the weight of his lover, who can be heard calling directions on the soundtrack. Each command is like a death sentence – he can barely stand up, much less do a bunny hop, in this humorous meditation on the impossibility of constantly meeting another's demands.

The quirky, inventive spirit of contemporary performative Video art reinforces the influence of pioneer artist-performers such as Jim Dine, Claes Oldenburg, Allan Kaprow, Carolee Schneemann, Robert Rauschenberg, the electronic engineer Billy Klüver, Georges Mathieu, and Joseph Beuys.[14] Video is the enduring link between dance, Performance art, visual art, media art and installation. The cross-fertilization between art and technology, in the performances of Cunningham, Rauschenberg, et al., set the groundwork for contemporary multimedia performance.

The video artist who has been at the center of dance-based media art is Charles Atlas (b. 1949, United States). Atlas worked with Merce Cunningham as protégé and collaborator for more than thirteen years (from 1970 to 1983), during which time they directed more than twenty videos together and invented what Atlas calls 'mediadance.' Neither pure dance nor pure video or film, mediadance is perhaps best understood by what it isn't: it is not documentation of a dance nor a film about dance. It is dance conceived for the filmed image, dependent as much on camera work and editing as it is on choreography. Cunningham explained her own way of approaching a new work to Atlas in the following way: 'Ask yourself, "What are the possibilities of this situation?" Go as far as possible. Work with all the possibilities.'

The best example of mediadance remains one of Atlas's first works with Cunningham, *Blue Studio: Five Segments* (1975–76), named for the blue screen used in film technology that disappears in the editing room so that the director can insert whatever background is desired. In the final cut Cunningham appears to float through a galaxy of colors and sculpted forms designed solely by technology.

Atlas has created scores of videos, films, performances, and set and lighting designs for opera, theater, and dance. Amongst the highlights of his work are collaborations in film and video with such artists as Bill Irwin, Marina Abramovic, Karole Armitage, Leigh Bowery, best known as a model for British painter Lucian Freud, and a collection of tapes made for the *Martha @ Mother* performances. They were organized by Martha Graham impersonator Richard Move at the former New York nightclub, Mother, in the 1990s.

Atlas's association with Belgrade-born artist Marina Abramovic has yielded to date a number of daring videos and performances, including *Delusional* (1994), produced in Belgium and Germany, which featured a glass-enclosed set within which Abramovic, wearing only a sheer plastic costume and black stiletto heels, at one point lets loose four hundred rats that were hidden under a rug. A meditation on death and decay in war-torn Bosnia, this theater piece followed the two artists' 1989 video, *SSS*, in which Abramovic wore a Medusa-style headdress made of real snakes.

Atlas explored the humorous edges of human endurance with Leigh Bowery in several tapes made before the performer's death in 1994. In one, Bowery, decked out in garish drag, à la John Waters's star Divine, pierced his cheeks with large safety pins, to which he attached fake red lips and then struggled to mouth the words to

Charles Atlas

207–210 It was with Leigh Bowery, Lucian Freud's former model and a Performance artist, who died in 1994, that Charles Atlas found a theatrical soul mate. With him he celebrated artifice and the joy of unbounded performance. In *Mrs Peanut Visits New York* (1999), Bowery, dressed up in a drag version of the Planter's brand 'Mr Peanut,' struts through New York's meatpacking district, home to a wild combination of macho truckers and meatpackers as well as drag queens and hustlers. Atlas and Bowery make the city a stage set for their outrageous insistence that we are all costumed to one degree or another.

Aretha Franklin's 'Take a Look.' Touching and discomforting, the tape celebrates artifice as Atlas leaves unedited his own guffaws and comments from behind the camera, while Bowery, a study in vulnerability, performs close to the lens. Amongst Atlas's many influences are Warhol's films, especially *The Chelsea Girls* (1966), Hollywood romances from the 1930s and 1940s, and mainstream television. His devotion to the poetry found in both dance and popular culture have been evident from a brief sketch with actors and a cat performed in a downtown loft, *Little Strange* (1972), to a 15-channel video installation that filled a castle, *The Hanged One* (1997).

The pervasive emphasis on Performance in contemporary video is undeniable. The 2001 Venice Biennale, heralded by some, deplored by others, as 'the Video Biennale,' contained a plethora of video installations, most of them performative in nature. From the cinematic battle of the sexes, *Flex* (2000) by Chris Cunningham (b. 1970, Great Britain), to the meditative *Snow White* (2000) by Berni Seale (b. 1964, South Africa), to *Wall Piece* (2000) by video pioneer Gary Hill, in which the artist repeatedly and forcefully threw himself against a wall, Performance was the primary material in the videos. Performative influences will only grow stronger as artists of our era continue to concentrate on ideas more than materials. Materials are in service to ideas, which, as the next chapter reveals, makes materials, even video, secondary concerns in the practice of art.

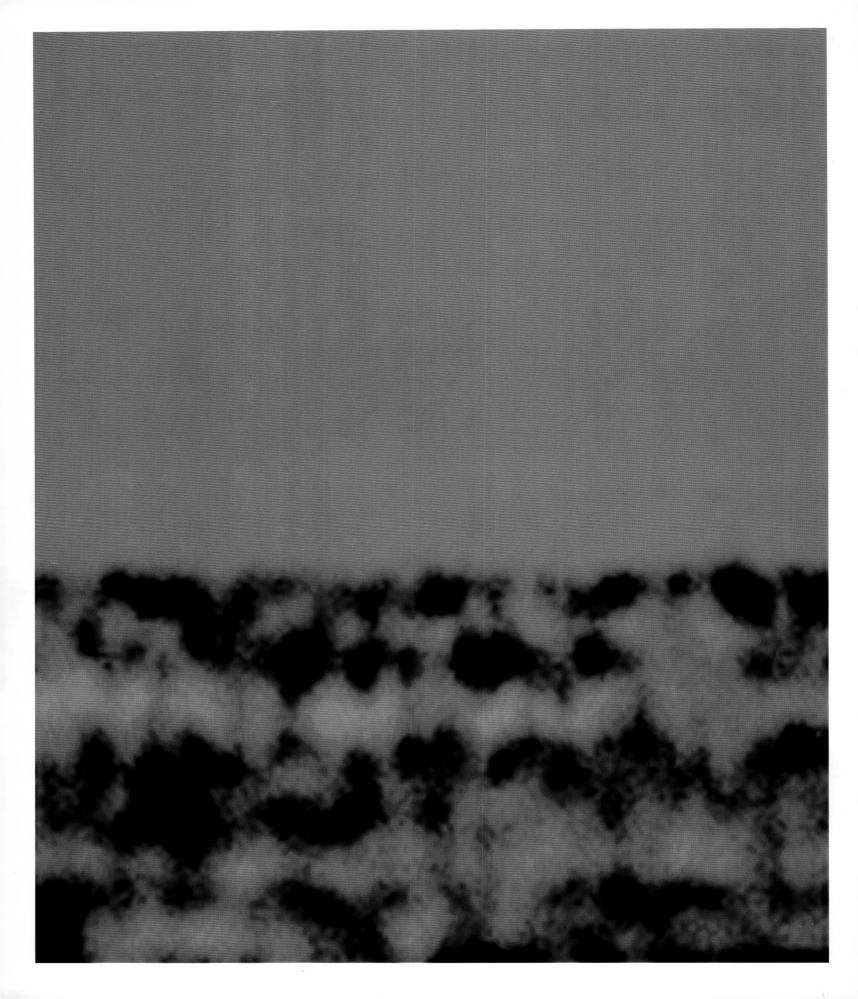

chapter 3

Video and the New Narrative

Michal Rovner
LEFT
211 *Overhanging* (1999)

New Narratives

Artists have always told stories, even in the studied markings of Impressionism or the indecipherable strokes of abstraction. Matisse encouraged young artists to discover what story it was that they, and they alone, could tell, and to tell it. Video artists are no exception, from the lyrical compositions of Bill Viola and Mary Lucier to the battle of the sexes in the work of Smith and Stewart and the political attacks in the videos of Zhang Peili, Yau Ching, and Wang Jianwei. Since its earliest days, video has been an intensely personal medium. Artists, attracted to its immediacy,

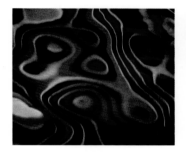   

Seoungho Cho
ABOVE LEFT
212 *Cold Pieces* (1999) by Seoungho Cho is a meditation on water, from drops to huge waves. Cho's palette becomes an abstract canvas on which one of the basic elements of nature performs for the viewer.

ABOVE CENTER LEFT
213 Seoungho Cho (b. 1959, Korea) creates painterly tapes that can resemble the workings of the unconscious mind. In *The Big Sleep* (1992), he tries to visualize in images the dream state in an attempt to control what is ordinarily uncontrollable.

Yau Ching
ABOVE CENTER RIGHT
214 *The Ideal Na(rra)tion* (1993)

ABOVE RIGHT
215 The day before Hong Kong reverted to Chinese rule, June 30, 1997, Ching filmed 'celebrations' for *June 30, 1997* (1997) around the city, which, for many, were veiled protests against the transfer of power.

could use the camera like a writer uses a pen (or a pencil, as John Baldessari said), with instant, visible results. From linear and non-linear narratives to futuristic fantasies, video stories have injected new life into the story of story-telling.

Twentieth-century audiences grew up with cinematic narratives mostly produced by Hollywood studios. Art viewers, a subsection of this larger audience, were nurtured on abstraction and the many other forms of perception-bending art practices of the century, including Minimalism and Conceptualism. Thus, when these art viewers were offered Video art, they did not necessarily expect the same type of narrative found in movies, though, at first, it was difficult for them to permit the moving image the same type of fluid palette as the still image on a canvas. Viewers of the avant-garde cinema of Stan Brakhage or Bruce Conner were certainly comfortable with abstraction, yet, despite the link between experimental film and video, the audiences did not necessarily overlap. The separation between 'art film' houses and galleries was, and remains, wide, though, as the final chapter shows, the story of the moving image has entered a radically new phase. Art film houses are rare now anyway. Video installations are to be found in galleries everywhere. However, digital technology is removing boundaries across the board and what was once considered experimental is finding its way on to large movie screens and what once appeared only in movie houses has been appropriated, reinterpreted, and channeled into video installations in galleries.

Gary Hill

BELOW LEFT AND RIGHT
216–17 Gary Hill has long explored
the relationships between the body
and language; languages and
personal psychologies. This video,
Incidence of Catastrophe (1987–88),
inspired by Maurice Blanchot's
novel *Thomas the Obscure* (1950),
equates the loss of innocence with
the entrance into literacy as Hill
records his daughter's early attempts
to speak.

OPPOSITE
218–23 In *Site/Recite (A Prologue)*
(1989) the camera weaves in and
out of various objects such as bones,
skulls, butterfly wings, comprising
what Hill calls 'little deaths that pile
up.' In the text accompanying the
images Hill speaks a long monologue,
part of which says: 'Nothing seems
to have ever been moved. There
is something of every description
which can only be a trap.... I
must become a warrior of self-
consciousness and move my body
to move my mind to move the words
to move my mouth to spin the spur
of the moment. Imagining the brain
closer than the eyes.'

Gary Hill

From the beginning Video art expanded the possibilities of narrative, especially personal and autobiographical stories. Though not a 'narrative' artist in the strict sense of the word, Gary Hill (b. 1951, United States) has struggled more than any other artist with the difficulties of constructing meaningful narratives, given the limitations language imposes on all of us. Since 1973, Hill has explored the elusive relationship between words and recorded images.

Hill found inspiration for his interests in language, poetry, identity, performance and sculpture in the vibrant artist community of Woodstock, New York, in the early 1970s. It was there that he had access to a Portapak camera. His first performance/media/sculpture was an action called *Hole in the Wall* (1973). He filmed himself blasting a hole in the wall the size of a television monitor at the Woodstock Artists' Association. In the newly carved orifice he placed a monitor which played a loop of the pre-taped action. In this piece, he laid out several issues that have preoccupied him ever since: time and the body as materials in art; the video image as language or text; the image as conduit for ideas.

In the late 1970s he became a journeyman artist-in-residence and instructor at various places in upstate New York, including the State University at Buffalo, which had a lively media program with Woody and Steina Vasulka and an experimental film community that included Hollis Frampton and Paul Sharits.

Trained as a sculptor, Hill transferred his interests in the materials of traditional sculpture to the electronic materials of video. In early works such as *Bathing* (1977), *Windows* (1978), and *Objects with Destinations* (1979), he manipulated everyday images such as bathers and windows into abstract landscapes. These works anticipated the digital alterations that are present everywhere in photography and video today. From 1987 to 1988 he made one of his most important videos, *Incidence of Catastrophe*, which was inspired by his own young daughter's attempts to form language and by Maurice Blanchot's novel *Thomas the Obscure*. At the end of the tape the naked, still body of a man lies before a wall of words. Here Hill succeeds in a seemless combination of poetry, theory, electronics, and sound.

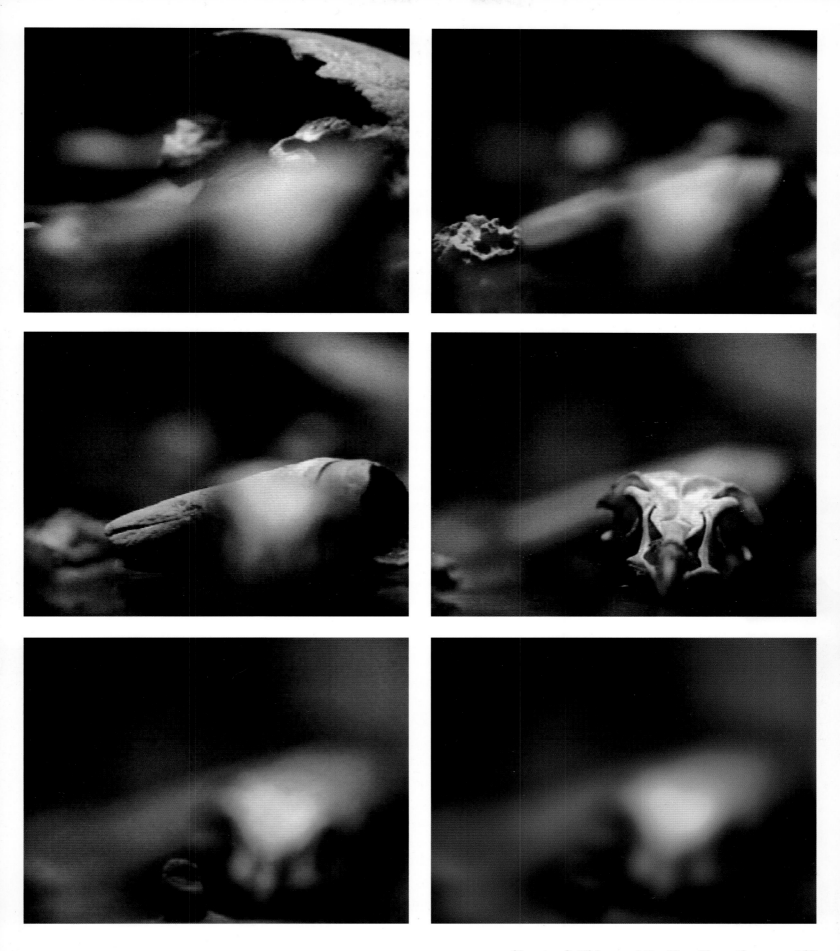

Hill's enduring interest has been to explore what he calls 'the never-ending process of attempting to communicate.' Such an enterprise might suggest a tentativeness or stuttering nature, but his video installations are remarkable for their formal beauty and fluidity as well as complexity. In *Why Do Things Get in a Muddle? (Come on Petunia)* of 1984, Alice in Wonderland jousts with her father about mismeanings or 'muddles' in dialogues rehearsed in reverse, then filmed backwards, resulting in a mind-boggling linguistic analysis.

By contrast, in the utterly silent, interactive work, *Tall Ships* (1992), viewers, walking into a darkened space, are confronted by ghostly images of everyday people coming towards them as in a dream. These specters do not speak but seem to want something that viewers cannot provide. Just as they approach, so do they recede into the darkness. Hill creates an ethereal video environment layered in multiple questions about the nature of daily encounters, the often unexpressed mutual needs of relationships, as well as the ersatz intimacy suggested by the filmed image. For Whitney curator Chrissie Iles this type of sophisticated techno-logical encounter is expressive of Hill's 'visceral art…based on the body and very sensual.'

Reminiscent of his 1992 installation *Cut Pipe*, which featured a tape of the artist running his hands over a speaker, *Language Willing* (2002) shows these same hands roaming over two strips of flowered wallpaper, one white, the other red, as Australian poet Chris Mann swiftly recites a barely intelligible poem about language, causality, and listening. Hill traces the origins of the piece to a memory of himself resting on a bed in a house in Lille, France, in the early 1990s. Next to his bed was some typical floral wallpaper. He started moving his hands over it in what for him became a very disturbing gesture. It has now evolved into a choreographed work with his hands 'interpreting' in movement the oral flow of the poet's words.

In the installation *Reflex Chamber* (1999), images are projected in a quiet staccato manner from the ceiling on to a tabletop. The viewer looks down at the camera moving ever closer to a gated window of what may be an abandoned house in the woods. Domestic objects (a bicycle, twin beds) come into view as a voice is heard mumbling fragmented phrases: 'I am going;' 'I am watching myself go.' Here the power of metaphor, achieved through image, sound, and clear concept strongly encourages the reflection that Hill seeks from his viewers.

Hill unearths the eerie in the everyday in *Still Life* (1999), a multi-screen *tour de force* that keeps the viewer's gaze shifting from large screens to small monitors. Computer-generated images (akin to the artist's 'liminal objects,' or other-worldly sculptures) of household goods (beds, tables, vacuum cleaners, televisions, a child's swing set) seem to sprout up in a dull, gray virtual space like weeds in a post-Armageddon garden. Hill records these images slowly from a serenely detached distance, thus heightening the terror of proliferating consumer goods stripped of their purpose. Seamlessly does this graveyard of machines and furniture appear and disappear within the installation space. Shadows are cast on to the large screens by viewers moving through the space, adding an ominous interactivity to the proceedings.

Accordions was filmed in an Algerian Arab neighborhood in July 2001. Consisting of five monitors showing 'portraits' of the locals filmed at a distance 'so the image doesn't quite arrive,' Hill acknowledges that this installation will have 'the unintended burden of 9/11.' Up until now his work has never been overtly political, but in this work it is, as cultures, languages, religious systems, television images and whatever else collide to radically alter the experience of this installation for a New York audience. Try as he does to understand and control them, the forces of language are forever subject to change.

Bill Viola

Personal narratives are represented in depth by Bill Viola whose substantial body of work from the 1970s to the present day represents a chronicle of personal and spiritual development. Unlike the influential diary-like films and videos of such artists as Jonas Mekas and George Kuchar (b. 1942, United States), Viola has chosen a narrative lyricism that resembles meditation more than personal picture albums.

Viola (b. 1951, United States) was attracted to art and technology from his earliest days as a student at Syracuse University in New York, where he helped found the Synapse Video Croup. His first videotape, *Wild Horses*, was made in 1972. He told an interviewer in 1997:

Something that has been apart of me as long as I can remember [is] the excitement of the new technique. I grew up in a postwar generation. A big influence on me was the World's Fair in New York in 1964–65, which was about as close to industrial Utopia as you can get. For me it was essentially a bunch of dark rooms with images projected in them, a whole series of installations, but cast in 'technology is good, the future is positive' kind of mode.[1]

Bill Viola

224 Bill Viola's unrelenting quest for understanding his own soul (or consciousness) as well as that of all humans has taken him and his camera to many parts of the world. In *I Do Not Know What It Is I Am Like* (1986), he uses a Sanskrit text as the basis to explore essential issues of life and death, birth and faith. In this stunning image he records his own reflection in the eye of an owl.

Viola's earliest tapes challenged the notion that technology is necessarily good, but he did so through exploration of the self, an enduring preoccupation in his work to the present day. In *Tape 1* (1972), a monitor contains the live image of a running camera facing a mirror, viewing its own image as it were. A man (Viola himself) enters the room, sits down, faces the camera and begins to stare, then starts to scream before turning the camera off. This Performance activity was characteristic of much of his early work, including *Playing Soul Music to my Freckles* (1975), in which he

performed for the camera with a loudspeaker superimposed on his back, and *A Non-Dairy Creamer* (1975). In this tape, his own image, captured in a coffee cup, gradually disappears as he drinks the coffee.

Viola's interests in video as a personal medium have been intertwined with his spiritual quests, at least since the mid-1970s when he began traveling, first to the Solomon Islands in the South Pacific, then Japan, Java, and Bali. While on a fellowship to Japan in 1980, he met Zen Master Daien Tanaka, who has remained a teacher for him. The search for unity, common to all mystical traditions, has found expression in Viola's earliest work, when he himself began uniting his interests in music, sound, and image within the framework

Bill Viola
LEFT
225 *Tape I* (1972)

Bill Viola
BELOW
226–34 *I Do Not Know What It Is I Am Like* (1986)

OVERLEAF
235 *The Stopping Mind* (1991)

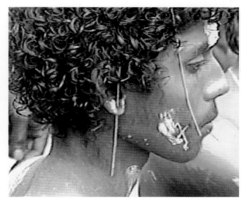
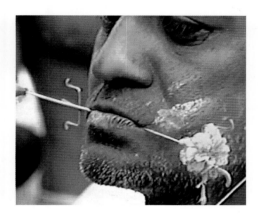

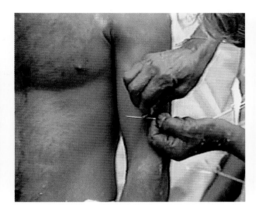

of video. In two tapes dating from 1975, *A Million Other Things (2)* and *Return*, light, sound, music, and a natural setting with trees, flowers, and water become the ingredients for meditations on time and memory, other themes that remain pervasive in his work.

Viola has found video the perfect medium for his personal explorations of time, memory, and the human spirit. It is in Video art, unlike any traditional form, that time can be manipulated, literally slowed down, sped up, erased, thus eliminating the boundaries of past, present, and future. For Viola, who grapples with nothing less than the basic elements of eastern and western spirituality (mystical solitude, egoless unity with nature, the life cycle), the technology of video is a means to an end, not an end in itself. Viola seeks a painterly sobriety in his work that is more akin to Romanticism than to electronic art.

For more than twenty years he has presented his work in the form of large-scale, full-wall installations as well as installations with objects. His *Chott el-Djerid (A Portrait in Light and Heat)* of 1979, filmed in a dry salt lake in the Tunisian desert, is an almost hallucinatory portrait of time passing, complete with mirages and ghostly figures that may, or may not, be passing before the viewer's eyes. In *Reasons for Knocking at an Empty House* (1983), a dark room contains a videotape of a man staring into the camera and a stark wooden chair that resembles an execution seat. On the monitor the man is struck on the head intermittently by another man who approaches him from the back. In *The Stopping Mind* (1991), a barely audible voice murmuring sentences about the body and loss of sensation emerges from four screens suspended from the ceiling. Beautifully colorful shots of red flowers in a large field seem to belie the narrators' words until these very images explode into images of violence.

In the monumental installations, *The Passing* (1991), *The Messenger* (1996), and *The Crossing* (1996), Viola maximizes video's potential to produce emotion-filled images of exquisite beauty and impact in a matter of minutes, while also managing to summarize his explorations of mystical waters. Taken as a trio, these works encompass a single man's struggle with earth, water, and fire as well as birth, death, and memory.

In another installation, *The Sleepers* (1992), seven metal barrels, filled with water, contain submerged monitors showing pictures of sleeping men, women, and children. There is an eerie serenity in these surveillance shots, with the subjects straddling that peculiar moment between life and death that sleep suggests.

Light, so intimate a companion for painters, photographers, filmmakers, and mystics alike, has clearly worked its magic on Viola. Especially in his darkened installation rooms, where images of babies sucking can collide with those of old women dying, it is light that links the passages in and out of life. Light and darkness compete in *Tiny Deaths* (1993). Human forms, barely silhouetted on the screen like huge negatives, take shape briefly and then, burning with light, disappear, never fully realized, into the dark. So, too, with mystical union, and the not so lofty existence that most people live: we catch glimpses of each other; perhaps we touch for a moment, and then we pass on into an unknown infinity that Viola attempts to materialize before our eyes.

To this day, Viola's work continues his life-long exploration of human consciousness and spirituality. *Memoria* (2000) is a single-channel projection on a silk cloth

Bill Viola
BELOW
236 Made after the death of a parent, this black-and-white tape, *The Passing* (1991), is a meditation on Viola's enduring investigations of memory, consciousness, life and death.

Video Art

Bill Viola

237 Reasons for Knocking at an Empty House (1983)

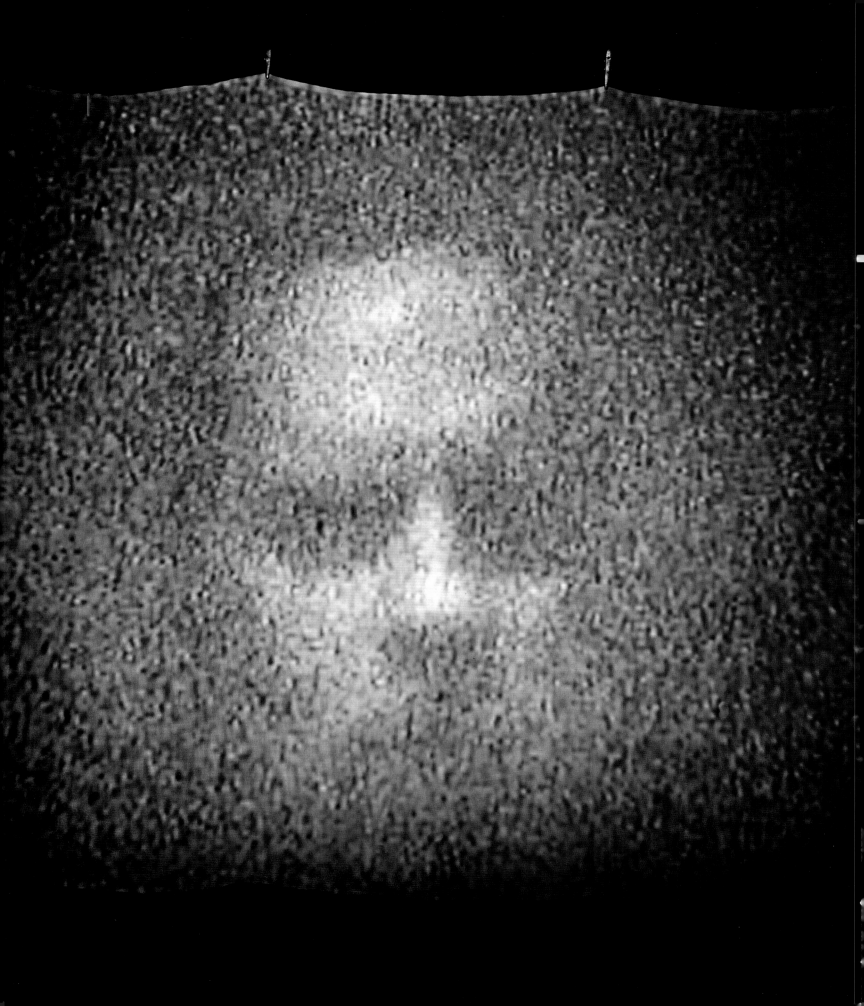

suspended from the ceiling. Filmed with an old black-and-white surveillance camera in very low light, the pained face of a man appears, then recedes from, the surface of the cloth, which now looks as delicate as a shroud. The face advances as if from the great beyond, the man struggling to communicate something of dire urgency to the viewer. However, just as his features can be made out, his image disappears again into a void, in an echo of Samuel Beckett's work. Using the silk as a projection surface, Viola grants video technology the same grainy timelessness achieved in such classic 16-millimeter films as those by Ronald Nemeth from the mid-1960s.

Ascension (2000) is a full-wall projection of a man fully clothed jumping feet first into some murky water. In slow motion his body, with arms extended like Christ's on the Cross, sinks, then rises almost to the top. Never able to breathe, the man sinks back down out of the camera's view. Viola's underwater camera deftly records the action as sparkling sunlight from above penetrates the water with a blue glow. As in *The Crossing* and *The Messenger*, Viola here combines greatly amplified sound and lushly filmed images to offer a brief narrative of an Everyman placed in an extreme situation, his body a reminder of the transient state of all our bodies.

In the mid-1990s Viola began attempting to bring to life medieval and early Renaissance paintings via Video art. Displayed as single projections, diptychs, or triptychs and often presented on flat LCD panels, each of these works is characterized by extremely slowed down movements of men and women in modern dress portraying 'characters' from the earlier paintings. Eyelids can take several minutes to close, as do arms rising up in supplication or extending in an embrace. One of these, *The Greeting* (1995), inspired by Pontormo's *Visitation* (1528–29), became the first work of Video art to enter the collection of the Metropolitan Museum of Art in New York when it was purchased in 2001.

For Viola the camera lens and the pupil of the eye offer means of self-reflection. In 1990 he wrote: 'Looking closely into the eye, the first thing to be seen, indeed the only thing to be seen, is one's own self-image. This leads to the awareness of two curious properties of pupil gazing. The first is the condition of infinite reflection, the first visual feedback.... The second is the physical fact that the closer I get to have a better view into the eye, the larger my own image becomes, thus blocking my view within.'[2] For video artist Bill Viola, the narratives he creates, the camera he uses, the meanings he probes form a continuous loop of investigations into the human spirit and the mysteries of creation.

Exploring Personal and Cultural Identity

German artist Marcel Odenbach (b. 1953) shares Viola's need to probe personal identity in his video work. His interests also extend to problems of vision and perception, using the camera as a metaphor for the human eye on the lookout for clues to self-understanding. His video *Die Distanz zwischen mir und meinen Verlusten* (**The Distance Between Myself and My Losses**) (1983) is an enigmatic video collage of appropriated images suggesting loss, especially lost innocence. Odenbach employs bands of black tape to mask the viewing image, a device that distances viewers from the footage, while at the same time making them appear to be gazing into private, forbidden territory. Historical references to bourgeois German culture, notions of sexual identity, and political involvement are considered briefly.

Willie Doherty

LEFT AND BELOW LEFT

240–41 Willie Doherty, born in Derry, Northern Ireland, in 1959, uses video to portray the darkness of war. Dimly lit streets, burnt-out cars and rubble populate his videos. *Somewhere Else* (1998), adopting the look of a documentary, investigates how the media is able to manipulate our perceptions of people and their conflicts. In his signature style, the beautiful landscapes we associate with Ireland bear the signs of war; the water of the ocean lapping on the sand reminds us of blood. As in most of his work, he uses multiple-screen projections to heighten the visual experience of the despair he depicts.

RIGHT AND BELOW RIGHT

242–43 *The Only Good One is a Dead One* (1993)

Philip Mallory Jones
ABOVE

Philip Mallory Jones
ABOVE
244 *Wassa* (1989) expresses Philip Mallory Jones's attempts to integrate his own experience as an African-American male in the United States with that of Africans in their own country. This tape was shot in Burkina-Faso, West Africa, and features the music of Houstapha Thiohbiano. Neither purely documentary nor music video, as we know it, *Wassa* is an experimental narrative that the artist calls a 'narrative structure based on emotional progressions.'

Philip Mallory Jones
BELOW LEFT
245 *First World Order* (1994)

Eder Santos
BELOW RIGHT
246 The videos of Eder Santos (b. 1960, Brazil) explore the African, Indian, and European roots of Brazil's people. In such technologically savvy works as *Nao Vou Africa Porque Tenho* (I Cannot Go To Africa Because I Am On Duty) (1990) and such poetic works as *Lies and Humiliations* (1988), he creates personal worlds revealing the struggles of many of his countrymen.

Even more elaborate is *In the Peripheral Vision of the Witness* **(1986), a video drama made originally as a three-channel installation for the Centre Georges Pompidou in Paris, which was filmed at the palace of Versailles. Odenbach again combines numerous images (original footage, Hollywood films) and dialogues in a multilayered examination of the self as viewer and voyeur, and the body seen as unique as well as connected to the world around it.**

Since the mid-1970s Odenbach has also used the platform of art videos to make heartfelt personal and political statements about military and cultural oppression, often focusing on the sins committed by his own country (Germany) in World War II. He favors direct, hand-held camera shots (crowds at a vigil at the Berlin Wall, runners finishing a race, children playing in a park) that lend an immediacy to his narratives and that stand in stark contrast to the dreamy (or nightmarish) archival footage of marching Nazis or stranded refugees that he inserts into the contemporary scenes. His work, embedded with a strong political sensitivity, has affinities with that of Juan Downey, Robert Cahen, Marina Abramovic, Stan Douglas, as well as filmmakers Rainer Werner Fassbinder, and Jean-Luc Godard.

In *The Idea of Africa* **(1997), a full-wall projection, archival images of a colonial celebration in an unspecified African country (white suited soldiers parading in front of rows of army brass and assimilated natives in suits and long dresses) are projected next to images of a contemporary African man repairing the shell of his dilapidated shack.** *United Colors* **(1990–92) features six monitors hanging unevenly along a wall. Single-channel videos show a black woman and five men (four Caucasian, one Oriental) engaging in daily activities. Elusive appropriated images float through these portraits at times, as Odenbach comments on the familiar Benetton advertising campaign.**

Odenbach employs these tactics of combining the archival with the contemporary to great effect in *Coming and Going* **(1995), which was filmed in a waterway (presumably in Germany). Odenbach weaves in shots of sleek leisure boats cruising on top of the water with newsreel footage of submarines surfacing in similar waters and Hitler boarding a large vessel and greeting his navy crew. Odenbach's camera, seamless editing, and unobtrusive sound go far to create the desired effect.**

X-PRZ

247–54 X-PRZ, a self-described 'bi-racial art band' (Tony Cokes, Doug Anderson, Kenseth Armstead, Mark Pierson), creates projects that engage critical issues in culture and politics. *No Sell Out…or I want to be the ultimate commodity machine* (1995) combines images of African-American leader Malcolm X with appropriated footage from advertisements, television shows, and other outtakes from popular culture. In this fast-paced collage the artists show how even controversial figures like Malcolm X become subsumed into the commodity culture of television and magazines.

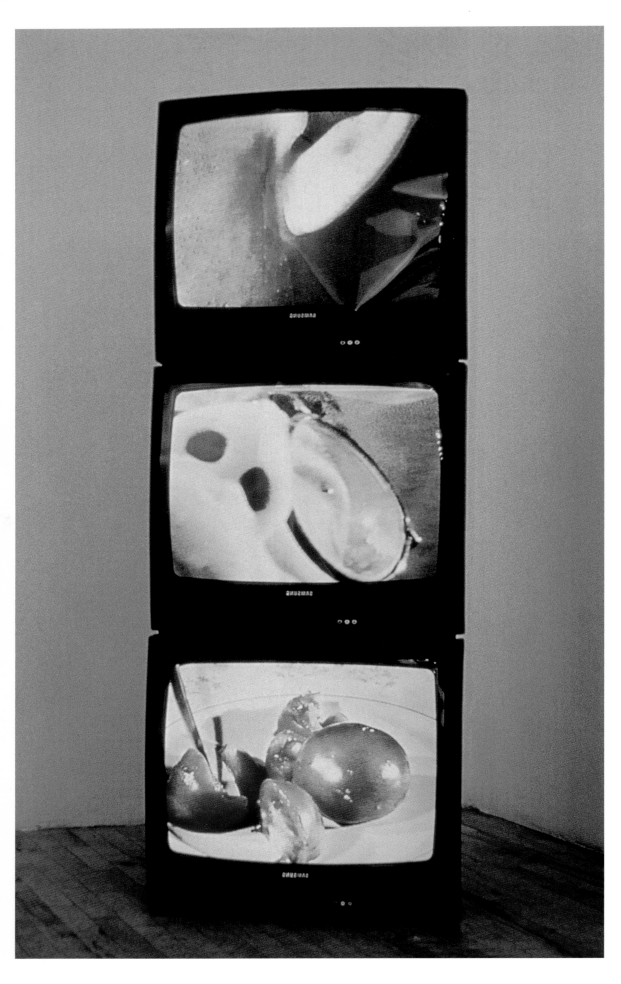

Zhang Peili
LEFT
255 *Eating* (1997)

Petér Forgács
OPPOSITE TOP
256 Petér Forgács (b. 1950, Hungary)
has been a central figure in
Hungarian video and film since the
1970s. Resisting the dangers of being
an artist under a repressive political
regime, Forgács made 'home movies'
of his own family and friends and
incorporated footage from others
into a retelling of life in dark times.
Wittgenstein Tractatus (1992) is a
personal narrative about the linguistic
philosopher, whose profound effect
on Conceptual art is most notable in
the work of Joseph Kosuth. Forgács
interweaves black-and-white home
movies from early in the 20th-century
with readings from the Wittgenstein
work (which was published in 1921).
The 'essays' become a meditation
on life and meaning, with a touch
of nostalgia for life before such
great repression.

Gusztáv Hámos

American artist Pier Marton (b. 1950), who also emerged from Performance and body art in the 1970s – his tapes *Performance for Video* (1978–82) are a record of this – explored personal and cultural identity in several tapes from the 1980s. The most poignant is *Say I'm a Jew* (1985), which is a story of the children of Holocaust survivors. Writing in the *New York Times* of this video, critic John Russell said: 'Not a moment is wasted, nor a word.... We leave convinced that – to quote from Mr Marton – "nothing short of complete healing is required of all of us." '

Issues of identity are also implicit in Video art in China, although most early Chinese video artists clearly inherited the mantle of Conceptualism. Due to lack of available materials, video was not much practiced in China until the early 1990s, though one artist, Zhang Peili, did make videos in the late 1980s. One of the first exhibitions of Video art by contemporary Chinese artists took place in the southern cultural capital of Hangzhou, which had been home to a group of experimental artists in the mid-1980s, including the collaborative group called Pond Association, one of whose members was Zhang Peili.

The 1994 Hangzhou exhibition, 'Image and Phenomena,' contained work from fifteen artists from all over China. Peili's installation, *The Focal Distance*, was described by Beijing-based curator and critic Karen Smith as 'a sequential distortion of a filmed cityscape across seven monitors, each subsequent image filmed from the previous monitor, effecting the degeneration in visual quality and clarity that occurs as each recording goes down one generation. The final image was a total abstraction of primary light, in blue and yellow forms, that danced across the screen like magnified atoms of energy.'[3]

Chen Shaotong's *Sight Adjuster III* (1996) featured video monitors within the black hoods of vintage bellows cameras. The artist created an intimate, voyeuristic environment showing rather mundane images of hands and bicycles cycling up the side of the screen. In this work, the old world collides with the new, but some things remain the same: the authorities are still spying on their people.

Yang Zhenzhong's *Fish Bowl* (1996) contained three monitors stacked in an aquarium. As the water circulated, large reddened lips announced, 'We are not fish,'

repeatedly. Crowded living conditions and attempts to impose conformity in Chinese culture seemed to be the desired theme. Qian Weikang's *Breath/Breathe*, a seven-monitor installation, recalled some tapes of Peter Campus. Weikang had eyes on the monitor staring at viewers' eyes, implying that both were engaged in a mutual ritual of spying.

Smith and Stewart

The struggles for identity in relationships characterizes the poignant single-channel and installation videos of the Scotland-based team Stephanie Smith (b. 1968, Great Britain) and Edward Stewart (b. 1961, Ireland). Since 1993, when they met during an artists' residency in Amsterdam, they have been creating video installations that graphically explore the tension and the tenderness that lie at the heart of human relationships, starting with their own. A married couple as well as an artist team, they have collaborated on more than a dozen projects featuring themselves biting, scratching, kissing, embracing, wrestling, even struggling to breathe inside plastic bags.

Gag (1996) is a double projection in which each of the two faces shown has a piece of colored fabric over the mouth. Methodically, the fingers or tongue of another person force the fabric into the mouth. Even more disturbing is *Breathing Space* (1997), a two-screen projection, in which each artist has a plastic bag tightly wrapped around his or her head. Microphones placed inside the bags record their struggle to breathe until one of the people (in this case Stewart) really starts to panic.

In each of their videos Smith and Stewart attempt to manufacture conditions that demand responses from the audience. This inclusion of viewers in the work of art has been a popular notion since Duchamp, but Smith and Stewart take it a step further. 'With *Breathing Space*,' Smith told the author in 2000, 'the viewer can't control his or her response. Watching someone struggling to breathe always makes us gasp for breath ourselves.' Though they deny any connection with Performance art or theater, precedents do exist for this type of 'extreme' Video art in some of the Performance-based work of video pioneers like Chris Burden (b. 1950). In his 1971

Chris Burden
259 *Shoot* (1971)

Shoot, for example, he is filmed being shot in the arm, while in *Through The Night Softly* (1973), he is seen lying on his bare stomach with his hands tied behind his back, pulling himself along a street full of broken glass. It is only a very cold-hearted viewer who would not have an emotional response to these videos.

Such comparisons only go so far, however. Chris Burden and other early video artists were concerned with the role of the artist's own body in creating art, while Smith and Stewart make compressed narratives suggestive of larger stories. 'Our work can be seen as outtakes from movies,' says Stewart. Indeed, the fractured scenarios of their videos do hint at psychological complexities more associated with the films of Hitchcock or the avant-garde cinema of Jean-Luc Godard and his longtime companion and collaborator

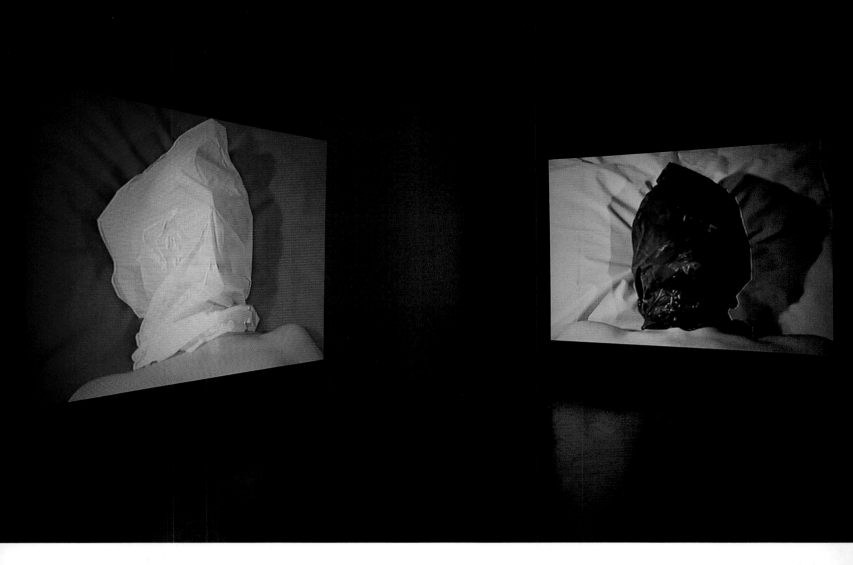

Smith and Stewart
260 *Breathing Space* (1997)

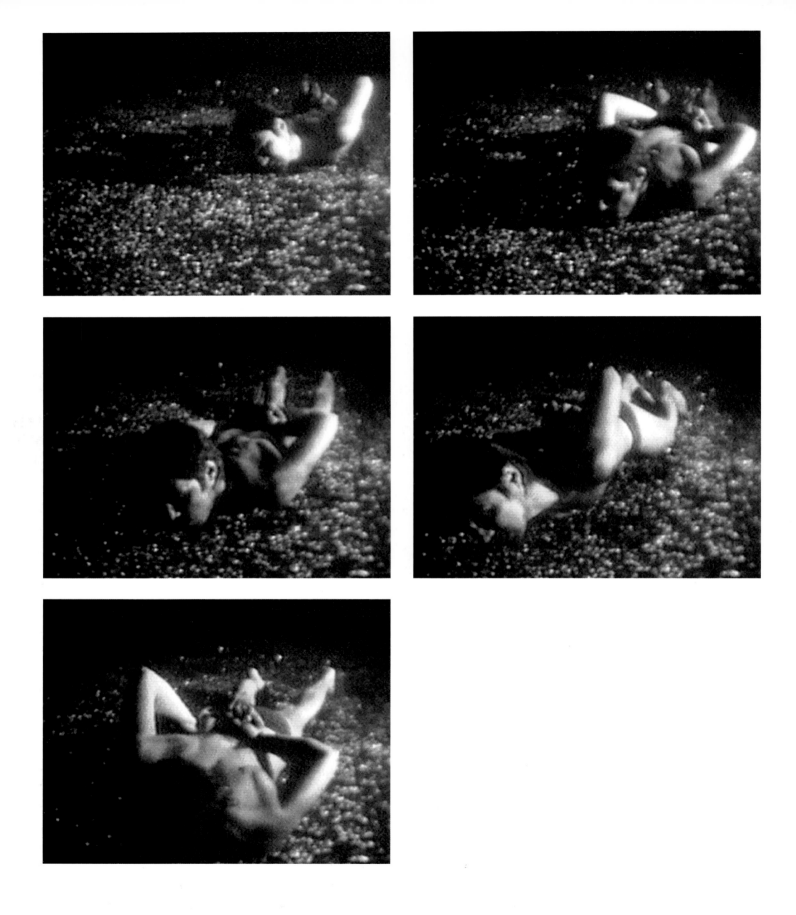

Video Art

Chris Burden
261–65 Chris Burden's body endured
frequent abuse as he allowed himself
to be shot, shocked, and crucified.
In *Through the Night Softly* (1973)
he forces himself across a stretch of
glass-strewn concrete. In filming
these performances and sometimes
broadcasting them on television,
he created an alternative to the
passive viewing we associate with
the television.

Anne-Marie Miéville. Smith and Stewart's techniques of fragmenting and displacing sound and image directly reflect Godard's and Miéville's signature experiments with sound and image (their film studio in Paris was called Sonimage or 'sound plus image'). Godard and Miéville have also made some of the most poignant studies of male/female relationships in works such as *Numéro deux* of 1975 and *Soft and Hard (A Soft Conversation on Hard Subjects)* of 1985. One significant difference between the two couples, however, is that Smith and Stewart have not thus far engaged in the humor that so often offers relief from the perils of relationships in the films of Godard and Miéville.

Mouth to Mouth (1995) is a particularly haunting video in which Stewart, fully clothed, lies at the bottom of water-filled tub staring longingly at Smith, who is leaning over him. She bends down to breathe into his mouth, and then resurfaces to catch her breath as he remains submerged. This peculiar scene leaves many questions unanswered: Is he really looking for help? Why doesn't she pull him out? Is this some kind of sadistic or masochistic game? How will it end? As in all of their work, *Mouth to Mouth* reveals the artists' keen visual control in the presence of psychologically aggressive interactions. The overall blue tint of *Mouth to Mouth*, the red pillow in *Breathing Space*, and the pink cloth in *Static*, to highlight but a few, are indicative of Smith and Stewart's reliance on aesthetic artifice to create beauty, even in the face of terrifying reality.

In Camera (1999) was filmed by a camera placed inside one of the artist's mouth. The extraordinary full-wall oral cavity that the viewer sees appears like an opening to a nether world one would do well to avoid. A voice is heard emanating from the mouth. 'I want to talk to you in the dark,' it says. Light flashes from inside the mouth, creating a kind of choreographed relationship between darkness and light, sound and silence. Reminiscent of Samuel Beckett's 1972 play, *Not I*, in which a disembodied mouth is seen on the stage spouting an avalanche of words, *In Camera* demonstrates the power of a single image to evoke an entire world.

Another artist team, Janet Cardiff and George Bures Miller, have created sophisticated multimedia installations that combine image, sound, and architectural space. Their presentation at the 2001 Venice Biennale, *The Paradise Institute*, consisted of a wooden 'movie house,' that seated only seventeen people who were invited to put on headphones as they watched a miniature theater screen containing a fractured narrative. Surrounded by haunting sounds accompanying disconnected images, visitors felt as though they had entered someone's disturbing dream.

Women Artists

Although the current landscape of Video art is populated by men and women alike, it is important to note that in the 1970s video gave women the opportunity to enter an art world that had often denied them access. The emergence of Video art coincided with the feminist movement and the increased availability of video cameras allowed women to participate in an endeavor that did not require a museum, or a gallery, for validation. Sonia Andrade (b. 1935, Brazil), Eleanor Antin (b. 1935, United States), Lynda Benglis (b. 1941, United States), Andrea Daninos (Italy), Anna Bella Geiger (b. 1933, Brazil), Rebecca Horn (b. 1944, Germany), Hermine Freed (b. 1940, United States), Julia Heyward (b. 1949, United States), Susan Milano (United States),

Ulrike Rosenbach (b. 1943, Germany), Ilene Segalove (b. 1950, United States), Nina Sobel (b. 1947, United States), Anne Tardos (United States), Ingrid Wiegand (United States) are some women linked with the rapid development of Video art in the 1970s.

In the United States the Los Angeles Woman's Building, a center for feminist programs, contained one of the earliest production facilities for independent video. Some of the above-mentioned artists worked there. As American curator JoAnn Hanley noted in her 1993 essay in *The First Generation: Women and Video, 1970–75*, 'Without the burdens of tradition linked with the other media, women video artists were freer to concentrate on process, often using video to explore the body and the self.'[4]

From the 1980s to the present day women artists have made such headway in Video art that their numbers at international exhibitions are virtually indistinguishable from men. Amongst major artists exhibiting internationally at this time are Jane and Louise Wilson, Gillian Wearing, Sam Taylor-Wood, Shirin Neshat, Rosemarie Trockel, Pipilotti Rist, Lorna Simpson, Diana Thater and Eija-Liisa Ahtila, some of whom will be discussed in the next chapter.

Remarking on the place of women in the history of Video art, Barbara London, a media curator at the Museum of Modern Art in New York since the 1970s, comments, 'People look at younger work and don't realize what went before. Recent work is not feminist like Martha Rosler's or Joan Jonas's because these women changed the world already. The younger ones are celebrating their womanhood, thanks to the older generation.'[5]

Lorna Simpson (b. 1960, United States) has created a compelling body of still and moving image work since the mid-1980s. Her characters are often placed in situations where communication is thwarted or impossible. Fragmented texts, whether spoken or written on the image, echo the artist's emphasis on the need to attempt communication, even if we fail. Her black-and-white films include *Recollection* (1998), in which memories are re-interpreted and misinterpreted, and *Call Waiting* (1997), in which two women attempt to communicate despite a series of ultimately very disruptive interruptions. *Interior/Exterior, Full/Empty* (1996) is a seven-screen film projection in which people may or may not be communicating with one another.

Mary Lucier

Video as a personal medium lends itself to not only narrative investigations of identity, but also lyrical narratives like those of Mary Lucier (b. 1944, United States). Emerging in the late 1960s and early 1970s with Conceptual performances and photographic works, Lucier has developed over the years a lush photographic style that she employs to explore memories, the natural world, and the struggle of human beings in the natural as well as unnatural, war-driven world.

Her career extends back to the late 1960s, when she began collaborating with her then-husband, musician Alvin Lucier. Though best known now for her lyrical multichannel installations, Lucier concentrated in her early work on conceptually based sound and photographic projections. In her *Polaroid Image Series #1: Room* (1969) Lucier, reflecting Alvin's technique of rerecording a text in a room and playing it until the words became unintelligible, rephotographed Polaroid photos until the

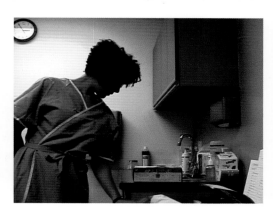

Lorna Simpson

266–74 The video *31* (2002), made for
Documenta 11, is a grid of thirty-one
screens on which are seen the daily
routines of a woman from the time
she wakes up until she goes to bed.
The monitors become like a light
board in which the bulbs illuminate
and then go off at different times.
The effect is mesmerizing for viewers
as they become accomplices in this
voyeuristic journey into the life of
a woman under surveillance.

Mary Lucier
ABOVE AND LEFT
275–79 *Ohio to Giverny: Memory
of Light* (1983)

OPPOSITE
280 *Oblique House (Valdez)* (1993)

OPPOSITE TOP
281 Mary Lucier, a pioneer of video installation, projected videos in *House by the Water* (1997) on to four sides of a house that was raised on stilts and surrounded by a cyclone fence. The work addresses the drama and mystery of living close to the primal forces of nature.

OPPOSITE BOTTOM
282 *Last Rites (Positano)* (1995)

images became indecipherable. These images were projected as an accompaniment to Alvin's thirteen-minute recording of his garbled text. Her projections took on a life of their own, looking in some cases like the Abstract Expressionist canvases of Robert Motherwell.

Lucier's experiments with Performance and technology soon became more conceptually sophisticated and linked with her interest in natural environments and ecology. Her *Salt* (1971), constructed in Portland, Connecticut, was a large multimedia 'installation' (at that time the word had not been adopted) that incorporated snow fencing, tobacco cloth, marble chips and amplified bird calls. The following year in Brooklyn she made a performance named *Journal of Private Lives*, which featured film and slide projections and writing on three large screens. By 1975 she was creating installations with live laser writing, video cameras, prerecorded texts, and multiple monitors, as in *Fire Writing*.

In common with several other video artists of her generation, Lucier spent her formative years working in Performance, sculpture and intermedia, elements that endure in her work today. She also retains her commitment to portraying the delicate balance between human beings and their habitats. For her, the personal, the political, and the poetic are one. Light and landscape (both internal and external) are metaphors of the essential connection between humans and their environments. They are also fragile components in cautionary narratives that reveal the destructive underbelly of both nature and the creatures who inhabit this earth.

Floodsongs (1998) was a multiscreen installation that investigated the town of Grand Forks, North Dakota, virtually destroyed by floods and fire in 1997. Included in the installation was a full-wall projection of a house's interior: Lucier's camera moved slowly through the drenched rooms, focusing on the discarded toys, upturned furniture, and personal effects that remained as silent reminders of a life once lived there. Attached to another wall were a chair, a stool, and a lit floor lamp whose single, exposed bulb created shadows on the floor of the darkened room. As she has done with objects from her own relative's homes in installations such as *Last Rites (Positano)* (1995), Lucier sculpted an architectural environment with these objects, highlighting them as monuments to a time that had passed, either violently or simply in the course of things. Bolted to the side walls were six large television monitors, each showing the talking head of one of the flood's victims: a priest, a singer, a married couple, etc. They spoke of watching their town burning on a television in the motel room where they had sought shelter, or of rebuilding their lives, or of moving on altogether. Their stories, issuing from speakers placed on the wall below the monitors, were amplified, running together in the small space like a discordant symphony, reminiscent of her very first piece, *Polaroid Image Series #1: Room*. Each element – the large central video, the monitors, the 'floating' furniture, and the sound – together encompassed the viewer in a high-pitched, sensual environment.

Unlike the passive experience of watching a film or a television news show, viewers could walk through this setting, approach the images that appeared and disappeared on the large and small screens and run their hands through the light of the lamp, joining their own shadows with those of the furniture. It is almost as if the viewers entered the homes of these mournful people, paying respects and offering understanding.

Mary Lucier
LEFT
283 *Forge* (2000)

BELOW AND OPPOSITE
284–85 *Migration (Monarch)* (2000)

Recent work, while continuing to explore these important themes, also testifies to the way Lucier has embraced new technologies. *Forge* (2000) features the raging flames of a forge where hardened materials were being shaped into industrial goods, steel shelves perhaps. Exposing both the usefulness and the devastation of heat, Lucier uses the forge as the place to examine the complex relationship between humans and the natural elements. Using a digital technique called 'nesting,' in which one image is placed inside another (like the 'picture in the picture' on a television set), Lucier intensifies the flaming activity inside the forge by multiplying it in front of the viewers' eyes.

In *Migration (Monarch)* (2000) an ageing monarch butterfly, which usually travels thousands of miles across North America to winter in Southern California or Mexico, is seen alighting on a human hand. It does not live very long, passing away after making this human contact. This digital video – along with the work of artists such as Michael Snow, Gary Hill, and Pipilotti Rist – was projected on a large screen in Times Square, New York.

Lucier has a conscience. Her lyrical narratives, sometimes painterly, sometimes enigmatic, are meant to inform. American critic Eleanor Heartney wrote of her work in 1993: 'For the last twenty-five years Mary Lucier has been engaged in a study of the meaning and implications of our metaphors for landscape.... She has focused on the contradictions inherent in the pastoral ideal which underlie so much American art and literature.'[6]

Lucier has much in common with a younger generation of video artists. She began as a still photographer as well as Performance artist. She also incorporated technological interventions in her work, as in her 1975 *Air Writing* and *Fire Writing*. Multiple video monitors, lasers, prerecorded audio texts and other elements contributed to energetic 'techno-performances' that reflected her profound and, as it turns out, enduring interest in air, fire, and earth.

Michal Rovner

One female artist who combines the technological savvy of video pioneer Steina Vasulka and the story-telling power of Beryl Korot with a singular vision that is at once political, personal, and sculptural is the Israeli artist Michal Rovner, whose single-channel tapes and large-scale installations represent the highest level of video practice at this time.

Michal Rovner (b. 1957, Israel), a photographer since the late 1970s, began using video in 1992 as an inspiration for her still photographs. Her first full-fledged video project, *Border* (1996), was filmed on the border between Israel and Lebanon during a time of war. Filmed with three hand-held cameras (hi-8, Digital Video, and Betacam), *Border* is a fictional narrative in which repetition, sliced dialogues, and surreal juxtapositions of texts and images result in a terrifying meditation on war and art.

Rovner films herself engaging in conversation with passers-by and, most dramatically, with a general in the Israeli army who keeps warning her 'to stay in your own reality' instead of trespassing into his. 'How famous you'd become if I died while you were filming,' he states in a characteristically challenging fashion. 'This film will help you in your world, will get you where you want to go, but what will it do for me?' As Rovner repeatedly asks him how her film will end – as if he were somehow

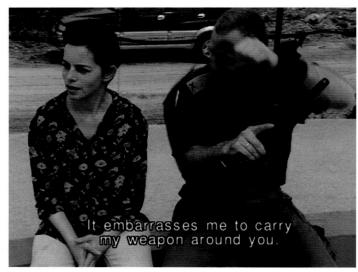

in control of the war's outcome – he replies mournfully, 'There is no ending to what you're filming.' Smoke from gunfire rises into the air a short distance away; a large number of birds swirl up and down in the blue sky beyond. Rovner's camera seeks out the danger in the commonplace.

Overhanging, mounted originally in 1999 in the Sandberg Wing of the Stedelijk Museum in Amsterdam and reconfigured and retitled *Overhang* for the 2000 presentation at the Chase Manhattan Bank on Park Avenue in New York, is a work of extraordinary ambition, complexity, and beauty. Filmed with three video cameras and projected on to adjoining scrim-covered windows (9 in Amsterdam, 17 in New York), *Overhanging* is a haunting, abstract work depicting what look like black-hooded figures making their way, with great effort, through an unidentifiable space. Above them, other human figures plod in white silhouette in a straight line across an equally barren landscape. They all move in painstakingly slow motion across what looks like a desert or a snowy tundra, walking endlessly toward no visible destination. It is as if these lonely souls were muttering the closing words of Beckett's novel *The Unnamable*, 'You must go on. I can't go on. I'll go on.' Rovner's figures move on continually. The projections fade from the palest white, to rouge, to black, and back to white. Rovner is clearly at ease with digital editing techniques that help her produce the images she wants. It is not the technology itself that is of interest, but its usefulness in creating a type of narrative abstraction.

In a single-channel version of this installation, also entitled *Overhang*, Rovner overlaid shots of swarms of insects on to the videotape. The dense, restless movement (its source is not at all clear from a casual viewing) on the screen at first makes the footage seem old, spotty, fading. After a while it seems timeless.

Given Rovner's nationality, associations with images of Holocaust prisoners and other victims of war come easily to mind. Rovner, however, refuses to be specific about the meaning of her work, preferring to allow her seamless mixture of realism and abstraction to address universal emotions. Like Beckett's characters, Rovner's figures are suspended somewhere between being and non-being, reality and fantasy. The ambiguous figures in her landscapes, marching endlessly toward an unspecified goal, speak to everyone who has ever asked the question 'Why?' and found no answers available.

Rovner's other short video installations, *Mutual Interest* (1997) and *Co-Existence* (2000), illustrate her enduring interest in the potential of abstract images to convey meaning about the natural world. She begins with this world and, through painstaking editing processes, arrives at her abstractions fully aware of their link to the original images. This working method finds particular resonance in her photographs, which often materialize as outtakes from her edited videos.

Rovner's *Notes* (2001) is a collaboration with composer Philip Glass. It opens with a shot of a row of odd-looking figures, resembling something like pods with skinny legs. As the video proceeds, more and more men, silhouetted in black, gather in packs and walk

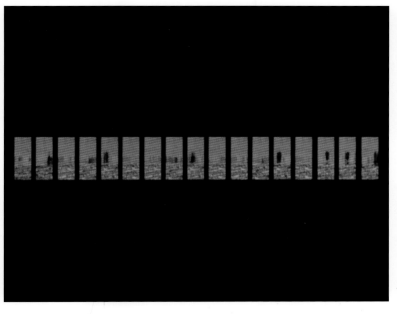

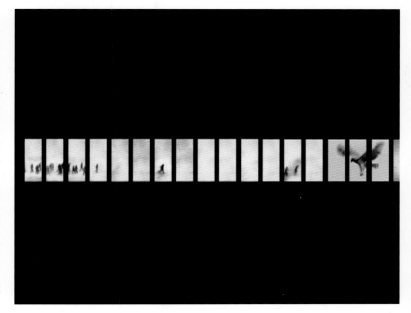

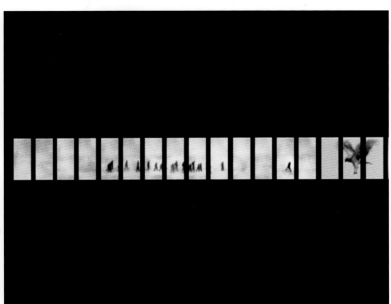

Michal Rovner

OPPOSITE AND OVERLEAF
292–95, 301 *Overhanging* (1999)

ABOVE AND LEFT
296–300 *Overhang* (2000)

302 Max Almy (b. 1948, United States) used sophisticated editing techniques in several videos in the 1980s to create futurist-looking tapes that were critical of the very technology she was using. *Leaving the 20th Century* (1982) is a science fiction travelogue in which people leave the earth, ending up in a place that feels like nowhere. Communication overload had resulted in a total lack of communication.

slowly toward nowhere in particular. As they proceed down the hill, Rovner makes a quick cut to five horizontal lines (like the 'bars' or 'clefs' on a sheet of music). These lines are made from cuts of very thin strips of earth upon which cluster more black figures. They move, sometimes separating, sometimes clinging together, like notes, first in a languorous Beethoven suite, then like frantic eighth notes in a Bach cantata. Glass's score moves determinedly forward with intermittent clanging sounds suggesting deep-seated conflict. At the end all the 'notes,' the dozens and dozens of men in black, stand on their assigned row and bow in unison. The camera fades to a snow-capped hill where a few men remain. They turn and walk down the hill away from the camera; the music stops, the screen goes black abruptly.

Rovner's work contains affinities with other media artists who have created poetic filmic meditations.[7] Her predecessors in this regard would be avant-garde filmmakers from the mid to late 20th century (Stan Brakhage, Hollis Frampton), worthy of mention also because of their broad importance to the field, and video artists like Shalom Gorewitz and Mary Lucier. Brakhage's film *Dog Star Man*, filmed from 1959 to 1965, is particularly relevant. In this multipart film, Brakhage offers a vast puzzle of images, sometimes at breakneck speed, that serve as poetic equivalents for his ruminations on the cycle of life and death, the seasons, and the progression from infancy to adulthood. What is important in the context of Rovner's work is Brakhage's physical manipulations of the film in order to create a lyrical handle for the viewer in the midst of arduous abstraction.

In Part One of *Dog Star Man*, following the dizzy-making fast cuts of the *Prelude*, Brakhage pictures his protagonist struggling to climb a snow-covered mountain. Shots fade in and out very slowly, sometimes melting into green or red. 'Part One is a *Noh* drama,' Brakhage has written, 'the exploration in minute detail of a single action and all its ramifications.'[8] Rovner manipulates her digitized video footage to the same effect. The Giacometti-thin figures of *Overhang* result from an almost obsessive removal process, in which Rovner whittles away all particulars from an image, leaving it barely discernible as a human being.[9]

For both Brakhage and Rovner, the 'person' in the film is an archetype and thus necessarily anonymous. The persons or figures exist as in a memory or dream, in a suspended state, wavering between the reality of the struggle they are in and the impossibility of emerging from the struggle. They are lost in an endless repetition, suggested by slow motion or a duplication of the image or the gesture multiple times. One of Brakhage's signature techniques is to lay images over one another several times. The resulting abstraction renders the original image virtually undetectable, leaving it only to the most attentive viewer to find the traces of an image buried within.

By adopting such intense abstraction, both Brakhage and Rovner demand that viewers relinquish their customary search for meaning in film and allow, rather, the altered sense of time and space to give a new relationship to what they are seeing. What they offer is an experience of the present moment shaped by color, gesture, sound (or, in Brakhage's case, silence), and mystery.

Rovner's use of digital editing techniques echoes the experiments of early video artists such as Ed Emshwiller, an Abstract Expressionist painter, who found in

Woody Vasulka

NEAR RIGHT

303 *Art of Memory* (1987) by Woody Vasulka, whose work developed separately from, and together with, his wife Steina from the mid-1970s, is a monumental narrative that combines footage of the sprawling American southwest (where the Vasulkas live) with images of war and the atomic bomb. Orchestrating these images with the processing techniques for which he is known, Woody creates a cultural and moral drama that relies on the power of the image to speak profoundly about human history and the horrors of war.

CENTER RIGHT

304 *The Commission* (1983)

Woody and Steina Vasulka

FAR RIGHT

305 *Golden Voyage* (1973)

  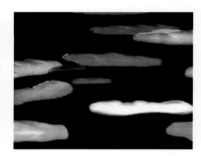

the new technologies animated equivalents for his canvases. Video synthesizers, computer systems, and a Moog audio synthesizer all came into play in his videos, especially *Thermogenesis* from the early 1970s. Keith Sonnier (b. 1941, United States), another painter, created sensuous multiple-image video collages that served as metaphors for the processes and materials of painting.

Most prominent amongst these early video artists (in addition to Nam June Paik and Jud Yalkut, who both worked with new electronics) were Woody (b. 1937, Czechoslovakia) and Steina Vasulka (b. 1940, Iceland), a husband-and-wife team, who pioneered digital processing and electronic image processing. In works such as *Home* (1973), in which colorizing and electronic imaging techniques are used to glamorize everyday objects, and *Golden Voyage* (1973), a homage to Magritte, the Vasulkas invented new means of electronic manipulation that altered viewers' perceptions in much the same as Pointillism and Impressionism had done in painting a century before. The Vasulkas remain very active with media projects. Recent large-scale installations by Steina – *Borealis* (1993) and *Orka* (1997) – were filmed in her native Iceland. Woody's work in progress, *Brotherhood*, is an assembly of six individual media constructions consisting of varied acoustic and visual structures containing projectors, speakers, screens, lights, and sensors.

Steina Vasulka

306 In *Orka* (1995) Steina Vasulka
returns to her native Iceland to record
images of haunting beauty. Birds and
waves seem to take this artist out of
time as she lets her camera linger
amid the elegance and force of nature.

Shalom Gorewitz

BELOW LEFT
307 *Empathy and Abstraction* (1998)

BELOW RIGHT
308 Shalom Gorewitz (b. 1949,
United States) explores historical and
political complexities in video work
marked by meticulous use of digital
after-image effects. *Dissonant
Landscapes* (1984–86) was made as
a response to the American invasion
of Granada in 1984. As in *Subatomic
Babies* (1983), Gorewitz manipulates
images of people and places, making
them appear other-worldly, not
because of art, but because of war.

Shalom Gorewitz (b. 1949, United States) used imaging devices like the Fairlight CVI and various components of the short-lived Amiga Computer to create his poetic meditations on landscapes in *Autumn Floods* (1979) and *Delta Visions* (1980) and on human relationships and longings in *Jerusalem Road* (1990) and *Promised Land* (1990). In some of his tapes the human figure appears erased or dissolved into some other type of reality. Gorewitz also shares Rovner's political determination, though his work can be much less optimistic.

Rovner is representative of the newest generation of video artists for whom digital techniques are paramount. She uses aftereffects with names like 'Symphony,' 'Flame,' and 'Inferno' to attain her haunting images. Just because they are 'digital' does not mean they are simple or fast. Rovner can take up to six months to edit a seven-minute tape, painstakingly erasing colors, fabrics or anything else to eliminate references to specific places and times. In filming she can also use 'incorrect' exposures to 'stretch' images before subjecting these images to even more manipulations in post-production.

'Post-production,' 'digital manipulations,' 'high-definition volumetric display,' 'film to video transfers,' these are not phrases associated with the early years of Video art. For artists like Rovner and virtually all other contemporary artists working with video, the medium is definitely not the message. There is nothing of particular interest about the flatness of video or even the real-time aspect of video as there had been in the late 1960s. Video, along with music and basic communication (the telephone, the computer) has gone digital. Images, both moving and still, can be captured by a camera worn on your wrist and manipulated endlessly on your desktop (and palm) computer. Video art, as a constituent part of the history (albeit recent history) of art, is slipping away from the grasp of art history as it has been known. It will not disappear from galleries and international exhibitions in the near future, but it will not be long before it will be beyond the grasp of current art-historical languages. Already Video art has become a subsection of Filmic art, a term better suited to the actual practice of most media artists today.

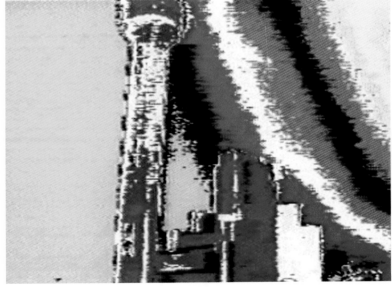

chapter 4

Extensions

Douglas Gordon
309 *Monument to X* (1998)

Adapting to New Technologies

While it is said that Video art has experienced important shifts roughly every ten years with the introduction of new technologies (Portapak, Betacam, VHS, 8-millimeter cameras) and working methods amongst artists (installations and projections in the 1980s as opposed to single channel in the 1970s), 1997 marked a sea change in the medium that altered it forever. In that year Sony Corporation, soon followed by Canon, introduced the first digital recorder in the United States, the DHR-1000. The previous year Sony had been the first to sell the Betacam SX, a sophisticated digital system for the broadcast industry, but the hand-held DHR-1000, like the Portapak over thirty years before, made digital moving-image recording accessible to a broad consumer public, including artists.

The late 1980s and early 1990s had witnessed the popularity of the hand-held 8-millimeter camera, but this product was short lived. Digital technology, which had existed for many years in telephone and other electronic industries, now began to dominate video. As computer software companies produced more and more editing tools (especially Avid Technology, which introduced digital nonlinear editing with the Media Composer® system in 1989) artists and others could retain complete control over their video work and not have to depend on 'editors' and other specialists for the final product.

More important for the purposes of this book, however, is the fact that, with digital technologies, the proper qualities of video itself that were so attractive to artists of the 1970s were no longer considered as crucial. It has become axiomatic that the moving image, or, rather, the 'movie' image, dominated the popular consciousness in the 20th century. The making of movies, however, is prohibitively expensive, and artists drawn to the moving image, especially those trained in art schools, have not been primarily interested in the story-driven, melodrama-based consumer films. However, having grown up with movies and television, they were naturally drawn to the moving image as a primary medium of expression for their artistic questions or, more accurately, as another means, amongst many available to them, of artistic expression. Some artists, like Julian Schnabel, Robert Longo and Cindy Sherman, have made Hollywood movies with varying artistic results. Conversely, some daring 'movie' directors are now filming in digital video and not using 35-millimeter film at all. Amongst the most critically successful video-films of this kind are Mike Figgis's four-screen mystery *Time Code* (2000) and Richard Linklater's *Waking Life* (2001). Noted director George Lucas shot his *Star Wars: Episode II – Attack of the Clones* (2002) entirely on digital video using Sony's 24P cameras (that cost US $100,000). This camera, unlike other video cameras, operates at 24 frames a second, the same as 35-millimeter film. Lucas was quoted in *The New York Times* (May, 13, 2002) as saying 'images shot with the 24P camera were indistinguishable from film.'

 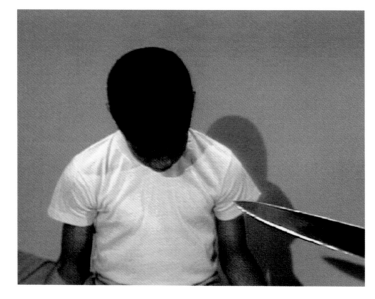

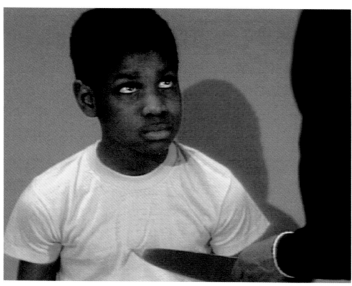 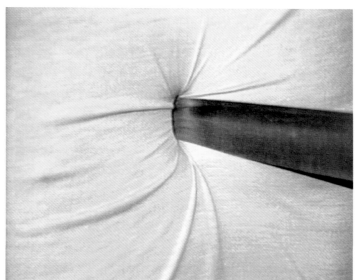

Robert Wilson

OPPOSITE

310–15 Robert Wilson, instantly recognizable for his elegant stage tableaux in theater and opera, turns in *Deafman Glance* (1981) to a video adapted from his five-hour performance of the same title. In a blindingly white house, a woman methodically performs the normal routine of washing dishes and pouring a glass of milk before she puts a knife to two young boys. For Wilson, who has been preoccupied with time since his first performances, video provides the perfect medium in which to experiment with dream states and the slow passage of time.

Tom Kalin

BELOW LEFT

316 Tom Kalin (b. 1962, United States) was a founding member of the AIDS activist group Gran Fury in the 1980s. He became known for his popular film *Swoon* in 1992. In his media work he moves from film to video freely. *That Poured Its Hot Breath* (1996) is a two-minute poetic video that uses home footage in the context of a diary. It is itself a non-narrative imagistic poem.

Ken Feingold

BELOW RIGHT

317 Ken Feingold (b. 1952, United States) began working in video and film in the early 1970s. Taking as his reference Lacanian psychoanalytic theory and semiotics, Feingold has, for many years, been exploring the notion of the Other through the complexity of the moving image. *The Double* (1984) is representative of his work. In this tape the chest of a man is opened while a voice belonging to Vito Acconci is heard reciting a text on the categories of human knowledge. Feingold has also traveled widely and made tapes in Bali, parts of India, and Southeast Asia.

As Video art enters its fifth, and perhaps final, decade (from the 1960s to the present), video, as a medium, is unimportant to artists. They are using whatever means of moving-image technology is available to them and often this means a combination of technologies. Nowadays most artists are shooting with digital cameras and transferring to DVD for projection; but others are shooting with 35-millimeter film as well as video, transferring to digital video for editing and transferring back again to 35-millimeter film for projection or using digital imaging that can approximate the 'look' of 35 millimeter film and so on. There are numerous possibilities and what emerges, as ever, is the triumph of concept and craft: those who are good at using whatever means they choose to communicate interesting ideas are those who are rising to the top of the field. This part of the story, at least, is not new.

No study of Video art would be complete without an attempt to place in context the many artists who now use a combination of video, digital video, film, DVD, computer art, CD-roms, and graphics in their work. While not strictly video artists (very few artists are), they use video as part of their larger practice. Matthew Barney (b. 1967, United States) is a prime example. From single-channel, performative videos to elaborate video and film combinations (the *Cremaster* series), Barney is representative of artists who move freely from video to film and beyond. At the opposite end of the spectrum, and tenaciously low-tech, is Kristin Lucas, whose performative videos and animations can involve toy cameras as well as at-home editing programs.

Video has become an essential component in what is imported into computers for digital art. Filmed moving (as well as still) images form the base of much early computer art from Cheryl Donegan's shots made in her studio to Gary Simmons's tapes of abandoned dance halls. A combination of video and animation makes up the ground of Tony Oursler's CD-rom *Fantastic Prayers* (1995), Bill Seaman's *Passage Set/One Pulls Pivots at the Tip of the Tongue* (1995), and the elaborate interactive work (with bicycle), *The Legible City* (1989–91), by Jeffrey Shaw (b. 1944, Australia).

Artists like Lynn Hershman, Ken Feingold, the group Dumb Type, and many others often rely on video imagery in the creation of their advanced technological art.

There is also the still quite young, and despite the controversy, inevitable realm of Virtual Reality, in which participants become immersed in worlds that feel totally real. In a sense, of course, they are. It's reality that's changing, and video technology is part of the extended body being shaped in this new world.

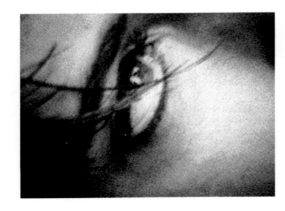

Pierre Huyghe

The French artist Pierre Huyghe (b. 1962) is one of a growing number of filmic artists whose video installations are well known to international art audiences. Not a typical 'appropriator,' he may at times incorporate Hollywood films into his work, or derive inspiration from the history of cinema (as many of his contemporaries do), but he does it in a totally fresh and personal way. While some artists like Douglas Gordon and Les Leveque manipulate actual films (Hitchcock's *Psycho* and *Vertigo*, respectively), Huyghe re-creates them with his own actors, sets, cameras, and other means. For Huyghe, the re-enactment allows him to tackle issues beyond cinema itself, certainly beyond cinema as a material. For him, the original film becomes a painted canvas that he erases, thus disclosing elements of identity and memory not evident (nor intended) in the film.

His *Remake* (1994–95) is just that: a remake of Hitchcock's film, *Rear Window* (1953). However, unlike typical Hollywood remakes (perhaps *the* great propensity of the moribund state of contemporary cinema: to redo what already proved successful in the past), Huyghe's films expose the structure of the original film by de-emphasizing the mystery of the narrative. His actors have difficulty remembering their lines, they behave in a way that does nothing to retain the tension of the original. Their very distance from the storyline allows Huyghe to expose Hitchcock's methods of cinema, in much the same way a post-modernist writer such as Bret Easton Ellis might dissect the act of murder in a novel like *American Psycho* (1991).

Huyghe's *The Third Memory* (1999) is a dual-screen installation based on the robbery of a Brooklyn bank in 1972 by a former bank clerk, John Wojtowicz, who wanted the money to help his lover, Ernest Aron, secure a sex-change operation. The event, protracted over eight hours while Wojtowicz and his partner, Salvatore Naturale, held bank employees hostage, was one of the first crimes captured live on television. So compelling were the images that they superseded Richard Nixon's renomination at the Republican National Convention, at least for awhile. It is reported that Nixon ordered the lights to be turned out in the bank so television coverage could return to the convention. The robbery, which resulted in Naturale's death by police gunfire, was the subject of Sidney Lumet's film, *Dog Day Afternoon* (1975), with Al Pacino as John Wojtowicz.

Fast-forward to the late 1990s, when Huyghe sees the film and notices at the end that it was based on a real story. He tracked down Wojtowicz, who had been paroled in 1979 and was living with his mother in Jersey City, and invited him to Paris, where Huyghe then reconstructed the movie set from *Dog Day Afternoon*. Hiring amateur

Pierre Huyghe
318 *The Third Memory* (1999)

Pierre Huyghe
319–20 *Remake* (1994–95)

Pierre Huyghe
321 *Two Minutes Out of Time* (2000)

actors and placing them in exaggerated 1960s wigs, Huyghe asked Wojtowicz to direct them in a re-enactment of the crime as he recalled it. Hence, the 'third' memory: the crime was performed in some form for the third time through the hazy lens of a very mediated history. Wojtowicz, now gray-haired and pudgy, took to the task with great gusto. 'I'll kill you, you motherfuckers,' he booms all too threateningly, as he performs for the actors what he actually said to the hostages over twenty-five years earlier.

What makes Huyghe's installation so compelling is how he grapples conceptually and visually with issues of memory and identity. Two projections placed side by side on one very wide white wall combine images from multiple digital cameras into a crisscross narrative that weaves from footage of the Lumet film to rehearsals for the current film, to actual scenes from the current film as well as shots of the film equipment, crew, and backstage curtains. This symphony of images serves Huyghe's probing critique of media spectacle. He reminds us of the real life and death that were sensationalized in the devouring gaze of the camera. Wojtowicz is no hero, but he becomes one in a perverse way as he performs for the viewer the memory of his fifteen minutes of fame.

Very little of the Lumet film is used here. Huyghe has too much energy and originality of his own to waste time on appropriation. He is more interested in the mechanisms of cinema and television interacting with the viewer's own mechanisms of memory. *The Third Memory* functions as a film loop, re-enacting over and over again scenes from life, scenes from a film and scenes from the filming of the re-enactment. As it wraps around itself, it becomes both an art and a critical experience. Huyghe functions as artist, critic, recorder, interpreter and conductor, leading viewers into their own questions about time and memory.

Huyghe's mastery of diverse media is evident in *Two Minutes Out of Time* (**2000**), an exquisite animated film about a digitally fabricated girl who was made as a back-ground character for a Japanese cartoon. 'While waiting to be dropped into a story,' the girl says about herself, 'she has been diverted from a fictional existence and has become…a deviant sign.' Huyghe gives her her own story and lets her tell of going to see a painting with 'waterlilies.' Pastel clouds float above her head as she delivers a paean to living, before disappearing into the ether. Full of pathos and wonder, it is a striking companion to the search for identity in *The Third Memory*.

Douglas Gordon

Scottish artist Douglas Gordon (b. 1966) has also explored identity and perception through a highly personal identification with films, especially those of Alfred Hitchcock. In *24-Hour Psycho* (1993), he digitally slowed down Hitchcock's 1960 classic film to twenty-four hours. In so doing he not only exposed the artifice of the filmmaker's trade by removing the immediate tension of the familiar horror scenes, but he also heightened tension in a way precisely because the film is so familiar. Gordon played with viewers' expectations as well as their memories and fears.

Rea Tajiri

322 Rea Tajiri (b. 1958, United States)
anticipated the predilection of several
artists in the 1990s to deconstruct the
films of Alfred Hitchcock with her
*Hitchcock Trilogy: Vertigo, Psycho,
Torn Curtain* (1987). She uses the
original scores by Bernard Hermann
from these movies and creates her
own repetitive, image collages from
appropriated still photos, newsreels,
and television shows.

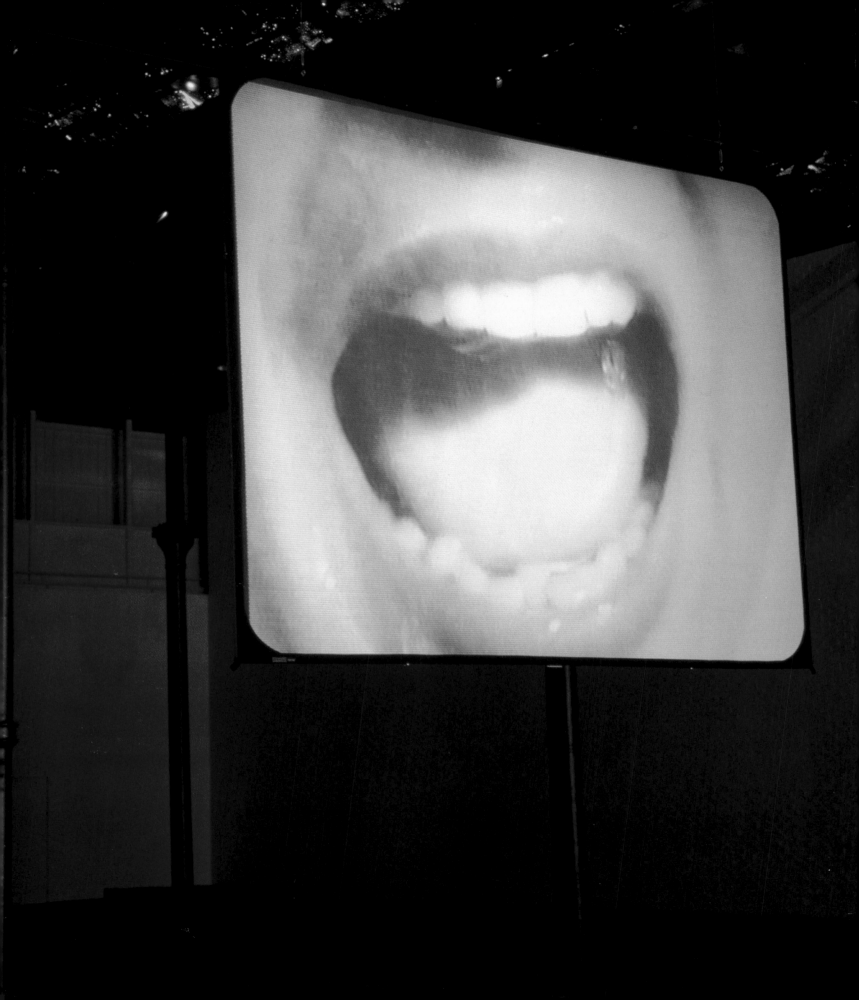

He often uses a two-screen or split-screen mode of presentation that allows for multiple perspectives, both psychologically and visually, for the viewer. In *through a looking glass* (1999), he appropriates a scene from Martin Scorsese's 1976 film *Taxi Driver* in which the lead character, the would-be assassin Travis Bickle, has a conversation with himself. Gordon digitally re-invents the 71-second scene on two opposite screens so that the paranoid and murderous Bickle (played by Robert De Niro) stares at himself, constantly repeating 'You looking at me?' The viewer, standing between the two images of Bickle, becomes implicated in Bickle's maniacal fantasies.

Rodney Graham

Canadian artist Rodney Graham (b. 1949) represents an earlier generation of Conceptual and video artists who have adapted to the new technologies. The utter beauty of Graham's *Vexation Island* (1997), a nine-minute film, owes its richness to its source: Cinemascope, a rich branch of 35-millimeter film that one suspects Graham could only afford to use for less than ten minutes. Nonetheless, here is Graham, dressed in an 18th-century, red British gentleman's costume, shipwrecked on a small strip of land in the British Virgin Islands, alone except for a blue parrot perched in a nearby tree. The sun burns brightly above shining white sands as the sea laps against the shore.

The camera, assured and fluid in the hands of director Robert Logevall, assumes a variety of close-ups and dolly shots that capture: Graham waking up; Graham spotting a coconut tree nearby; Graham shaking the tree, an act that makes a coconut fall on his head, so rendering him unconscious once again. The camera hovers over Graham's character (no names are used; the only sound comes from the waves and the wind), asleep on the shore, bleeding from a head wound; then it moves slowly along the beach, capturing every nuance of color and shading the waters have to offer. Then the camera looks up toward the coconut tree, statuesque against the clear sky, and finally shifts to Graham's back as he falls in slow motion to the ground after the coconut hits him.

In a sense, Graham's 'film,' made at a time when Cinemascope films had reached the technical heights of James Cameron's *Titanic* (1997) and Spielberg's *Close Encounters of the Third Kind* (1977), can look like the work of a poor artist trying to play with the big boys. His intentions, of course, are different from mainstream filmmakers. In this case his aim is to make visual one of French critic Gilles Deleuze's more obscure notions of animal and vegetative violence and one of Freud's lesser ideas on split consciousness, all through the falling coconut. Graham's strategies, familiar from the experiments of John Cage in music and Warhol and Brakhage in film, still cast their spell; altering perceptions and placing the viewing experience closer to the realm of dreams than waking life.

In his *Halcion Sleep* (1994), Graham literally entered a dream state after taking the sedative drug Halcion. He slept in the back of a van, dressed in pajamas, with a camera focused on him. The van drove through the streets of Vancouver at night as Graham slept in the dark with light appearing only from passing street lights. It could be said of Graham what Stan Brakhage said of himself: 'Like Cocteau, I was a poet who made films.'

Rodney Graham
BELOW AND OPPOSITE
324–25 *Vexation Island* (1997)

Video Art

Installation

All of the artists discussed here use the installation format in their work. The elements of what we now call 'installation' have been present in Video art since the 1960s, when Wolf Vostell and Nam June Paik used multiple monitors in their presentations. Installation art, by its very nature, suggests interactivity. Installation artists make environments for viewers to enter literally, thus creating a physical participation with the work. This in turn expands the perceptual and optical impact of the work. Installations, whether in museums, galleries, storefronts, or on street walls, video-walls, or any other possible surface, extend the experience of the moving image beyond not only the monitor, but also the darkened room. The possibilities of video installations were expanded as projection devices developed from the bulky tri-color VHS projectors to the trim, compact DVD projectors that can be placed anywhere.

Sam Taylor-Wood, Ugo Rondinone, Chris Cunningham, Iñigo Manglano-Ovalle, and Doug Aitken are amongst several international artists for whom large-format, multi-wall projections have made Video art an immersive experience. They are also representative of the contemporary artist for whom video is only one material amongst many at their disposal.

Iñigo Manglano-Ovalle

Born in Madrid in 1961, Iñigo Manglano-Ovalle was raised in Bogota and Chicago. His installation work has involved human genetic research, automobiles, sensory deprivation tanks, car sound systems, firearms, and designer apartment buildings. His video installations, inspired by his interest in architecture, especially that of Mies van der Rohe, are characterized by a sleek minimalism. In *Le Baiser/The Kiss* (1999), filmed at Mies's Farnsworth House, Plano, Illinois (completed 1950), thin polished steel poles and wire provide an imposing grid within which projection screens are suspended like sheets on a very upscale clothesline. Viewers become immediately drawn into the lush color of a projected autumn scene: huge trees with bright yellow leaves, seen through the open expanse of a glass-enclosed structure, sway gently in a breeze. Manglano-Ovalle shoots with a wide-format digital video camera, then transfers tapes to DVD for projection. The digital video footage, viewable from both sides of the screen, full of color and movement, feel like another being in the room.

The all-glass exterior of Mies's apartment house becomes a blank canvas upon which Manglano-Ovalle paints his scenario. A window washer in gray overalls and an orange hat works outside as an androgynous person in red inside the apartment gyrates to music coming in through headphones. Only separated by a sheet of glass, neither character acknowledges the other. Their worlds, for a moment close together, are far apart. An eerie silence permeates the viewing room. Anticipating doom, as cinema has trained the spectators to do when such bucolic scenes appear on a screen, the viewers fear for the home's thin occupant versus the robust workman. Nothing untoward happens, of course. In fact, nothing happens at all. If the laborer is trying to seduce the person in red with suggestive wiping movements, he gets no response.

For Manglano-Ovalle, as his other work shows, this separation virtually defines class distinctions in contemporary society. This polemic might be lost on viewers, however, because of the sheer beauty of the piece. His masterly use of the medium exposes how far Video art has come in terms of striking image.

Iñigo Manglano-Ovalle
330–35 *Climate* (2000)

Climate (2000) is an even cooler presentation of a mysterious narrative, or, in this case, three narratives. Three unrelated characters, whose identities are spelled out only in accompanying printed material (a surrogate birthmother, a futures analyst who predicts markets based on weather forecasts, and a gun fetishist) are filmed in another Mies building (Chicago's Lake Shore Drive Apartments, completed 1951). At times, looking at *Climate* feels as if one is watching all the apartments in Hitchcock's *Rear Window* that did not have a murder occurring: mundane, sometimes inscrutable activities of anonymous city folk.

A droning, musical soundtrack fills the viewing space; unfamiliar words are heard in voice-over. Gradually the fractured narrative appears to have something to do with global interactivity: a gulf-stream shift that will raise the water temperature of the Atlantic, and by a complicated chain of events, will result in favorable economic changes in Indonesia, while causing an environmental disaster in Argentina. Manglano-Ovalle's text refers to a not too distant future, in which Australia has ceased to exist and the Amazon region has become home to software conglomerates.

He also used 35-millimeter film transferred to a laserdisk for projection in his 2001 installation, *Alltagszeit (In Ordinary Time)*, which was filmed in the enormous glass central hall of the Mies-designed Neue Nationalgalerie in Berlin (completed in 1968). Manglano-Ovalle condensed a twelve-hour shoot into a sixteen-minute full-wall projection in which people are filmed entering and exiting the clean, spare space as the light changes dramatically from dawn to dusk. Inspired by Jacques Tati's 1967 film *Play Time*, in which a man becomes lost in the clean corridors of modernist buildings, Manglano-Ovalle's installation has the central character appearing and disappearing in the space as if he, too, were inseparable from the architecture around him.

The installation format does not allow for the neat ending of a feature film. Even Godard, who had an influence on both Manglano-Ovalle and Pierre Huyghe, sometimes permits the comfort of a denouement. But not filmic installations. At most they offer impressions to those who pass through them.

In his installations, Manglano-Ovalle creates what might be called one-act video-plays that continue his exploration of the fate of humanity as seen through very specific communities. Filmic technologies are a part, but only a part, of these explorations. They exist to serve his ideas. In themselves they are not of great interest to the artist. 'The idea is going to tell me what medium is appropriate,' he told the author in 2001, 'and the medium is going to be appropriate only because it's appropriate, not because it is the medium.'

William Kentridge

South African artist William Kentridge (b. 1955) works with film and video to expose the tangled web of South African apartheid. Kentridge is a modernist poet whose chosen medium, the animated film (often shot on 16 millimeter and then transferred to video for projection), is a playing ground of repetitions, fragments (often Surrealist-inspired flights of fancy), and deeply romantic imaging.

Kentridge's films derive from charcoal drawings; but how single drawings can unfold into such dizzy-making imagery is a sleight of hand worthy of an illusionist. Three of his films, *Felix in Exile: Geography of Memory* (1994), *History of the Main Complaint* (1996), and *Weighing…and Wanting* (1997), are disquieting meditations on the state of individuals and nameless groups caught in the grasp of hatred, paranoia, isolation, and senseless, brutal death.

Felix, an undistinguished, white, middle-aged man, naked and alone, paces aimlessly around a drab room, obsessively repeating meaningless actions. He shaves, and his image disappears in the mirror as the face of a handsome black woman appears. She looks through a telescope into Felix's blank eyes; then she turns toward the stars, looking up to the sky for relief from the carnage she sees

William Kentridge
RIGHT
336 American critic Rosalind Krauss says of his work, such as *History of the Main Complaint* (1996): 'In Kentridge's practice filmic animation is a support or ground for what takes place within or on top of it, namely a type of drawing that is extremely reflexive about its own condition, that savors the graininess of the clouds of charcoal or pastel as they are blown onto paper, that luxuriates in the luminous tracks of the eraser that open on to Turneresque fogs.'[1]

Iñigo Manglano-Ovalle
OVERLEAF
337–42 *Alltagszeit (In Ordinary Time)* (View 2) (2001)

on the streets of the East Rand, a mining area near Johannesburg. Her image, now drawn on pieces of paper, falls like the pages of a calendar ripped away when the month is finished. Stars swirl to form a faucet, which spills water into Felix's sink, eventually flooding his room in blue tinted liquid, and so on: images melting into one another, faces of poor miners staring at the viewer before some are murdered, with blades left in the chest, and abandoned.

Without any sense of the artist repeating himself, but only going deeper into the myths he is unearthing, *History of the Main Complaint* opens with another middle-aged man, large, fully dressed in striped suit and tie, lying unconscious in a hospital bed. Men with stethoscopes, first three, then ten, poke at him, trying to rouse him from a death-like sleep. He dreams of the trappings of his bureaucratic past: official stamps, telephones, adding machines. His innards, viewed through CAT scans, MRIs, and X-rays, consist of office detritus that gave him a sense of power once upon a time. He dreams of driving along a deserted road and seeing a black man being kicked and killed; he drives on.

Kentridge works in a stream of consciousness that allows impressions and momentary flashes to take form and then yield to new images, without any loss of momentum; indeed, quite the opposite; momentum builds with each frame.

Doug Aitken

Doug Aitken (b. 1968, United States), more than most filmic artists, desires – and has succeeded in creating – sweeping cinematic experiences in the context of video installations. His works, from *monsoon* (1995) to *electric earth* (1999), are so exquisitely filmed (he uses 35 millimeter and digital video) that it is difficult to tell the difference between them and studio films, although the content, of course, is not the same. 'In my installations I don't see the narrative ending with the image on the screen,' he told publisher and critic Amanda Sharp. 'Narrative can exist on a physical level – as much through the flow of electricity as through an image.... I don't wish to control and experience, nor do I want to make something that's merely experiential. I'd rather attempt to set up a system that brings a set of questions to the viewer. I'd like my work to provide nutrients.'[2]

Despite the elegance of his images, Doug Aitken is a restless artist, eager to break down standard cinematic barriers and common ways of formulating narratives. 'I am fascinated by film, but I'm even more interested in breaking it apart. I think of the format itself and how limiting it has become, which is why I use multiple screens.... I want to expand the realm of perception. My working process is changing constantly. I'm never illustrating a story or following a script. I let circumstances inform me.'

Like a true post-medium artist, Aitken says of his work: 'I make forms of communications. I use mediums as they suit the concepts.' In common with some others in this chapter, Aitken shoots primarily on film and transfers to video for projection. 'A lot of my attraction to film is because of light. There is something less tangible about film, something more hidden in it.... By contrast, video is flat, revealing everything at once.'[3]

Aitken, known, like Taylor-Wood, for both richly colored photographs and multi-surface installations, began making films and showing in galleries and alternative spaces in the early 1990s. His film, *autumn* (1993), starred the now well-known actress Chloë Sevigny. Though he has shot films in many parts of the world – in Guyana for *monsoon*, in the Namib desert for *diamond sea* (1997), in Montserrat for *eraser* (1998), amongst other places – his work retains a strong American preoccupation with landscape as well as a very contemporary interest in personal identity and time. 'I am constantly piecing things together, finding fragments of information, splicing them, collaging them, montaging them to create a network of perceptions,' he has said.[4] His very choice of words demonstrates his keen awareness of cinematic language and activities (especially editing) on contemporary art practices.

This 'splicing' and 'collaging' is most evident in *electric earth* (1999), a color film transferred to eight laserdisks for projection, that extends into four different 'rooms' created by scrims. With its late night shots of an African-American youth dancing solo down abandoned Los Angeles streets, *electric earth* becomes an elegy for a life lived in the shadows. 'I dance so fast I become what's around me,' the young man

Doug Aitken

343 *electric earth* (1999)

OVERLEAF

344 *electric earth* (1999)

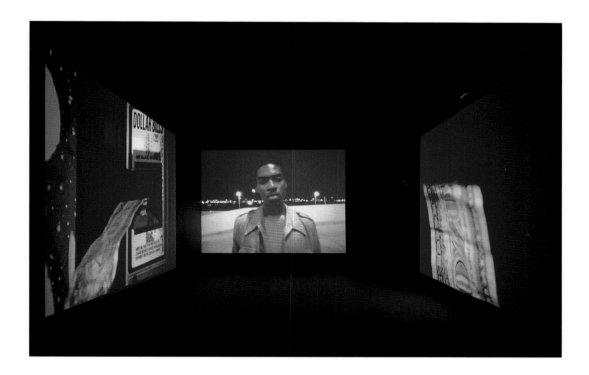

says. 'I absorb the information. I eat it. It's the only "now" I get.' Aitken films him in front of a closed trophy store and then facing a towering Coca-Cola machine; in a parking lot, empty, apart from a silvery shopping cart; and in a bedroom, as he holds a remote control in front of a flickering TV set. Viewers move through the installation, confronting walls and corners where sharp, color images are projected. Aitken's poetic aspirations are captured beautifully in a shot of a tattered piece of fabric caught in the openings of a steel fence.

There is no passive way to experience *electric earth*. If viewers enter into it, the young man's nocturnal ramblings become a part of them. His image is projected on all the walls around them, spliced in with shots of streets and digital clocks announcing the time, and its passing. If he is in his small room, viewers feel claustrophobic; if he is walking down a dark quiet street, viewers feel scared: not because

Aitken has set up a narrative for viewers to follow. He has not. Rather he has created a kind of surveillance environment in which viewers are thrust into this man's life without his knowing it.

The solitariness and confinement of *electric earth* pales in comparison with the utter desolation of *eraser*, filmed on the island of Montserrat after it was devastated by a volcano from 1996 to 1997. Totally void of life, the island is a ghostly reminder of nature's dominance. Aitken moves his camera slowly through the now-dead environment as if he were a time traveler discovering a long-lost civilization.

Aitken's influences, especially Bruce Nauman – evident in works like *bad animal* (1996) and *these restless minds* (1998) – become less apparent with each new large-scale installation. He is inventing a singular body of work that, while rooted in the cinematic tradition of Eisenstein and more contemporary films with the grandeur of *Doctor Zhivago* and *Lawrence of Arabia*, takes personal video making and expands it into filmed environments that retain the complexities of Conceptual video.

'Filmic' art

As Video art enters its fourth decade, moving ever closer to cinema on the digital highway, artists, as has been shown, are no longer concerned with preserving video's unique characteristics. In the 1970s, video as a time-based art was favored for both its immediacy and its affordability. In fact, the lush images of 35-millimeter film were not only felt to be too expensive for most artists, they were also regarded with suspicion. They did not present life as it was. Video, by contrast, was filmed and could be presented in 'real time.' In those rebellious years of early Video art, such a notion was important.

Now the dense textures previously associated only with film are available in digital technologies.

Eija-Liisa Ahtila

Like Aitken and recently Manglano-Ovalle, Finnish artist Eija-Liisa Ahtila (b. 1959) shoots on film and transfers the footage to video for DVD projection. This technique results in a gray area that is neither film nor video, which is why the word 'filmic' has been adopted to cover these hybrids. Perhaps an even more accurate name would be 'filmic digital art.'

Ahtila's installation, *Consolation Service* (1999), is a twenty-three-minute, two-screen narrative projected side by side on the same white wall. What are usually quick 'reaction shots' (someone responding with a look or a short sentence) in cinema are here given their own screen, so, as the action takes place on one side, the other side shows close-ups of people's faces, or of furniture, or anything else the director finds interesting. In Ahtila's scenario a young couple is seen going to a therapist with their infant. They communicate poorly, fight loudly, and decide to divorce. They then go through the motions of a birthday party with friends, afterwards taking a walk across a frozen lake which cracks, claiming the lives of the husband and the friends. In the final scenes, the wife is at home with the baby and the husband appears in a post-death state. He bows several times then is gone, presumably forever.

Ahtila's tale, which echoes in feeling the desperation of couples seen in work by Bergman or Godard, is told in rich colors and poetic asides. Shadows from candles,

Eija-Liisa Ahtila

345 In *The House* (2002), a three-screen projection, a woman living in isolation in the country begins to have aural and visual hallucinations. In time they take over her life and she becomes increasingly paranoid. Ahtila based her abstract narrative on conversations she had with women who had suffered some form of psychosis. The viewer's attention passes from screen to screen as images of self-delusion become more and more apparent. The split-screens echo the woman's state of mind. The artist intends to disrupt the normal flow of cinematic logic, replacing it with an empathetic rather than rational appeal.

snow kicked up by puppies at play, flickering images of running horses on a television set – all add up to a very satisfying viewing experience. According to critic Ulrike Matzer, *Consolation Service*, 'like all of Ahtila's films, touches upon a fund of shared human experience. The events could take place anywhere. They are both personally and universally applicable. She draws upon styles and effects from such conventional genres of film as the short feature, the commercial, the documentary, the music video, and the Hollywood fiction, weaving these elements together to form new worlds of images that defy clear categorization.'[5]

Her *Anne, Aki, and God* (1998) is an elaborate installation with a theatrical setting: an empty bed, a reading lamp and five monitors arranged within a large wooden structure. Above is a large projection of two actors playing the role of 'God' in this melancholic narrative of a man, Aki, who is descending into the isolated darkness of schizophrenia and is unable to leave his apartment. Media curator Chrissie Iles writes of *Anne, Aki, and God*, 'Ahtila interweaves the charge of live Performance with the fictional and documentary modes of filmmaking, into a multi-layered spatial narrative which deconstructs both the anguish of insanity and the thin line between imagination, hallucination, and reality.'[6]

The House (2002) takes a similar theme. In much of her work Ahtila explores the plight of women who find themselves in very difficult situations resulting from not only harsh circumstances, but also mental illness. There is a lyrical beauty to the piece. Ahtila's brilliant colors and fanciful direction have the seductive feel of a benign hallucination, even though we know the woman is suffering deeply.

Ahtila echoes the practices of early video artists in her three-part installation *Me/We; Okay, Gray* (1993), although the videos in this three-monitor installation were also originally shot on 35-millimeter film. Three television sets – two on wooden tables and one on the floor (with DVD players on chairs next to them) – show imaginary, black-and-white 'television commercials' concerning the sexes, radiation leaks, and people feeling left out of the reality around them. Mimicking the style of television commercials, Ahtila portrays women in a variety of unflattering, if comic, situations. She does what several early video artists did: present one fully realized and intimate idea, a moment in a life, or a thought too personal and fleeting to be given much attention. That she does it with film is another indication that the same importance is no longer attached to certain mediums by media artists. Artists such as Ahtila suggest that Marshall McLuhan's dictum has not survived the test of time: the medium, it seems, is not the message, at least to these artists.

Eija-Liisa Ahtila
346 *Consolation Service* (1999)

Eija-Liisa Ahtila

347 *Me/We; Okay, Gray* (1993)

Matthew Barney

348 *Field Dressing (orifill)* (1989)

Matthew Barney

Matthew Barney (b. 1967, United States), like many other artists in this category, can hardly be called a 'video artist,' as his work is far removed from the 'pure' practice of Video art. However, neither is he an 'experimental film' artist: he started in galleries and now shows in both galleries and cinemas. He shoots on video, then transfers to film for projection. His concerns certainly echo the performative videos addressed in Chapter 2, but the filmed scenarios of his masterwork to date, the *Cremaster* series, have such elaborate costumes (including prosthetic devices), scenery, visual effects, and animation that they comprise a personal filmic art unlike any other.

From his earliest video work, *Scabaction* (1988), in which Barney cuts his irritated skin with a razor and medicates the wound with substantial amounts of Vaseline and a gel pack, and *Field Dressing (orifill)* (1989), in which he scales the walls of his studio naked, Barney has been interested in male effort, bodily functions and fluids, and sexuality. With the *Cremaster* films,[7] dating from 1994 to the present, these themes became dramatized through a fantastical image machine of hybrid human/animal beings with exposed genitalia; underwater nymphs; majestic queen bees and a host of other characters inspired equally by Wagner, the American dance director Busby Berkeley, and the novelist Truman Capote, who wrote *In Cold Blood* (1964).

He has been filming the five-part series out of order since the early 1990s and releasing them as they are made. Hence, *Cremaster 4* was shown in 1994, *Cremaster 1* from 1995 to 1996, *Cremaster 5* in 1997, *Cremaster 2* in 1999, and *Cremaster 3* in 2002. In this and other ways, Barney reflects the methods of experimental theater artist Robert Wilson, whose project, *The Civil Wars*, was also unveiled in five parts over several years in the 1980s. Like Wilson, Barney did not release his series in sequence, partly to emphasize the non-naturalistic nature of the enterprise. Barney shares Wilson's phantasmagoric imagination: both populate their surreal scenarios with gods and goddesses, pop stars, and cultural icons. Barney has Harry Houdini, Gary Gilmore, Norman Mailer, The Queen of Chain, while Wilson uses Abraham Lincoln, Giuseppe Garibaldi, Robert E. Lee, and Hercules. However, where Wilson favors exotic birds and people on stilts, Barney prefers medical devices, prosthetic limbs, gooey fluids and the like. His worlds are a fetishist's dream in which private body parts (the cremaster is the muscle in the male genitals to which the testicles are attached) assume center stage in exaggerated form in magnificently, if bizarrely, clad hybrid bodies. In *Cremaster 4*, for example, Barney himself (he stars in all his videos) is seen with orange hair, floppy ears, long, hoofed legs, and a sparkling white suit.

The *Cremaster* series cannot be viewed as different parts of the same 'story' as, say, the three parts of *The Godfather* films can. These *Cremaster* films are linked only by the central muscle of their title, suggesting a male-centered universe that dissolves under the power of strong female presences like The Queen of Chain in *Cremaster 5* and the mysterious queen-bee type with the honey dripping from her nose in *Cremaster 2*. In each of these, Barney plays with sexual mores, sexual

identities (he acts a character called the Queen of Chain's 'Diva' in *Cremaster 5*) and a host of personal, abstracted themes honored by many contemporary artists. If references can be made for Barney's unique cosmology, they would include the art of Eva Hesse, Kiki Smith, and the films of Jack Smith – *Flaming Creatures* (1963) – Mike Kuchar, especially *Sins of the Fleshapoids* (1965), and Kenneth Anger – *Inauguration of the Pleasure Dome* (1966) and *Invocation of My Demon Brother* (1969).[8]

Aleksander Sokurov

Russian artist Aleksander Sokurov (b. 1951) also stands out amongst artists who are extending the use of video into new and sophisticated terrain. Is he a film director, video artist, 'poet with a camera?' Known as a filmmaker in the tradition of the great Russian director Andrei Tarkovsky, Sokurov also makes art videos shown at video festivals, for instance, *Mother and Son* (1997). Whether personal interpretations of literary classics – *Save and Protect* (1989), based on *Madame Bovary*, and *Whispering Pages* (1993), loosely associated with *Crime and Punishment* – or simply personal meditations on life and death – *The Second Circle* (1990) and *Mother and Son* – Sokurov's films (some shot on 35-millimeter film, some on video) are characteristically dreamlike and intensely beautiful. Is he a video artist? The answer hardly matters, though he did make cinematic history with his 2002 film, *The Russian Ark*, which is a single-shot, ninety-minute movie filmed with a digitial video camera.

The New Wave of Women Artists

It is clear from many of these examples of media artists that Video art opened up vast new possibilities for women artists from many countries. Tracey Moffatt (b. 1960, Australia), for example, photographer, video artist, and filmmaker, suspends boundaries in her use of materials. In a single exhibition she can present a suite of photographs, a videotape, and a 35-millimeter film, all with considerable confidence. In both still and moving images, she spins tales derived from her fascination with the commonplace (roller derby races and surfers) and the aesthetic.

Remarkable in its compositional beauty and restraint is her *Night Cries – A Rural Tragedy*. Filmed in 1989 in 35 millimeter and transferred to laserdisk for projection, *Night Cries* is a seventeen-minute pastiche of fluid, painterly images that recount the interaction between a middle-aged daughter who feels trapped and her dying mother, whose life has been reduced to sleeping fitfully, eating, and making assisted trips to the outdoor lavatory. A palette of desert oranges, blues, and cloudy whites permeate the set of the sound stage where Moffatt has created a surreal vision of the Australian outback. In contrast to her photos, tight compositions in the midst of an expansive natural landscape, *Night Cries* is a moodscape that unabashedly announces its artifice. This controlled, staged environment reflects the daughter's claustrophobia and allows Moffatt maximal directorial control. In mostly silent rage, the daughter goes about her daily tasks of feeding her mother, wheeling her to the outside lavatory, and listening to her nocturnal squirmishes with encroaching death.

Both women are completely self-centered, and the viewers' sympathies shift from one to the other. At times the daughter seems neglectful, even cruel, though the mother has lost all affection, all sense of gratitude to her. Black-and-white scenes from a distant childhood inserted in the film are the only indication of a once real, if

Aleksander Sokurov

352–54 *Mother and Son* (1997), an elegy to the devotion of son to mother, is a companion piece to Aleksander Sokurov's film, *The Second Circle* (1990), in which a young man returns to Siberia to bury his father. Though long estranged from him, he dutifully takes care of all the 'final things' like washing the body and making the funeral arrangements. *Mother and Son* observes another young man taking very special care of his mother in her final days. Few words are spoken, but their gestures and their eyes convey great meaning.

Tracey Moffatt
355–56 *Night Cries – A Rural*
Tragedy (1989)

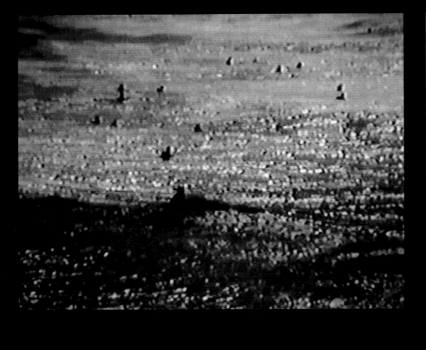

complicated, relationship between the two women. Particularly prophetic, perhaps, is a sequence where a girl and her brother are at the beach with their mother. Some seaweed attaches itself to the girl's throat, choking her, as the mother, who is some distance from her daughter, stares out to sea, not hearing the screams of her child. Years later, the daughter lies on her bed late at night smoking a cigarette; a train passes in the distance; the mother cries out a dry, nightmarish howl that is unheard.

The tragedy here does not result from the sudden death of a child, a flashback, or a mother taken too soon from her children. Rather it is the slow tragedy of a life perceived as useless and empty; a daughter robbed of horizons, rocking her dead mother, and crying like a baby.

In a radical shift in tone, Moffatt's videotape, *Heaven* (1997), is a sexy, feminist romp in the parking lots of surfers' beaches, where Moffatt insinuates her camera in the midst of the private rituals of young male athletes. In a humorous reversal of customary voyeurism, it is the boys who are being watched. Moffatt is part of the new wave of women media artists, who, like Joan Jonas, Carolee Schneemann, and Marina Abramovic before them, are giving contemporary art a bold new face.

Lynn Hershman (b. 1941, United States) also creates fictional characters at times, but they now tend to inhabit the virtual worlds of altered reality. Emerging from the San Francisco Performance scene in 1970, Hershman created the character Roberta Breitman who, for nine years, was her alter ego, her performance character. Roberta had her own life, complete with her own residence, wardrobe, credit cards, and the like. Other additional identities adopted by Hershman have included the agoraphobic Lorna (1979–82) and the wired CyberRoberta (1997–2000), an updated version of the earlier Roberta. Hershman says she has been concerned with the 'articulation of identity' throughout her career. She has kept an 'electronic diary' since 1984, video-taping and submitting the footage to various editing techniques that fragment the narratives. A pioneer of computer-based, interactive art, Hershman has created work that engages and challenges the identity issues now paramount in the computer age.

She anticipated the ubiquitous practice of creating new identities in chat rooms long before AOL and Yahoo were invented. Her works of digital art, which often incorporate video, have included *Room of One's Own: Slightly Behind the Scenes* (1990–93), an installation triggered by viewers' eye movements, and the film *Conceiving Ada* (1996–97), based on the life of Ada Byron, Countess of Lovelace, who is credited with inventing an early prototype of the computer.

Lynn Hershman

LEFT AND BELOW LEFT

363–64 *Teknolust* (2002), shot on high-definition video, is a cyber comedy about three women who live in colorful isolation when one of them decides she requires sperm. Taking Lynn Hershman's long-time interests in women's issues and technology, *Teknolust* is both a winning fantasy and a cautionary tale about having all of one's needs (including make-up) met by digital means.

Kristin Lucas (b. 1968, United States) has inherited the performative art of Hershman and others in her critiques of a society gone to extremes with technology. In numerous short videos and performances made since 1996, Lucas creates characters adrift in a world of gadgets, radio waves, and overstimulation. *Cable Xcess* (1996), a typically humorous as well as cautionary video, incorporates several images on to a split screen. The artist describes it as 'a public service announcement/infomercial which informs viewers about the consequences of long-term exposure to electromagnetic fields. I perform as both spokesperson and case study, transmitting a pirate broadcast through my body (body as satellite), educating viewers about early signs of exposure, and sharing alternative methods for coping with contamination.'[9]

In a similar manner her video *Host* (1997) involves a young woman, played by the artist, who is seen in an online therapy session directed by the system operator of a 'multimedia kiosk' imagined by Lucas. *Drag and Drop* (1999), a phrase that refers to a computer task, is an interactive video Performance in which Lucas plays tennis with an opponent who is just a video projection on a screen opposite her. She rigged sensors under the court that controlled the movements of her 'opponent.' It is notable that Robert Rauschenberg's *Nine Evenings: Art and Technology* (1969), one of the primary examples of multimedia Performance, also made use of wired tennis rackets.

Lucas's work, known for its sophisticated use of low-tech instruments like toy cameras, has grown increasingly complex and interactive. Her *Simulcast Mobile Kit*

Kristin Lucas

ABOVE LEFT

365 *Screening Room* (1998)

ABOVE CENTER LEFT, CENTER AND RIGHT

366–68 Kristin Lucas is representative of a new breed of artists at home with all manner of new technologies, from toy cameras to video to computers. Her work often takes shape in street performances. She invites viewers to take a critical stance towards technology, which plays such a ubiquitous presence in their lives. In this work, *Cable Xcess* (1996), she informs viewers about the long-term consequences of exposure to electromagnetic fields from televisions to cell phones.

#1 (1998–present) can involve numerous performers using a modified video-mixer on a toy guitar, helmets with adjustable antennae, and hand-made satellite dishes. Dressed in orange overalls in the original 'intervention,' as she called it, participants moved through the streets of Tokyo interacting with onlookers in this mock-futuristic game of electronic toys. 'I find myself more and more interested in a dialogue and in collaboration with artists, athletes, engineers, musicians, programmers and writers,' Lucas says, emphasizing her self-understanding as an artist who uses technology, including video, only as a means for expressing her concerns.[10] Video is a component of a much larger critique of technology.

Shirin Neshat (b. 1957, Iran) is a filmic artist for whom installation is the best-suited mode of presentation for her short, visually graphic explorations of cultural repression and sexual politics in her native Iran. In a few short years, the artist has received extraordinary international attention (including a prize at the 1998 Venice Biennale) with her installations *Turbulent* (1998), *Rapture* (1999), *Soliloquy* (1999), *Fervor* (2000), *Possessed* (2001), and *Pulse* (2001). Each one was shot on film (usually 16-millimeter) and transferred to DVD or laserdisk for projection.

In common with many of the artists examined in this book, Neshat's earliest work was Performance-based photography. Living in the United States since the

1970s, she made, in the early 1990s, her *Women of Allah* series, in which she donned the black head-to-toe cover worn by women in many Islamic cultures, the chador, and wrote militant feminist poetry on the exposed parts of her body (bare feet, palms of her hand) in Persian. In one, *Allegiance with Wakefulness* (1994), she is seated on the ground with her painted bare feet facing the camera, the barrel of a gun placed ominously between her feet.

Her short films, made in Morocco in black and white, are characterized by classically framed and exquisitely conceived shots (like the men in white shirts and black pants running up stone steps and the women draped in black walking toward the sea in *Rapture*) that encapsulate in a very few moments entire worlds of emotion and conflict.

The first film she made in color, *Passage* (2001), was commissioned by Philip Glass for the series that also included *Notes* by Michal Rovner, discussed in Chapter 3. In a rocky landscape a young girl kneels before a pile of stones, black-clad figures huddle together on the ground, funeral possessions pass by, a long, winding path of stones suddenly ignites, sending black smoke into the vast, empty sky. In this meditation on

Shirin Neshat

OPPOSITE TOP LEFT AND BOTTOM LEFT
369–70 *Passage* (2001)

ABOVE LEFT
371 *Turbulent* (1998)

ABOVE RIGHT
372 *Rapture* (1999)

death, burial rites, and violence, Neshat's camera (in this case 35-millimeter film transferred to DVD for projection) expertly surveys a desolate land populated by the sons and daughters of war.

The Future of Video Art in the Digital Age

At the end of this study of Video art, enter artist Perry Hoberman (b. 1954, United States), an avant-garde artist whose work in media and art in the early 1980s anticipated media's ubiquitous presence in the art world ten years later, while, at the same time, suggesting its demise twenty years from then. His first installation in 1982 (he worked in theater and Performance in the 1970s as well), *Simulcast #2*, consisted of multiple screens (projection surfaces) with translucent plastic megaphones protruding from them. Images were projected through the megaphones on to the screens, resulting in a cacophony of fractured pictures. Multiple associations were present at once: the overkill of television images on society; the varying ways different viewers

Perry Hoberman

ABOVE

375 Perry Hoberman might have
used video in his installation work;
in fact viewers are often seduced into
thinking he does. However, Hoberman
is interested in what has become
another material in art, 'interactivity,'
as *Cathartic User Interface* (2000)
shows. Fulfilling the Duchampian
dictum that the viewer completes
the work of art, Hoberman and others
rely totally on viewers or participants
to complete the art: without them it
does not exist.

Christoph Draeger

OPPOSITE TOP AND BOTTOM

373–74 The work of Christoph
Draeger (b. 1965, Switzerland) often
involves human tragedies and
disasters. He will sometimes re-enact
tragedies in miniature in his studio
and film them. *Ode to a Sad Song*
(2001) is situated in an abandoned
trailer park. Draeger and his crew
set fire to an RV (recreational vehicle)
and filmed it, projecting the footage
on multiple screens. The installation
became a metaphor for a wasteland,
a formerly thriving civilization that
has incinerated itself. Draeger's work
took on a particular poignancy after
the events of September 11, 2001,
when New York (where the artist lives)
was attacked by al-Qaida terrorists.

see different images; the 'unreality' of what is seen on the screen, and so on. In a sense, Hoberman's first work prefigured the end of the projected image.

His second piece, *Out of the Picture* (1982), was an early type of appropriation in which Hoberman remade the book and film of *The Invisible Man*. He created an installation environment in which viewers walked through the projected images amidst clothing, shadows, test tubes, and a sound track in which the Invisible Man exposed his designs to conquer the world. For more than twenty years now, Hoberman has been incorporating advanced, interactive technology into a massive critique of technological culture. Despite appearances, he has not used video at all, except in one installation, *The Empty Orchestra Café* (1991–93). All of his fast-moving images have been 3D projections and digitally manipulated pictures. His aim is to seduce the audience into involvement with the installation.

Perhaps the best summary of his work is his *Cathartic User Interface* (2000), in which viewers (or rather 'participants') are invited to throw fist-sized beanbag balls at a large, blinking keyboard wired with words expressive of many people's frustrations with computer technology: 'You have no new mail, you have no friends, you have no life.' He might have used video, but he did not. His aim was to expose the futility in trying to overcome technology. The medium he chose was a secondary consideration.

Despite certain indicators amongst artists, it is too early to suggest the end of Video art, even though the Video art with which this study began, the unedited tapes that ran in artists' studios until they were finished, is long gone. Digital video has completely changed the landscape and digital video is only beginning its ascendance. It has been discovered by Hollywood and young filmmakers are finding it an attractive, affordable alternative to 35-millimeter film. A foot of film costs approximately US $1 to buy and process compared with 1.5 cents for digital tape. Of the 107 films in the 2001 Sundance Film Festival, the American film world's equivalent of a debutante ball, almost twenty-five percent of the entries were shot on digital video, twice as many as the year before.

One of the more intriguing, if overly zealous, developments in the use of video in filmmaking, mentioned briefly above, is the Dogma group formed in 1995 by Danish film directors Lars Von Trier and Thomas Vinterberg. The two created a 'vow of chastity' that prohibits Dogma members from using standard movie-making materials and techniques like film stock, artificial lighting, music scores, make-up, props, or costumes. All films must be shot with hand-held video cameras and emphasize story line and 'real' performances. Two films to emerge in the late 1990s that received critical acclaim were *The Celebration* and *The Idiots*. How many more will appear is not clear.

What is happening in digital art is supplanting video as it has been known. Software is replacing editing machines. In the future, virtual reality will re-define our experience of 'reality'. '*Start-stop* technology,' as new media curator Magdalena Sawon says, 'is no longer viable.' The linearity (even of non-linear, abstract videos) of videos, as played on a tape or projected on to a wall, will be replaced by increasingly interactive viewer/participant manipulations. There is already evidence of this in the

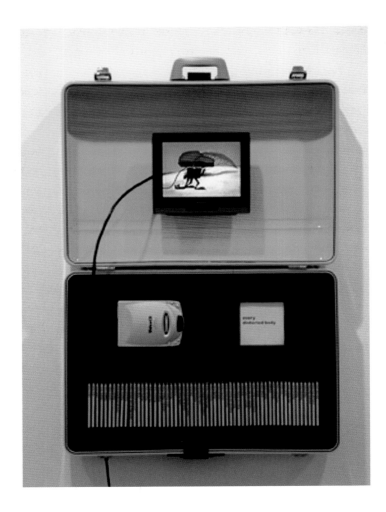

work of many artists, like the team Jennifer and Kevin McCoy, who, though they use video footage, create elaborate, even obsessive, interactive installations that are the next phase of appropriation-based interactivity.

Every Anvil (2001) is a video database of shots from over one hundred episodes of *Looney Toons* cartoons from the 1940s and 1950s. Each shot is indexed according to categories of violence and physical extremism such as 'Every Explosion,' 'Every Flattened Character,' and 'Every Scream.' The McCoys devised an interactive installation in which visitors (or participants) choose which disks to play according to the 'action' or 'emotion' they want to see.

Similarly, *Every Shot, Every Episode* (2001) contains literally that: every shot of every episode of the 1970s television show, *Starsky and Hutch*, which viewers can watch according to their own tastes for the content of certain scenes. The computer now rearranges the dramatic content for prime emotional impact according to the desires of the viewer. Control of the work has shifted from the creators and producers to the consumers.

Grahame Weinbren (b. 1947, South Africa, lives in United States) and his collaborators have mastered this shift in their creation of a truly interactive cinema. Weinbren and Roberta Friedman collaborated on *The Erl King* (1984), a touch-screen interactive cinema installation exploring several overlapping narrative threads, including Freud's famous 'burning child' dream and the Goethe/Schubert piece 'ErlKönig.' Participants encounter a vast array of imagery (stock car racing, palm trees, Hawaiian shirts) as they wander through a landscape of 19th-century Romanticism and 1980s cultural excess.

Even more elaborate is Weinbren's *Sonata* (1991–93). The biblical story of Judith decapitating Holofernes to save her home town and Tolstoy's short story 'The Kreutzer Sonata' form the backdrop of images in an interactive installation. Participants can look at each story from multiple points of view (by pointing at a projection screen) and navigate through the dense imagery as if they were in a dream. In *Tunnel* (2000), Weinbren, James Cathcart, and Sandra McLean created an interactive installation in the city of Dortmund, Germany. Visitors walking through an enclosed, claustrophobic space, like a coal tunnel, set off ghost-like images that appear beneath their feet. The images, 'ghosts' or 'avatars' as the creators call them, follow the visitors, moving when they move, stopping when they stop until they reach the end of the tunnel.

This type of image-manipulation provides a much more sophisticated and intellectually-based interaction than the familiar video games found in stores and arcades throughout the world. While not embraced under the rubric of 'art,' video games have developed over the years and today are as popular as cinema. In fact, movies and television shows now use popular video-game personalities as the basis for some of their shows.

The future of Video art is best told in the following tale of two cities. In 1989, in Liverpool, a group of young collaborators founded Video Positive, a festival of Video art that, in a short period of time, became a respected European venue. In 2000, Video Positive became 'history,' as the founder Eddie Berg pronounced. 'Ten years ago,' Berg writes in *The Other Side of Zero: Video Positive, 2000*, 'at the dawn of the last

Grahame Weinbren and James Cathcart with Sandra McLean

377–82 Tunnel (2000)

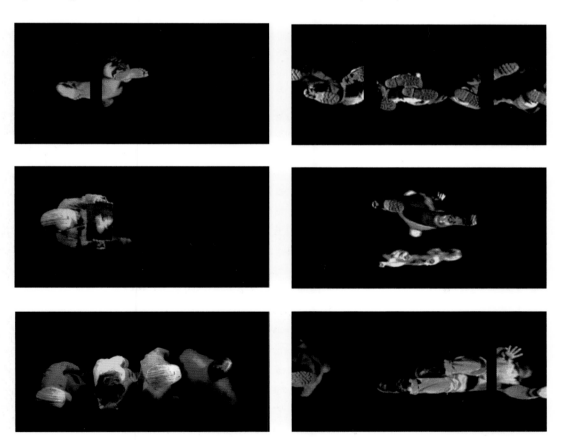

decade of the old century, a century dominated by technological developments and the cultural impact of moving image media, most of Britain's galleries and exhibitors had yet to declare a significant interest in artists working with video or emerging technologies…. However, once it was "discovered" they just couldn't let it go. But let it go we must.'

The final Video Positive (the festival is being reborn with a new name and new emphasis) did indeed have a number of video installations, but there were more non-video based 'projects,' a word that has emerged to describe all manner of artists' mixed-media works and ideas. Included were a sound installation by Swiss artist Ugo Rondinone (also known for his large video installations), an 'online environment and video/sound installation' by British artists Sonia Boyce and 'the Liverpool Black Sisters,' and 'an online multimedia and streaming web community site' by the Danish group Superflex. The once new technology of video had now taken its place beside other, more computer-driven media.

In Boston, Massachusetts, curator George Fifield founded VideoSpace in 1991 at the height of popularity for Video art. For most of the 1990s Fifield organized video exhibitions in Boston area spaces and museums until he noticed profound changes. 'I followed the art form,' he says, ' and it was moving into the digital era. Computers and other digital technologies were changing the playing field.' Fifield proceeded to create the Boston CyberArts Festival, which, while including some forms of Video art, presents a full range of digital arts from webart to Virtual Reality. It has become the largest festival of its kind in the United States.

Similar events occur all over the world in cities like Seoul, Korea, which hosts an international biennial event exploring the convergence of media technologies and the contemporary arts. Another sign of the times is the noted Video Art Festival in Locarno, Switzerland, founded 1980, which now includes 'the electronic arts.'

It is, of course, too soon to make any firm statements about the end of, or future of, Video art. Art historians will have their way with the medium in due time. What can be stated is that, like any technology-based medium (including television, radio, film), video is no longer what it was before the digital age. Then it was a clear alternative to film, loved for its immediacy, its availability, its potential as a community tool for social change, its affordability for artistic exploration.

Video technology is now in a hybrid stage, combining all manner of digital technologies in the creation of what is likely to be a new medium. It is time for video to assume its place as simply a 'filmic' medium, now that the word 'filming' refers to the many ways in which the moving or animated image is created. The golden age for Video art took place in the 1990s, when every festival, biennial, contemporary gallery, and alternative space projected videos on to walls, screens, chairs, cathedral ceilings, and everywhere else. It has been done, and, as with cinema, the next phase is to come.

Notes

Introduction

1 William Anastasi interviewed by the author, September 2001.
2 Rosalind Krauss, 'Video and Narcissism', *October*, No. 1, spring 1976, p. 51.
3 Vito Acconci, quoted in Lori Zippay (ed.), *Electric Arts Intermix: Video*, 1991, p. 12.
4 Rosalind Krauss, *A Voyage on the North Sea: Art in the Age of the Post-Medium Condition*, 1999, pp. 31–32. Curiously, despite this affirmation of video's heterogeneity on p. 31, Krauss reiterates her 1976 position here on video as 'decidedly narcissistic' on p. 30.

Chapter 1
Shaping a History

1 Hermine Freed, 'Where do We Come From? Where Are We? Where Are We Going?' in Ira Schneider and Beryl Korot (eds.), *Video Art: An Anthology*, 1976.
2 For lively histories of the intrigues involved in the founding of television, see David E. Fisher and Marshall Jon Fisher, *The Tube*, 1997, and Evan I. Schwartz, *The Last Lone Inventor*, 2002.
3 *Troisième Biennale de Lyon*, 1995, p. 71.
4 In Douglas Davis and Allison Simmons (eds.), *The New Television: A Public/Private Art*, 1977, pp. 179ff.
5 Marshall McLuhan, *The Mechanical Bride: The Folklore of Industrial Man*, 1951.
6 Frank Gillette interviewed by the author, June 2001.
7 Paul Ryan interviewed by the author, New York, June 2000.
8 For more information on the exhibition 'TV as a Creative Medium', see Ben Portis at www.eai.org.
9 Ben Portis, *The Fulcrum: TV as a Creative Medium*, Electronic Arts Intermix, 2001.
10 Quoted in Paul Ryan, 'A Genealogy of Video,' *Leonardo*, Vol. 21, No. 1, 1988, pp. 39–44.
11 See Dee Dee Halleck, *Hand-Held Visions: Uses of Community Media*, 2002. Also Deirdre Boyle, *Subject to Change: Guerilla Television Revisited*, 1997.
12 Julia Scher interviewed by the author, July 2000.
13 Julia Scher in *TEN 8*, Vol. 2, No. 2, September 1991, pp. 64–65.
14 In Douglas Davis and Allison Simmons (eds.), *The New Television: A Public/Private Art*, 1977, p. 186.
15 Ibid., pp. 192–93.
16 See also Wolfgang Becker in Douglas Davis and Allison Simmons (eds.), *The New Television: A Public/Private Art*, 1977, p. 194.
17 A. L. Rees, *A History of Experimental Film and Video*, 1999, p. 88.
18 Ibid., p. 90.
19 Wheeler Winston Dixon, *The Films of Jean-Luc Godard*, 1997, pp. 95 and 99.
20 Jenny Lion (curator), *Magnetic North*, catalogue of the exhibition at the Walker Art Center, Minneapolis, and Video Pool, Inc., Winnipeg, 2000.
21 Gene Youngblood, *Expanded Cinema*, 1970, p. 318.
22 John Alan Farmer, 'Pop People' in *The New Frontier, Art and Television, 1960–1965*, 2000, p. 64.
23 This information was obtained during interviews by the author with Richard Ekstract (February 28, 2003) and Paul Morrissey (March 1, 2003). Information about this party and photos of it appeared in *The New York Herald Tribune*, October 3, 1965. <mhtml:mid://00000018/#_ftnrefl>
24 John Alan Farmer, 'Pop People' in *The New Frontier, Art and Television, 1960–1965*, 2000, p. 65.
25 For further information on the history of Video art and video artists, see: www.eai.org; www.newmedia-arts.org; www.davidsonfiles.org; www.centreimage.org; www.vdb.org.
26 Lucy Lippard, *Six Years: The Dematerialization of the Art Object from 1966–1972*, 1973.
27 Chrissie Iles, 'Between the Still and Moving Image,' in Chrissie Iles, *Into the Light: The Projected Image in American Art, 1964–1977*, 2001.

Chapter 2
Video and the Conceptual Body

1 Quoted in Pepe Karmel, *Pollock at Work: The Films and Photographs of Hans Namuth* in *Jackson Pollock*, 1998.
2 Paul Schimmel, *Leap into the Void: Performance and the Object* in *Out of Actions: Between Performance and the Object, 1949–1979*, 1998, p. 18.
3 David Sylvester, 'The Supreme Pontiff' in *Francis Bacon*, 1998.
4 For further information on Fluxfilms, see Bruce Jenkins, 'Fluxfilms in Three False Starts' in *In the Spirit of Fluxus*, 1993, pp. 122–39.
5 John Hanhardt, *The Worlds of Nam June Paik*, 2000, pp. 116–17.
6 See Joseph Kosuth—*Art After Philosophy and After: Collected Writings, 1966–1990*, 1991.
7 Arthur C. Danto, *After the End of Art*, 1997.
8 Peter Wollen, 'Global Conceptualism and Northern American Conceptual Art' in *Global Conceptualism, Points of Origin, 1950s to 1980s*, 1999, pp. 73–85.
9 For more on the role of the 'heroic male artist' see Anne Edeb Gibson, *Abstract Expressionism: Other Politics*, 1997. She resurrects unsung female artists working at that time, such as Jeanne Miles (b. 1908), Alice Trumbull Mason (1904–71), Irene Rice Pereira (1907–71), and many others.
10 Martha Rosler interviewed by the author, autumn 2000.
11 Robert Fleck, 'The Evidence in Pictures' in Kurt Kren, *Kurt Kren: Film Photography Viennese Actionism*, 1998, p. 27.
12 VALIE EXPORT, *Woman's Art*, 1972, reprinted in *Split: Reality VALIE EXPORT*, 1997, p. 205.
13 See Reinhard Braun, *Video. TV. Telecommunication. The Early Projects* in *Re-Play, Beginnings of International Media Art in Austria*, 2000, p. 401ff.
14 For a full exploration of worldwide Performance art and its roots in Action painting, see Paul Schimmel, *Out of Actions: Between Performance and the Object, 1949–1979*, 1998.

Chapter 3
Video and the New Narrative

1 David A. Ross, *Bill Viola*, 1998, p. 152.
2 Bill Viola, 'Video Black – The Mortality of the Image' in Doug Hall and Sally Jo Fifer (eds.), *Illuminating Video: An Essential Guide to Video Art*, 1990, pp. 477–86.
3 The author is indebted to Karen Smith for describing this exhibition in a personal interview, December 2001.
4 Quoted in Laura Cottingham, 'New Wine in Old Bottles: Some Comments on the Early Years of Art Video' in John B. Ravenal (ed.), *Outer and Inner Space*, 2002, p. 8.
5 Barbara London interviewed by the author, February 2002.
6 Eleanor Heartney, '*Noah's Raven* and the Contradictions of Landscape,' originally published in Sandra Knudsen (ed.), *Noah's Raven: A Video Installation by Mary Lucier*, 1993, reprinted in Melinda Barlow (ed.), *Mary Lucier*, 2000, p. 169.
7 'Filmic' seems a useful word to describe the moving image medium, embracing both video and film. Videotape and 35-millimeter film are both used 'to film' images; hence, the word filmic.
8 Stan Brakhage, *Metaphors on Vision* in *Film Culture*, No. 30, autumn 1963, quoted in P. Adams Sitney, *Visionary Film: The American Avant-Garde 1943–1978*, 1979, p. 174.
9 Rovner's figures in *Overhanging* do indeed echo Giacometti in all his existential spareness. For a comparison between Giacometti's sculpture and Beckett's writings (whom Rovner also resembles), see Matti Megged, *Dialogue in the Void: Beckett and Giacometti*, 1985.

Chapter 4
Extensions

1 Rosalind Krauss, '*The Rock*': William Kentridge's Drawings for Projection, *October*, No. 92, spring 2000, p. 3ff.
2 Interview with Amanda Sharp in Daniel Birnbaum, Amanda Sharp, and Jörg Heiser, *Doug Aitken*, 2001, p. 6ff.
3 Doug Aitken interviewed by the author, 2002.
4 Interview with Amanda Sharp in Daniel Birnbaum, Amanda Sharp, and Jörg Heiser, *Doug Aitken*, 2001, p. 13.
5 Ulrike Matzer, 'The Fragile Nature of Normality' in *Eija-Liisa Ahtila, Consolation Service*, 2000.
6 Chrissie Iles in *Seeing Time: Selections from the Pamela and Richard Kramlich Collection of Media Art*, 1999.
7 Are Barney's works videos or are they films? Some say the means or methods of projection define the medium, others believe the shooting source does. Barney shoots on video and projects on film. I favor the latter definition: they are videos only if shot with a video camera.
8 In *Seeing Time: Selections from the Pamela and Richard Kramlich Collection of Media Art*, 1999, Chrissie Iles also notes the influences of film directors Stanley Kubrick (*2001: A Space Odyssey*, 1969), David Cronenburg (*Dead Ringers*, 1988), and Busby Berkeley.
9 Kristin Lucas, *Temporary Housing for the Despondent Virtual Citizen*, 2000, p. 16.
10 Quoted in Kristin Lucas, *Temporary Housing for the Despondent Virtual Citizen*, 2000, p. 39.

Select Bibliography

Introduction

Krauss, Rosalind, *A Voyage on the North Sea: Art in the Age of the Post-Medium Condition*, 1999
Zippay, Lori (ed.), *Electric Arts Intermix: Video*, 1991

Chapter 1
Shaping a History

Armstrong, Elizabeth, and Joan Rothfuss, *In the Spirit of Fluxus*, 1993
Boyle, Deirdre, *Video Classics: A Guide to Video Art and Documentary Tapes*, 1986
Breitwieser, Sabine (ed.), *Re-play: Beginnings of International Media Art in Austria*, 2000
Cubitt, Sean, *TIMESHIFT on video culture*, 1991
Davis, Douglas, and Allison Simmons (eds.), *The New Television: A Public/Private Art*, 1977
Delehanty, Suzanne (ed.), *Video Art*, 1975
Farmer, John Alan, *The New Frontier, Art and Television, 1960–1965*, 2000
Fast>>Forward: New Chinese Video Art, 1999
Frueh, Joanna, Cassandra L. Langer, and Arlene Raven (eds.), *New Feminist Criticism*, 1993
Gill, Johanna, *Video: State of the Art*, 1976
Hanhardt, John, *Video Art*, 1986
— (ed.), *Video Culture: A Critical Investigation*, 1990
—, *The Worlds of Nam June Paik*, 2000
Hillier, Jim (ed.), *The 1950s: Neo-Realism, Hollywood, the New Wave*, 1985
Iles, Chrissie, *Into the Light: The Projected Image in American Art, 1964–1977*, 2001
Levin, Thomas Y., Ursula Frohne, Peter Weibel (eds.), *CTRL Space*, 2002
McLuhan, Marshall, and Quentin Fiore, *The Medium is the Message: An Inventory of Effects*, 1967
Rees, A. L., *A History of Experimental Film and Video: From Canonical Avant-garde to Contemporary British Practice*, 1999
Renov, Michael, and Erika Suderburg (eds.), *Resolutions: Contemporary Video Practices*, 1996
Rush, Michael, *New Media in Late 20th-Century Art*, 1999
Schneider, Ira, and Beryl Korot (eds.), *Video Art: An Anthology*, 1976
Shamberg, Michael, and Raindance Corporation, *Guerilla Television*, 1971
Troisième Biennale de Lyon, 1995
Van Assche, Christine (ed.), *Vidéo et après, La collection vidéo du Musée national d'art moderne*, 1992
Youngblood, Gene, *Expanded Cinema*, 1970

Chapter 2
Video and the Conceptual Body

Braun, Reinhard, *Video. TV. Telecommunication. The Early Projects* in *Re-Play, Beginnings of International Media Art in Austria*, 2000
Danto, Arthur C., *After the End of Art: Contemporary Art and the Pale of History*, 1997
de Zegher, Catherine (ed.), *Martha Rosler: Positions in the Life World*, 1988
EXPORT, VALIE, *Woman's Art*, 1972
Gibson, Anne Edeb, *Abstract Expressionism: Other Politics*, 1997
Global Conceptualism: Points of Origin, 1950s–1980s, 1999
Hanhardt, John, *The Worlds of Nam June Paik*, 2000
Hopps, Walter, and Susan Davidson, *Robert Rauschenberg: A Retrospective*, 1997
Jenkins, Bruce, *In the Spirit of Fluxus*, 1993
Karmel, Pepe, *Pollock at Work: The Films and Photographs of Hans Namuth* in *Jackson Pollock*, 1998

Kosuth, Joseph, *Art After Philosophy and After: Collected Writings, 1966–1990*, 1991

Kren, Kurt, *Kurt Kren: Film Photography Viennese Actionism*, 1998

Schimmel, Paul, *Out of Actions: Between Performance and the Object, 1949–1979*, 1998

Sylvester, David, *Francis Bacon*, 1998

Wollen, Peter, *Global Conceptualism, Points of Origin, 1950s to 1980s*, 1999

Chapter 3
Video and the New Narrative

James, David E., *Allegories of Cinema: American Film in the Sixties*, 1989

Hall, Doug, and Sally Jo Fifer (eds.), *Illuminating Video: An Essential Guide to Video Art*, 1990

Ravenal, John B. (ed.), *Outer and Inner Space: Pipilotti Rist, Shirin Neshat, Jane and Louise Wilson and the History of Video Art*, 2002

Ross, David A., *Bill Viola*, 1998

Sitney, P. Adams, *Visionary Film: The American Avant-Garde 1943–1978*, 1979

Chapter 4
Extensions

Birnbaum, Daniel, Amanda Sharp, and Jörg Heiser, *Doug Aitken*, 2001

Danto, Arthur C., *After the End of Art: Contemporary Art and the Pale of History*, 1997

Druckrey, Timothy (ed.), *Electronic Culture: Technology and Visual Representation*, 1996

Guldemond, Japp, and Marente Bloemheuvel (eds.), *Cinéma, Cinéma: Contemporary Art and the Cinematic Experience*, 1999

Iles, Chrissie, *Seeing Time: Selections from the Pamela and Richard Kramlich Collection of Media Art*, 1999

Lucas, Kristin, *Temporary Housing for the Despondent Virtual Citizen*, 2000

Masséra, Jean-Charles (ed.), *Pierre Huyghe: The Third Memory*, 2000

Matzer, Ulrike, *Eija-Liisa Ahtila, Consolation Service*, 2000

Weibel, Peter, and Timothy Druckrey (eds.), *net_condition: art and global media*, 2001

010101: Art in Technological Times, 2001

Chronology

The Chronology is excerpted, in large part, with permission, from the following sources: The New Media Encyclopedia (www.newmedia-arts.org), produced by the Centre Georges Pompidou, Musée National d'Art Moderne, Paris; the Museum Ludwig, Cologne; and the Centre pour l'image contemporaine Saint-Gervais Genève, Geneva; Electronic Arts Intermix, New York (www.eai.org); The Experimental TV Center, Troy, New York (www.experimentaltvcenter.org); Davidson Gigliotti's Video History (www.davidsonsfiles.org).

1963
Artists

Nam June Paik exhibits *Electronic TV*, a piece consisting of thirteen monitors with distorted broadcast images, at Galerie Parnass, Wuppertal, Germany

Wolf Vostell, *TV Dé-coll/age* at Smolin Gallery, New York; also at Galerie Parnass, Wuppertal, Germany

Exhibitions

New York Annual Avant-Garde Festival (1963–80). The curator, Charlotte Moorman, and many of the regular participants – Nam June Paik, John Cage, Yoko Ono and John Lennon, the Hendricks brothers, Alison Knowles, Phil Corner, Yoshi Wada – were identified with Fluxus

1964
Artists

Fred Barzyk produces *Jazz Images*, one of the earliest experimental programs made at the public television station, WGBH-TV, Boston

Marshall McLuhan's *Understanding Media* is published in the United States

1965
Artists

Andy Warhol is given a Norelco slant-track video recorder by Richard Ekstract, publisher of *Tape Recording* magazine to help promote Norelco's new personal video equipment. Warhol presents first public showing of artist-made videotapes on September 29 at an 'underground' party held in the large railroad siding underneath the Waldorf-Astoria hotel in New York. The party itself was videotaped and played back to the guests. This information was obtained during interviews by the author with Richard Ekstract (February 28, 2003) and Paul Morrissey (March 1, 2003). Information about this party and photos of it appeared in *The New York Herald Tribune*, October 3, 1965. <mhtml:mid://00000018/#_ftnref1>

Nam June Paik buys one of the first Sony Portapaks on the American market with a grant from the Rockefeller Foundation. On October 4 he shows tape accompanied by a text entitled 'Electronic Video Recorder' at the Café Au Go-Go, New York

Wolf Vostell's exhibition 'Phänomene, Verwischungen, Parituren' and *TV Dé-coll/age* organized by the Autofriedhof and the Galerie René Block in Berlin, Germany

Wolf Vostell's *24 Stunden*, *dé-coll/age* at Galerie Parnass, Wuppertal, Germany

Nam June Paik, *TV Chair*, video sculpture by Nam June Paik, presented at the third annual Avant-Garde Festival in New York, organized by Charlotte Moorman

'Nam June Paik: Electronic TV,' Paik's first gallery show in the United States, at Galeria Bonino, New York

'Nam June Paik: Electronic TV, Color TV Experiments, 3 Robots, 2 Zen Boxes & 1 Zen Can', at The New School for Social Research, New York

Les Levine makes his first video, *Bum*, in New York

Exhibitions

'New Cinema Festival 1' at New York Cinémathèque, organized by John Brockman with videotapes by Nam June Paik and Charlotte Moorman. Festival explores uses of mixed-media projection

Political

Rockefeller Foundation begins to fund artists for experimentation with video

Legislation creates the National Endowment for the Arts, which establishes The American Film Institute (AFI). One of its goals is to preserve the heritage of film and television

Technology

Sony introduces ½-inch CV-2000, the 'first' consumer video format

Sony brings out its first portable ½-inch black-and-white videotape recorder

1966
Artists

Wolf Vostell, 'Verwischungen. Happening-Notationen,' presentation of works, performance and happenings, at Kunstverein, Cologne, Germany

Ken Dewey, *Selma Last Year*, New York Film Festival at Lincoln Center, Philharmonic Hall Lobby, New York City. Multichannel video installation with photographs by Bruce Davidson, music by Terry Riley

Exhibitions

'Nine Evenings: Theater and Engineering' at the 69th Regiment, New York City. Organized by Billy Klüver and EAT. Mixed-media performance events with collaborations between ten artists and forty engineers. Video projection used in works of Alex Hay, Robert Rauschenberg, David Tudor, and Robert Whitman

Innovation

Vidéo Production Company is created by Jean-Christophe Averty with Igor Barrère, François Chatel, Pierre Tchernia, and Alexandre Tarta in France

Experiments in Art and Technology (EAT) founded by Billy Klüver. Influential collaborations between engineers and artist, including Robert Rauschenberg, Jasper Johns, John Cage, and Andy Warhol. Some collaborations were exhibited at the World Expo '70 in Osaka, Japan

Electronic Paintings by Ture Sjölander and Bror Wilkstrom commissioned by National Swedish Television

1967
Artists

Electronic Blues by Nam June Paik in 'Lights in Orbit,' Howard Wise Gallery, New York City. Viewer participation video installation

Luciano Giaccari presents videotapes at Studio 971 in Varese, Italy

Exhibitions

'American Sculpture of the Sixties,' Los Angeles County Museum. Includes video installation by Bruce Nauman. The same museum starts the Art and Technology Program

'Light/Motion/Space,' Walker Art Center, Minneapolis in collaboration with Howard Wise Gallery, New York City. Travels to Milwaukee Art Center. Includes video works by Nam June Paik, Aldo Tambellini, and others

Innovation

Aldo Tambellini opens the Black Gate in New York, the first 'Electromedia Theater,' where he organizes screenings and creates environment-actions using video

Political

Rockfeller Foundation awards first video fellowship

Technology

Portapak (Sony) becomes available in France

Television

KQED-TV in San Francisco sets up an experimental workshop on the initiative of Brice Howard and Paul Kaufman, with a grant from the Rockefeller Foundation. In 1969 it was named 'National Center for Experiments in Television at KQED-TV' and funded by the Corporation for Public Broadcasting and the National Endowment for the Arts. WGBH-TV in Boston initiates its artists-in-residence program through a grant from the Rockefeller Foundation, directed by Fred Barzyk

1968
Artists

Jean-Luc Godard develops project for broadcast entitled 'Communications' for Radio-Nord. Several programs, recorded in video, are transferred to film for the broadcast; the quality of the result is deemed inadequate and the project is abandoned, Quebec, Canada

Danish artist William Louis Sørensen conceives his first video installation, *Any Magnetic or Magneto-Optical Recording System That…* a magnetic tape loop with live recording and nearly simultaneous playback of the image, Denmark

'Bruce Nauman: Corridor,' Nicholas Wilder Gallery, Los Angeles

Limbo, an electronic ballet by Alwin Nikolais that was produced at WCBS-TV, is one of the earliest creative uses of chroma-key

Sorcery by Robert Zagone and Loren Sears and produced at KQED-TV, San Francisco, uses dense special-effects imagery

The Big Eye by Les Levine, at the Architectural League, New York, included prerecorded tapes shown to an audience whose responses were taped and displayed simultaneously

Exhibitions

'The Machine as Seen at the End of the Mechanical Age,' the first exhibition to include Video art at the Museum of Modern Art in New York, curated by Pontus Hulton, contained work by Nam June Paik

'Cybernetic Serendipity,' The Computer and the Arts,' exhibition at The Corcoran Gallery, Washington, D. C. Exhibition organized at Institute of Contemporary Arts, London; American showing augmented by work selected by James Harithas. Includes video work by Nam June Paik. Travels to Palace of Art and Science, San Francisco. Director of exhibition, Jasia Reichardt

'Intermedia '68,' Brooklyn Academy of Music. Nam June, Paik, Ken Dewey, Les Levine, Aldo Tambellini, Terry Riley, Jud Yalkut. USCO, etc. curated by John Brockman. This show traveled in New York State, and included occasional live performances by Nam June Paik, Trisha Brown, and Simone Forti, and films by Jud Yalkut

Innovation

The Video Workshop at Haslev Teachers College started by Torben Søborg, Denmark

Creation of the GRI (Groupe de Recherche Image) at the ORTF in France under the direction of Pierre Schaeffer. François Coupigny develops the *truqueur universel* (universal special effects device), which is used by Martial Raysse, Peter Foldès, and Jean-Paul Cassagnac to color black-and-white video images

Jean-Luc Godard creates Sonimage Company in Paris, then moves it to Grenoble
Chris Marker creates the SLON (Service for Launching New Works) group with André Delvaux
Godard and Marker use the first Sony 2100 ½-inch black-and-white cameras to create rough documents that will be distributed in the form of a counter-culture magazine called *Vidéo 5* in François Maspéro's bookstore, France
Zero Group under Otto Piener collaborates with an American, Aldo Tambellini to create a live broadcast for WDR entitled 'Black Gate Cologne.' Art dealer, Gerry Schum, sees this show, Germany
Creation of Ant Farm, a San Francisco based art group, started by Chip Lord, Doug Michels, and Curtis Schreier
Land Truth Circus, an experimental video collective founded by Doug Hall, Diane Hall, and Jody Proctor, San Francisco
Video collective, Commediation, created by Frank Gillette, Harvey Simon, David Cort, Howard Gutstadt, and Ken Marsh
Founding of Centro de Arte y Communicación (CAYE) in Buenos Aires, Argentina, and video distribution center

1969

Artists

Peter Weibel shows two videotapes at Multi Media, Vienna: *Prozess als Produkt*, the preparations for the exhibition, and *Publikum als Exponent*
Katsuhiro Yamagushi creates the video installation *Image Modulator*, Japan
Bruce Nauman shows his first neons, videotapes, and a closed-circuit video installation, *Live/Taped Video Corridor*, at the Leo Castelli Gallery, New York
'Dennis Oppenheim' at the John Gibson Gallery, New York
'Corridor' exhibition by Bruce Nauman at the Nicholas Wilder Gallery, Los Angeles. Installation with video
Catalan artists Joan and Oriol Durán Benet carry out the first experiments with closed-circuit video (*Daedalus Video*), Spain

Exhibitions

Harold Szeemann organizes the exhibition 'When Attitudes Become Form' at the Bern Kunsthalle in Switzerland. Among the sixty-nine artists invited to this event are Joseph Beuys, Hans Haacke, Robert Morris, Bruce Nauman, Dennis Oppenheim, Richard Serra, Lawrence Weiner, and Gilberto Zorio
'TV as a Creative Medium' exhibition at Howard Wise Gallery, May 17–June 14, Serge Boutourline (*Telediscretion*); Frank Gillette and Ira Schneider (*Wipe Cycle*); Nam June Paik (*Participation TV*); Nam June Paik and Charlotte Moorman (*TV Bra for Living Sculpture*); Earl Reiback (*Three Experiments within the TV Tube*); Paul Ryan (*Everyman's Moebius Strip*); John Seery (*TV Time Capsule*); Eric Siegel (*Psychedelevision in Color*); Thomas Tadlock (*The Archetron*); Aldo Tambellini (*Black Spiral*); Joe Weintraub (*AC/TV – Audio Controlled Television*). In the introduction to program notes Howard Wise cites the obsolesence of the machine and the overwhelming effects of TV on culture and society

Innovation

Gerry Schum opens TV Gallery in Berlin and, shortly afterward, inaugurates the Videogalerie in Düsseldorf, the first in Europe. Videotapes he shows include not only his own productions (he invites, among others, Daniel Buren for a video installation produced in 1971, Wolf Knoebel, and John Baldessari), but also other works (Bruce Nauman)
Global Village, New York City, begins as video collective with information and screening center. Founded by John Reilly, Ira Schneider, and Rudi Stern. Directors John Reilly and Julie Gustafson. Becomes media center devoted to independent video production, with emphasis on video documentary
Raindance Corporation, New York City, a collective formed for experimental production. Members included: Frank Gillette, Michael Shamberg, Steve Salonis, Marco Vassi, and Louis Jaffee; soon after Ira Schneider and Paul Ryan, and then Beryl Korot
Videofreex founded in New York. Experimental video group, whose members included Skip Blumberg, Nancy Cain, David Cort, Bart Friedman, Davidson Gigliotti, Chuck Kennedy, Curtis Ratcliff, Parry Teasdale, Carol Vontobel, Tunie Wall, and Ann Woodward

Political

With the end of the decade, political video collectives, action groups, and research workshops are created in New York and San Francisco (Televisionary Associated, the Alternate Media Center, Open Channel, the Media Bus). Political and community organizations use video as a means of communication and activism (Vietnam Veterans Against the War, Gay Activist Alliance, Environmental Protection Agency, etc.)

Television

Land Art by Gerry Schum. First Program, ARD-TV, Germany. Included Boezem, DeMaria, Dibbets, Flanagan, Heizer, Long, Oppenheim, Smithson
Dilexi, produced by John Coney, KQED-TV, San Francisco. Twelve programs made in collaboration with the Dilexi Foundation, including *Music with Balls* (Terry Riley and Arlo Acton) and *The Empire of Things* (Philip Makanna)
KQED-TV, San Francisco, Experimental Television Workshop renamed National Center for Experiments in Television (NCET), funded by the Corporation for Public Broadcasting and the National Endowment for the Arts (NEA). Paul Kaufman, Director. NCET published a series of reports: *Video Feedback, Direct Video* (Stephen Beck); *Reflections on Values in Public Television* (Paul Kaufman); *Communication, Organizations and John Stuart Mill* (Richard Moore); *About Television Reality and Performance* (Brice Howard); *Television and Reality* (Paul Kaufman); *Talking Faces, Eating Time and Electronic Catharsis* (Marvin Duckler); *Suggestions Toward a Small Video Facility* (Richard Stephens and Don Hallock); *Reflections on Two Media* (Bill Gwin); *An Ancient Gift* (Brice Howard)
The Medium is the Medium, WGBH-TV, Boston. Produced by Fred Barzyk, Anne Gresser, and Pat Marx. First presentation of works by independent video artists aired on television. Thirty-minute program with works by Allan Kaprow, Nam June Paik, Otto Piene, James Seawright, Thomas Tadlock, and Aldo Tambellini. Broadcast of 'The Medium is the Medium' by WGBH TV in Boston on March 23, 1969
Subject to Change, SQN Productions for CBS, New York. Produced by Don West. Program of videotapes initiated by Don West with CBS and produced by Videofreex and other members of the video community. Videotapes produced on all aspects of the counterculture (alternative shoots, communes, radicals, Black Panthers, riots, demonstrations, etc.). Never broadcast

1970

Artists

Split Reality, the first video installation by VALIE EXPORT, Austria

Exhibitions

Exhibition at the Whitechapel Art Gallery in London, '3>ï: New Multiple Art,' featuring Joseph Beuys, Robert Filliou, and Bruce Nauman. Their works are also shown at two international exhibitions, Expo '70 in Osaka and the Sixth Tokyo Biennale, organized by art critic Yusuki Nakahara
'Vision and Television' at the Rose Art Museum, Brandeis University, Waltham, Massachussetts, organized by Russell Connor. First exhibition incorporating video in a US museum. Includes Frank Gillette and Paul Ryan, Les Levine, Nam June Paik, John Reilly and Rudi Stern, Ira Schneider, Eric Segal, Aldo Tambellini, Videofreex, and Joe Weintraub
The Jewish Museum in New York presents an exhibition entitled 'Software-Information Technology: Its New Meaning for Art'
'Body Works,' Museum of Conceptual Art, San Francisco, first video exhibition on the West Coast. Organized by Willoughby Sharp. Videotapes by Vito Acconci, Terry Fox, Bruce Nauman, Dennis Oppenheim, Keith Sonnier, and William Wegman
The Museum of Modern Art, New York, presents 'Information,' curated by Kynaston McShine, on different currents in Conceptual art. Artists include Vito Acconci, Art & Language, Joseph Beuys, Gilbert and George, Dan Graham, Hans Haacke, Bruce Nauman, and Lawrence Weiner

Innovation

Birth of artists' collectives in Montreal, including Véhicule, committed to new forms of expression like Performance and video. Creation of alternative production and exhibition spaces (A Space in Toronto, Western Front in Vancouver)
At the Ecole des Beaux-Arts in Paris, Paul and Carole Roussopoulos set up the Vidéo Out collective. Its first video, featuring Jean Genet speaking about Angela Davis, is a kind of counter-television. A series of political videos defend the cause of women and workers
Harald Szeemann and Hans Sohm organize 'Happening Fluxus,' Kunstverein, Cologne
New multimedia groups emerge in Japan, including Video Hiroba and Video Earth, created by Ko Nakajima
First issue of *Afterimage*, edited by Simon Fields and Peter Sainbury
Willoughby Sharp founds the magazine *Avalanche* in New York. Devoted to avant-garde activities and particularly Video art, it continues publication until 1976
Creation of the Synapse Video Center in Syracuse, New York, a group for production and distribution of videotapes (Gary Hill, Bill Viola, etc.)
Tom Mariani founds Museum of Conceptual Art, San Francisco, an alternative space presenting performances and multimedia artworks
Museum of Conceptual Art (MOCA), San Francisco, founded by Tom Marioni. An alternative museum created for Performance and multimedia art
Raindance Foundation, New York, publishes *Radical Software*. Co-editors, Phyllis Gershuny and Beryl Korot. Published by Ira Schneider and Michael Shamberg from 1970 to 1974, Vols. 1–2. Alternative video magazine and information channel for distribution and exchange of video works
First book publication to cover Video art, *Expanded Cinema* by Gene Youngblood, in New York
People's Video Theater, with Ken Marsh, Howard Gutstadt, and Elliot Glass

Technology

Sony announces ½-inch color portable videotape recorder
Nam June Paik and Shuya Abe develop Paik/Abe synthesizer while artists-in-residence at WGBH-TV, Boston
Eric Siegel builds Electronic Video Synthesizer with financial assistance from Howard Wise, New York
Stephen Beck builds his Direct Video Synthesizer

Television

Violence Sonata by Stan Venderbeek. Artist-in-Residence Program, WGBH TV, Boston. Exploration of theme of violence, using videotape, film, live performers, and studio and phone-in participation from audience
A 'guerilla television' project, aimed at combatting the ORTF monopoly with local TV, is set up by ACT and a group from the Beaux-Arts in France. They work out of a Montparnasse apartment in Paris, with two video cameras and a control panel
'Identification' broadcast on Westdeutscher Rundfunk I from Gerry Schum's TV Gallery with artists Giovanni Anselmo, Joseph Beuys, Alighiero e Boetti, Pierpaolo Calzolari, Jan Dibbets, Gilbert and George, Mario Merz, Ulrich Rückriem, Reiner Ruthenbeck, Lawrence Weiner, and Gilberto Zorio
Experimental Television Center (ETC), Binghamton, New York, founded. Director Ralph Hocking. Originally Community Center for Television Production. Production/post-production center emphasizing synthesized and computer-generated imagery through Artist-in-Residence Program. Equipment access to portable technology. Cable series, workshops and exhibition series 'Video by Videomakers.' Ken Dominick, Coordinator. Other people later associated with the ETC: Sherry Miller Hocking, Robert Diamond, David Jones, Brian Byrnes, Paul Davis, Don McArthur, Peer Bode, and Hank Rudolph

1971

Artists

Gina Pane films herself with a video camera to document her action *Nourriture/ Actualités TV/Feu* in a Paris apartment, France
Martial Raysse makes a ¾-inch video with Alain Jacquier, *En prime Pig Music*, France
Juan Downey: With Energy Beyond These Walls, Everson Museum, Syracuse, New York. Video installation
Keith Sonnier, *Projects Room*, Museum of Modern Art, New York, curated by Riva Castleman

Exhibition

'Artists' Propositions for Closed-Circuit Television,' presented at the Yellow Now Gallery in Liège, is the first video event in Belgium. The minimal setup consists of a camera and a monitor. Guy Jungblut invites some fifty artists to offer their ideas on information. Among those participating are Jacques Lizène, Jacques-Louis Nyst, and Jean-Pierre Ransonnet
At the Seventh Paris Biennale, the artists' films section curated by Alfred Pacquement includes works by Vito Acconci, Dan Graham, Bruce Nauman, Dennis Oppenheim, Richard Serra, and Keith Sonnier
First Spanish installation of TV screens is presented at the Galería Vandrés in Madrid: 'Espacio (Acción/

Interacción)/Space(Action/Interaction)' by Muntadas, a member of the first generation of Spanish video artists

'New American Filmmakers Series: Videoshow' at the Whitney Museum of American Art, New York, curated by David Bienstock Davis. Artists featured include Nam June Paik, Aldo Tambellini, Steina and Woody Vasulka, and others

'Tapes from All Tribes' at the Pacific Film Archive. Berkeley, California, curated by Video Free America. Video Free America was an early West Coast video collective based in San Francisco

'Ten Video Performances' at the Finch College Museum of Art, New York, curated by Elayne Varian. Featured artists include Vito Acconci, Peter Campus, Douglas Davis, Simone Forti, Dan Graham, Alex Hay, Bruce Nauman, Claes Oldenburg, Nam June Paik, Robert Rauschenberg, Steve Reich, and Eric Siegal

'The Television Environment' by William (Billy) Adler and John Margolies at the University Art Museum, Berkeley

Innovation

Jean-Pierre Boyer creates the Montréal Vidéographe in Montréal, Canada, a space for creation and distribution that invites city residents to make videotapes and distribute them upon request. Grants from the National Film Board will allow 140 projects to be carried out

Vidéogrammes de France is set up by the ORTF and the publisher Hachette for the manufacture and distribution of mass-market videotapes

Establishment of Travens Video Workshop, a video group in Munich, including Neinhardt Franke, Charly Rosch, and Brian Wood

The Lijnbanncentrum in Rotterdam opens a video studio producing documentaries and educational tapes. Shows tapes by Dutch artists (Van Elk, Ben d'Armagnac, Jan Dibbets) as well as Americans (notably Terry Fox, Dan Graham, and Dennis Oppenheim)

Steina and Woody Vasulka create The Kitchen Live Audience Test Laboratory (now called The Kitchen) in New York. It presents, produces, and distributes artists' works, notably in video

Howard Wise founds Electronic Arts Intermix, funding other organizations like The Kitchen and the annual New York Avant-Garde Festival. EAI becomes a locus for collecting, preserving and distributing artists' videotapes

T. P. Video Space Troupe, New York City, founded by Shirley Clarke; experimental workshop exploring two-way video. Original members include Wendy Clarke, Bruce Ferguson, and Andy Gurian

The Everson Museum in Syracuse inaugurates first Video art department in a museum with curator David Ross. He organizes *Westcoast Video #1,* with works by George Bolling, Terry Fox, Howard Fried, Joel Glassman, Paul Kos, and William Wegman

Political

Anne Couteau and Yvonne Mignot-Lefebvre create the Paris video collective Vidéo 00

Television

Scottish television retransmits ten works by video artist David Hall. This program, *TV Interruptions,* is the first artistic broadcast on British television

Establishment of Artists' Television Workshop by WNET-TV, New York, renamed Television Laboratory in 1972, directed by David Loxton

Electronic Hokkadim by Douglas Davis at Corcoran Gallery of Art and WTOP-TV,

Washington, D. C. First live two-way telecast – viewers telephone in with sounds that modify visual images broadcast

Non-Camera Images by Stephen Beck, National Center for Experiments in Television, San Francisco, KQED-TV. Program produced on Beck's synthesizer

1972
Artists

Peeling Off, Richard Kriesche's first video presentation, at the Innsbrucker Galerie in Innsbruck, Austria

First appearance of Video art at the Palais des Beaux-Arts in Brussels with a performance-video installation by William Wegman for the group exhibition 'Onze Artistes de la West Coast'

First presentation of Gerry Schum's *Land Art and Identification,* organized by Annie Lummerzhzim in Liège, Belgium

Gina Pane uses a video camera to tape the reaction of the public during *Le lait chaud,* an action in a Paris apartment

Daniel Buren develops a project for a video installation before Gerry Schum's TV Gallery in Düsseldorf is closed. *Recouvrement-effacement,* presented in Venice in 1973 and in Florence in 1974, was later dedicated to Schum

Gerry Schum presents videotapes at Documenta 5 in Kassel, Germany, and at the Venice Biennale

The House Gallery in London presents *60 TV,* the first video installation by David Hall and Tony Sinden, in 'A Survey of the Avant-Garde in Britain,' including objects, performances, films, and conceptual works

Ed Emshwiller's *Scape Mates,* computer drawings and tapes of actors, is produced in the laboratories of WNET-TV, New York

'Keith Sonnier,' an exhibition of videotapes at the Leo Castelli Gallery, New York

Concerto for TV Cello/TV Bra at the Everson Museum, Syracuse, comprising videotapes and installation by Nam June Paik with Performance by Charlotte Moorman

Music Image Workshop by Ron Hays, WGBH-TV, Boston. An attempt to produce tapes, working with the Paik-Abe synthesizer, in which music and image are uniquely suited to each other

'Peter Campus' at the Bykert Gallery, New York, curated by Klauss Kertess

Exhibitions

'Projektion' at Louisiana Museum of Modern Art, Humlebaek, Denmark

'Women's Video Festival' at The Kitchen, New York, organized by Susan Milano

'First Annual National Video Festival' at the Minneapolis College of Art and Design, curated by Tom Drysdale, includes Peter Campus, Ed Emshwiller, Nam June Paik, Ira Schneider, and Aldo Tambellini. Panelists include Russell Connor, Barbara Rose, George Stoney, and Gene Youngblood

'St Jude Video Art Invitational' at the de Saisset Gallery and Art Museum, Santa Clara, California, curated by David Ross, with work by John Baldessari, Lynda Benglis, Douglas Davis, Taka Iimura, Shigeko Kubota, and William Wegman

'Works from the Experimental TV Center' at Binghamton, Everson Museum, Syracuse, curated by Ralph Hocking

'White, Black, Red, and Yellow' at The Kitchen, Mercer Arts Center, with work by Mary Lucier, Shigeko Kubota, Cecilia Sandovar, and Charlotte Warren

Innovation

The group General Idea starts its own magazine, *File,* in Toronto

Political

Top Value Television (TVTV), founded in San

Francisco. Independent documentary production group providing alternative coverage of the Democratic and Republican conventions in Miami; the first use of ½-inch videotape on broadcast television. Original production by Hudson Marquez, Allen Rucker, Michael Shamberg, Tom Weinberg, Megan Williams, and members of Ant Farm, Raindance, and Videofreex collectives; other members of TVTV include Wendy Apple, Michael Couzens, Paul Goldsmith, Betsy Guignon, Stanton Kaye, Anda Korsts, Andy Mann, and Elon Soltes

Technology

Sony markets a standard portable ½-inch color videotape recorder and introduces standard system for ¾-inch videotape cassettes

Television

Fred Forest begins interventions on state-run television. Broadcasts 'one minute of white' in the middle of the news on Télé-Midi in France

The Everson Museum in Syracuse organizes 'Douglas Davis: An Exhibition Inside and Outside the Museum', including videotapes and projects for communication by television

Take Out!, by Douglas Davi, a collaboration between Everson Museum and WCNY-TV, Syracuse, and the Intermedia Institute consisting of three-and-a-half-hour dialogue with the public, who responded by telephone to a broadcast museum exhibition

1973
Artists

Toshio Matsumoto makes *Mona Lisa,* the first Japanese work to use the Scanimate synthesizer, Japan

Nam June Paik completes *Global Groove* at WNET-TV, New York, a tape made from TV images with the Paik/Abe synthesizer

'Shigeko Kubota' at the Wabash Transit Gallery, School of the Art Institute, Chicago

The Irish Tapes by John Reilly and Stefan Moore at The Kitchen, Mercer Arts Center

Electronic Video by Nam June Paik at The Kitchen, Mercer Arts Center

Videotapes from the Perpetual Pioneer of Video Art by Nam June Paik at The Kitchen, Mercer Arts Center

'William Wegman' at the Los Angeles County Museum of Art, Los Angeles, curated by Jane Livingston

'Frank Gillette: Video Process and Meta-Process' at the Everson Museum, Syracuse (built and installed by Bill Viola). One of the first of the big multichannel installations. Gillette was a pioneer of the form

Peter Beyls begins his projects for televisions, involving the generation of abstract images with analog computers, with the installation *TV Tower* at the IPEM in Ghent

Exhibitions

The first major video exhibition in Austria, 'Trigon: Audiovisuelle Botschaften,' organized by Austria, Italy and Yugoslavia, is held in Graz. Features works by Austrian, Italian, and Yugoslav artists, American video retrospectives, and video workshops

'Video' at the Lijnbaancentrum, Rotterdam, shows international artists, with a focus on Dutch artists like Joepat and Tajari

Everson Museum organizes 'Circuit: A Video Invitational,' a traveling exhibition featuring video works by sixty-five artists

'Women's Video Festival' at the University of Illinois, Circle Campus, Chicago

'International Computer Arts Festival' at The Kitchen, Mercer Arts Center, curated by Dmitri Devyatkin

'Whitney Biennial' at the Whitney Museum of American Art, features Peter Campus, Joan Jonas, and others

Innovation

Flor Bex opens a video department at the Internationaal Cultureel Centrum (ICC) in Antwerp. It then becomes the main center for video production and distribution in Belgium and Europe

Maria Gloria Biccochi founds Art/Tapes/22 in Florence, a center for the production of artists' videos and their distribution in Europe as well as in the United States and Japan

1974
Artists

Using Sonimage video editing equipment, Jean-Luc Godard and Anne-Marie Miéville complete the film *Jusqu'à la victoire,* shot in the Middle East in 1970, now renamed *Ici et ailleurs,* France

Thierry Kuntzel makes his first videotape, *La Rejetée* (now lost), based on Chris Marker's film *La Jetée,* France

Performance video by Vito Acconci, *Command Performance,* created at 112 Greene Street in New York

Exhibitions

'Art Vidéo Confrontation 74,' presented by the Musée d'Art Moderne de la Ville de Paris and the Centre d'Activités Audio-Visuelles (CNAAV)

'Art vidéo couleur' exhibition at the American Center in Paris, featuring videotapes by Ed Emschwiller, Bill and Louise Etra, Nam June Paik, Woody and Steina Vasulka, and others

'Projects: Video,' beginning of a series of presentations of video works curated by Barbara London, at the Museum of Modern Art, New York

'Art Now: A Celebration of the American Arts' at the John F. Kennedy Center for the Performing Arts, Washington, D. C. Video artists include, among other fine artists: Vito Acconci, Lynda Benglis, Peter Campus, Douglas Davis, Juan Downey, Terry Fox, Hermine Freed, Frank Gillette, Joel Glassman, Nancy Holt, Joan Jonas, Beryl Korot, Paul Kos, Shigeko Kubota, Andy Mann, Nam June Paik, Ira Schneider, Keith Sonnier, Bill Viola, and William Wegman

'New Learning: Spaces and Places' at the Walker Art Center, Minneapolis. Artists include James Byrne, Peter Campus, Juan Downey, Frank Gillette, Andy Mann, Ira Schneider, University Community Video, and William Wegman

'Women in Film and Video' at SUNY Buffalo, New York. Artists include Shirley Clarke, Hermine Freed, Julie Geiger, Jenny Goldberg, Sami Klein, Beryl Korot, Shigeko Kubota, Joan Jonas, Susan Milano, Steina Vasulka, and Jane Wright

'Electronic Art IV' at Bonino Gallery (Galeria Bonino), New York. Artists include Nam June Paik

'Collector's Video' at the Los Angeles County Museum of Art, curated by Jane Livingston. Artists include John Baldessari, Peter Campus, Terry Fox, Frank Gillette, Nancy Holt, Joan Jonas, Paul Kos, Dickie Landry, Andy Mann, Robert Morris, Bruce Nauman, Richard Serra, and Keith Sonnier

Innovation

The Provinciaal Museum voor Moderne Kunst in Ypres, Belgium, acquires its first videotapes

Formation of the feminist video group Vidéa, France

In Florence, opening of the Art-Tapes

Gallery, which publishes tapes by Italian artists (Chiari, Vaccari), other European artists (Christian Boltanski), and Americans (John Baldessari, Joan Jonas, and Paul Kos)

Anthology Film Archives in New York, the first film museum, founded in 1970 by Jonas Mekas, opens its collection to videos

'Open Circuits: The Future of Television,' a conference at The Museum of Modern Art, New York. Artists include Fred Barzyk, Douglas Davis, Gerald O'Grady, and Willard van Dyke

'Video and the Museum,' a conference at The Everson Museum, Syracuse, New York. Artists include Jim Harithas and David Ross

1975
Artists
Nam June Paik retrospective at the Stedelijk Museum in Amsterdam

'Bill Viola: Installation,' his first museum show, at the Everson Museum, Syracuse, New York

Exhibitions
'Artists' Video Tapes' organized by Michel Baudson at the Palais des Beaux-Arts in Brussels, with Joseph Beuys, Christian Boltanski, Allan Kaprow, Nam June Paik, and Wolf Vostell. Belgian artists include CAP group, Jacques Charlier, Leo Copers, 50/04 group, Mass Moving, Danny Matthijs, Hubert Van Es, and Mark Verstockt

Jan Veercruysse organizes 'Kunst als Film' at Elsa Von Honolulu Gallery, Ghent. The video section includes Jacques Charlier, the CAP group, the 50/04 group, Leo Copers, Eddy Devolder and Carl Uytterhaegen, Lili Dujourie, Danny Matthijs, Guy Mees, Hubert Van Es, and Mark Verstockt

'Video International' exhibition at the Arhus Art Museum, Copenhagen

At the 'Ninth Paris Biennale' Douglas Davis presents a video section with twenty-eight artists, including Christian Boltanski, Pierre-Alain Hubert, Gordon Matta-Clark, Misloslav Moucha, Muntadas, Keith Sonnier, and Bill Viola. Spanish artists show their first video-tapes

'Radical Software' at the Kölnischer Kunstverein, Cologne, Germany

'Video Show' at the Serpentine Gallery, London. The main artists include Roger Barnard, David Crichtley, David Hall, Brian Hoey, Steve James, Tamara Krikorian, Mike Legget, Peter Livingstone, Stuart Marshall, Alex Meigh, Steve Partridge, Liz Rhodes, Tony Sindon, and Reindeer Werk

'First International Exhibition of Video Art' in Italy takes place in Milan, organized by Tamasso Trini

'Arte de Video,' an exhibition at Museo de Arte Contemporaneo de Caracas. Artists include Ralph Hocking, Woody and Steina Vasulka, and Walter Wright

Group show consisting of tapes and instal-lations. Travels to five cities, including Sao Paulo, Brazil. Features works by Frank Gillette, Joan Jonas, Steina Vasulka, and others

'Everson Video 75' at the Everson Museum, Syracuse, New York. Curator is Richard Simmons.

Ant Farm, Community Video/Cast, David Cort, Dance Media, Dimitri Devyatkin, Electron Movers, Dieter Froese, Beryl Korot, Shigeko Kubota, Andy Mann, Paul Ott and Fred Kesler, Peter Van Riper, and Bill Viola

'Media Burn,' a Performance and media event at Cow Place, San Francisco, Ant Farm

'Americans in Florence/Europeans in Florence' at Long Beach Museum of Art. Curated by David Ross and Maria Gloria Bicocchi

'Commissioned Video Works,' curated by Jim Melchert. Artists include Antin, John Baldessari, John Fernie, Dennis Oppenheim, Bob Watts, and William Wegman

'First Ithaca Video Festival' at Ithaca, New York. Curated by Philip Mallory Jones. Annual traveling video show

'Projected Video' at the Whitney Museum of American Art, New York. Artists include John Baldessari, Lynda Benglis, Peter Campus, Douglas Davis, Bill Etra, Hermine Freed, Shigeko Kubota, Nam June Paik, Richard Serra, Keith Sonnier, Steina and Woody Vasulka, and William Wegman

'Moebius Video Show' at the San Francisco Art Festival, San Francisco. Artists include Ant Farm, Terry Fox, Phil Garner, Joanne Kelly, Darryl Sapien, and Skip Sweeney

'Video Art' at the Institute of Contemporary Art, Philadelphia, curated by Suzanne Delehanty

Innovation
The magazine *Parachute* is founded by Chantal Pontbriand and France Morin in Canada on the basis of an idea by René Blouin and Chantal Pontbriand

Heure Exquise! collective is founded near Lille for the promotion of Video art. In 1982 the collective began to specialize in the distribution of videotapes. In 1985 it became a video station, an alternative to TV broadcasting, and, in 1992, a training and documentation center

Numerous artists employ television as object, in installations or actions, or as a base of serial works, such as Károly Halász s series, *Modulated TV*. (Reproductions are made of this in Géza Perneczky's *Important Business*, and in 1977 this is also presented at the exhibi-tion, 'Serial Artworks' at the István Király Múzeum in Székesfehérvár)

Technology
Sony develops Betamax, allowing TV programs to be recorded on video

1976
Artists
Paik retrospective, organized at the Kunstverein in Cologne

Gábor Bódy's *Psychocosmoses* (also on 35-millimeter film) is the first Hungarian computer film produced

Exhibitions
'Video Show' at the Tate Gallery, London, featuring works by Roger Barnard, Brian Hoey, Tamara Krikorian, Stuart Marshall, and Steve Partridge

Third Eye Centre in Glasgow presents exhibition 'Video: Towards Defining an Aesthetic'

'Video Art: An Overview' at the San Francisco Museum of Modern Art, San Francisco, California, curated by David Ross. Twenty-nine artists' tapes and installations

Innovation
Founding of London Video Arts (LVA), artists' organization for the promotion and distribution of video

First issue of *Videography*, a magazine devoted entirely to video

Television
Arena, a special program of British and American artists' videotapes, is broad-cast on BBC2. Program is presented by David Hall and produced by Mark Kidel and Anna Ridley. For the occasion, Hall makes *This Is a TV Receiver*, with Richard Baker

1977
Artists
First video by French artist Orlan, documenting performance entitled *Mesurage*. Artist uses her 'Orlan-corps' (Orlan-body) unit to measure the Centre Georges Pompidou, Paris

Exhibitions
'Art, Artists, and Media,' a retrospective in Graz, Austria. International artists and theorists participate in the conference organized in conjunction with this event

Jean Dupuy tapes *Artists Propaganda II (Paris)* at the Centre Georges Pompidou, Paris. Among the artists whose short performances are recorded are: Roy Adzack, Christian Boltanski, André Cadere, Béatrice Casadesus, Jacqueline Dauriac, Charles Dreyfus, François Dufresne, Robert Filliou, Gérard Gassiorowski, Alain Germain, Raymond Hains, Bernard Hiedsieck, Joël Hubaut, Françoise Janicot, Piotr Kowalski, Bruno de Lard, Emile Laugier, Annette Messager, Jacques Monory, Jacques de Pindrey, Guy de Rougemont, Richard Texier, Martial Thomas, Claude Torey, and Nil Yalter

'Vidéo en film manifestatie,' an inter-national exhibition and colloquium, at the Bonnefantenmuseum, Maastricht, Netherlands. Includes British artists Roger Barnard, David Crichley, David Hall, Tamara Krikorian, Stuart Marshall, and Steve Partridge

Eighth International 'Video Encounter,' organized in Lima, Peru, by the Centro de Arte y Communication (CAYC) of Buenos Aires

Innovation
Creation of the first Danish Video Workshop in Haderslev and the Danish Film Workshop in Copenhagen, both funded by Danish Film Institute. They provide equipment for persons seeking to express themselves via film and video

At the Centre Georges Pompidou, Paris, Pontus Hulten creates a 'photo-film-video' department, which is headed by Alain Sayag. Between 1976 and 1978, Mnam buys about fifty videotapes by Jean Dupuy, Paul-Armand Gette, Suzanne Nissim, Teresa Weinberg, and Robert Wilson

The first international Video art program is presented by Peter Weibel in Budapest at the Ganz Cultural House. A publica-tion is produced for this occasion, which includes texts by László Beke, Tibor Hajas, Dóra Maurer, and László Najmányi. (The texts are republished in 1988 by the Kossuth Cinema entitled, *Video Art*.)

An independent art course is conducted by Miklós Erdély and Dóra Maurer, also at the Ganz Cultural House, in which the participants have access to video

Several works and projects are realized and planned directly involving video, of which the majority, however fragmen-tary, remain today, such as tapes of Tibor Hajas's *The Guest*, *The Jewels of Darkness*, and several works by László Najmányi and Gergely Molnár (*Ezra Pound*, *Flammarion Kamill*, *David Bowie in Budapest*), Hungary

At the Venice Biennale, a seminar on 'Art, Artist, and the Media' is organ-ized by Richard Kriesche, Peggy Gale, Wulf Hersogenrath, and Marshall McLuhan

1978
Artists
Robert Wilson makes *Video 50*, 50 thirty-second videos conceived as interludes,

in the Centre Georges Pompidou's studio (co-produced by INA, CNAC-CGP, NIRT, ZDF), Paris

Nam June Paik retrospective at the ARC, Musée d'Art Moderne de la Ville de Paris in France includes the installations *Moon Is the Oldest TV* and *TV Clock*. In conjunction with the retrospective, the American Center shows his recent tapes (*Global Groove*, *Guadalcanal Requiem*, *Merce by Merce*, etc.) and organizes interventions by Paik and Charlotte Moorman

The lecture by Gábor Bódy entitled 'Infinite Mirror-Tube' is presented at the Tihany Semiotics Congress, Hungary. This lecture is connected to the last part of his 35-millimeter film entitled *Four Bagatelles*, which can also be considered as the first Hungarian video piece. Bódy presents a more detailed version of this lecture, 'Infinite Image and Reflection Total Expanded Cinema,' in Edinburgh in 1978

Exhibitions
First 'International Video Encounter,' organized by Walter Zanini at the Museu da Imagen e do som in São Paolo, Brazil

'Video Art '78' at the Herbert Art Gallery and Museum, Coventry. International exhibition of installations, performances, tapes, and films organized by Steve Partridge. Works by Kevin Atherton, Roger Barnard, Lindsay Bryfton, David Crichley, Keith Frake, David Hall, Brian Hoey, Tamara Krikorian, Stuart Marshall, Alex Meigh, Marceline Mori, and Steve Partridge. European and American artists include Marina Abramovic, Nan Hoover, Friederike Pezold, Ulrike Rosenbach, Bill Viola, and Peter Weibel

Innovation
Creation of Arhus Film Workshop, Denmark, which, during the 1980s, organizes video festivals and exhibitions

Nam June Paik's installation *TV Garden* is presented at the Centre Georges Pompidou, Paris

The Espace Lyonnais d'Art Contemporain (ELAC), Lyons, France, sets up a depart-ment for promotion of video and art films (artistic director, Georges Rey). The ELAC is the first such institution in France to present video on a weekly basis (documents touching on visual arts, television, dance, music, architecture, and society in relation to contemporary art), as well as installa-tions and events involving state-of-the-art technology

Television
Gábor Bódy's two television plays are realized (*Soldiers* and *Chalk Circle*), in which he develops the potential of electronic image and sound, a first for Hungarian television

1979
Exhibitions
'Ars Electronica '79' festival in Linz, Austria, on the theme of *Kunst und Technik* (art and technology)

Exhibition in homage to Gerry Schum at the Stedelijk Museum in Amsterdam

'British Video Art in Canada,' curated by David Hall, features a selection of videotapes by British artists (traveling exhibition to Toronto, Halifax, and Queens University in Kingston)

Innovation
A number of more comprehensive essays are published in the field of electronic image and sound, such as György Somogyi's Video-Visions. A 'video team' commences operation within the Balázs Béla Studio, Hungary

Video Art

1980

Exhibitions

'Videokunst in Deutschland 1963–1982,' first major exhibition devoted to video, is held at the Kunstverein, Cologne, with works by Klaus vom Bruch, Barbara Hammann, Peter Kolb, Marcel Odenbach, Friedericke Pezold, Frank Soletti, and Ulay

'About Time: Video, Performance and Installation by Women Artists,' Institute of Contemporary Arts, London, and Arnolfini Gallery, Bristol. Works by Catherine Elwes, Rose Garrard, Roberta Graham, Susan Hiller, Tina Keane, Rose Finn Kelcey, Alex Meigh, Marceline Mori, and Jane Rigby

'Japanese Experimental Film 1960–1980,' organized by the American Federation of Arts in Japan

'Video, el temps y l'espai. Sèries informatives 2/Video, Time and Space,' organized by the Barcelona Architects' Association, Barcelona. Works by Spanish and foreign artists, including Juan Downey, Dan Graham, Wolf Kahlen, Shigeko Kubota, and Muntadas

First Video art festival of Locarno, organized by Rinaldo Bianda, director of the Galerie Flaviana, Switzerland

The Kitchen in New York presents 'French Video Art – Art vidéo français,' a week of French video. Curated by Don Foresta of the Center for Media Art in Paris, the program surveys video creation in France through productions of four major institutions: the Center for Media Art at the American Center, the Centre Georges Pompidou, the Institut national de l'audiovisuel, and the Ecole Nationale Supérieure des Arts Décoratifs in Paris. Artists represented include: Roland Baladi, Dominique Belloir, Robert Cahen, Roman Cieslewicz, Nicole Croisset, Colette Deblé, Olivier Debré, Catherine Ikam, Thierry Kuntzel, Chris Marker, Hervé Nisic, Suzanne Nissim, François Pain, Slobodan Pajic, Patrick Prado, Pierre Rovère, Claude Torey, Teresa Wennberg, and Nil Yalter. A parallel exhibition with the same title is presented at the American Center in Paris

Innovation

The plan is drafted for *INFERMENTAL* (the first international video magazine), the first issue realized by Gábor Bódy in 1982 in Hungary

Gábor Bódy institutes the MAFILM K* (experimental) Section in Hungary, which organizes a large-scale 'hair and make-up festival' in 1981

1981

Exhibitions

First Franco-Latin American video arts festival is held in Santiago, Chile

'Performance, Video, Installation,' Tate Gallery, London, with films by Vito Acconci, Stuart Brisley, Robert Morris, and Bruce Nauman, and videos by Ian Baum, David Hall, Tina Keane, et al.

1982

Artists

Nam June Paik's *Tricolor Video*, installation with 384 color TVs, is presented in the Forum of the Centre Georges Pompidou, Paris

Following the release of his film *Passion* in 1981, Jean-Luc Godard makes *Scénario du Film Passion* in video, France

Wolf Vostell creates *Dépression endogène* in Los Angeles – an installation of live turkeys making their way among gutted video monitors that have been filled with cement. One monitor in working condition continuously plays a videotape made by the artist in San Francisco and shows different neighborhoods and freeways encircling the city

Nam June Paik retrospective at the Whitney Museum of American Art, New York

Exhibitions

'1. Danske Symposium on Videokunst,' the first Danish symposium on Video art, is organized by Niels Lomholt and Torben Søborg (director of the Haslev Video Workshop) at the Huset in Copenhagen. Four issues are addressed: forms of creation through the video medium, production strategies, the role of video as art in relation to Danish institutions, and exhibition possibilities in Denmark and abroad

First International New Images Forum in Monte Carlo, Monaco

The Center for Media Art at the American Center in Paris organizes evening programs with videotapes by American artists Gary Hill, Nam June Paik, Woody and Steina Vasulka, and Bill Viola

The first 'San Sebastián Video Festival,' held in Spain, this festival was parallel with the 30th San Sebastián International Film Festival. Focus programs feature Kit Fitzgerald, Muntadas and Nam June Paik. Selections by The Kitchen in New York, the Centre Georges Pompidou in Paris and Vidéographe (RTBF). Installations by Michel Jaffrenou and Patrick Bousquet, Marie-Jo Lafontaine, Joan Logue, and Muntadas, and a performance by Jean-Paul Fargier and Philippe Sollers. Eugènia Balcells presents her first video installation in Spain, *Atravesando Lenguajes/Crossing Through Languages*

Innovation

Antenne 2 broadcasts the first installment of the program 'Juste une image,' shot in video and prepared by Thierry Garel, Louisette Neil, and Philippe Grandrieux. Produced by the Institut National de l'Audiovisuel in France, this monthly program helps to make the tapes of American video artists such as Dara Birnbaum, Gary Hill, Joan Logue, Nam June Paik, Steina Vasulka, Bill Viola, and Bob Wilson known in France. It also presents interviews with Robert Cahen, Joëlle de la Casinière, Jean-André Fieschi, and Philippe Quéau

Creation of the International Video and Television Festival by the Centre d'action culturelle in Montbéliard (biennial competition among some forty video works, one artist retrospective, talks), directed by Pierre Bongiovanni. The first year's festival includes videos by Dominik Barbier, Dominique Belloir, Alain Bourges, Robert Cahen, Nicole Croiset and Nil Yalter, Philippe Demontant, Michel Jaffrenou and Patrick Bousquet, Jean-Louis Le Tacon, Pierre Lobstein, Hervé Nisic, Yann N'Guyen Minh, and Teresa Wennberg

Carole Roussopolos, Delphine Seyrig, and Iona Wiener found the Centre audiovisuel Simone de Beauvoir in Paris in order to assist women in the creation and distribution of audiovisual works

Television

Channel 4 goes on the air, in Britain. The Workshop Declaration establishes an agreement between TV technicians of the Union Act and those of Channel 4 for the creation of open workshops. These workshops serve the production of films and videos and allow the broadcasting of programs outside the usual union agreements

1983

Artists

Bill Viola exhibition at the ARC, Musée d'Art Moderne de la Ville de Paris. For his first solo exhibition in Europe, the American artist shows two video sound installations: *An Instrument of Simple Sensation* and *A Room for Saint John of the Cross*, along with a selection of tapes from 1977 to 1983

John Sanborn creates the video opera *Perfect Lives* with writer Robert Ashley

Exhibitions

'Recent British Video,' programmed by The Kitchen in New York, includes works by John Adams, Ian Bourn, Catherine Elwes, Mick Hartney, Steve Hawley, Tina Keane, Richard Layzell, Antonio Sherman, Margaret Warwick, and Jeremy Welsh

Television

A collaboration between Channel 4 and London Video Arts results in Access Funding to facilitate video post-production

1984

Exhibitions

'Ars Electronica '84,' festival in Linz, Austria. Participants include Glen Branca, Jürgen Claus, Herbert W. Franke, Isao Tomito, Peter Weibel, Gene Youngblood, and others

'1. Videonale,' Bonn, the city's first international art video festival, is organized by Dieter Daniels, Bärbel Moser, and Petra Unützer

First National Video Festival, organized by the Circulo de Bellas Artes in Madrid, which opens a new era in the history of Spanish video. Video installations by Carles Pujol (*Alicia*), Concha Jerez (*Trepan, descienden por la escalera o*), Eugènia Balcells (*Color Fields*). Foreign artists include Inge Graf and Zyx, Dan Graham, Michel Jaffrenou (*Circus*), Marie-Jo Lafontaine, Woody and Steina Vasulka, Wolf Vostell, and Peter Weibel

'Video Art, A History' organized by Barbara London at the Museum of Modern Art in New York

Innovation

A group of Danish video artists create the private gallery Tretanken in Copenhagen as a production co-operative with its own equipment

Creation of 'Network 1, Travelling Video Library,' a videotape collection temporarily stored in video libraries and accessible to the public in Bristol and Newcastle. Organized by the Arnolfini Gallery in Bristol and Project UK, Newcastle, under the direction of Mike Stubbs

Television

The Centre Georges Pompidou, Paris, and WNET/Thirteen's Television Laboratory in New York coproduce Nam June Paik's *Good Morning Mr Orwell*, a live broadcast by satellite hookup. French artists Robert Combas, Pierre-Alain Hubert, Sapho, Studio Berçot, and Ben Vautier participate in the project from Paris along with foreign artists Joseph Beuys, John Cage, Merce Cunningham, Peter Gabriel, Allan Ginsburg, and Charlotte Moorman

1985

Exhibitions

First International Video-Biennale at the Museum Moderner Kunst in Vienna. Participants in the symposium held during the Biennale include Chris Dercon, Anne-Marie Duguet, Barbara London, Ulrike Rosenbach, Jean-Paul Tréfois, and others. A retrospective of women's videotapes presents works from Quebec, Hamburg, and Australia

'Nouvelles Fictions dans la vidéo en France' is presented at the Musée d'Art Moderne de la Ville de Paris with works by Emma Abadi, Dominique Belloir, Alain Bourges, Jean-Christophe Bouvet, Jean-Yves Cousseau, Jean-Paul Fargier, Danielle Jaeggi, Agathe Labernia, Eric Maillet, Anne Raufaste and Denis Couchaux, Wonder Products, and Teresa Wennberg

'The New Pluralism,' a selection of films and videos made between 1980 and 1985, curated by Michael O'Pary and Tina Keane at the Tate Gallery in London, includes British artists John Adams, Catherine Elwes, David Finch, Sandra Goldbacher, Tamara Krikorian, Margaret Warwick, Jeremy Welsh, Mark Wilcox, Graham Young, and others

Time Based Arts (an Amsterdam producer and distributor with its own projection site) presents a three-part program of British art videos, 'Subverting Television: Deconstruct/Scratch/After Image.' Among the artists included are Georges Barber, the Duvet Brothers, Catherine Elwes, the Flying Lizards, David Hall, Steve Hawley, John Maybury, John Scarlett-Davies, Jeremy Welsh, Mark Wilcox, and Graham Young

'Video Encounter' exhibition organized by the Circulo de Bellas Artes in Madrid, featuring video installations by Gabriel Fernández Corchero, Mary Eugenia Funes and Mareta Espinosa, Sento Bayarri, Maldonado and Os Iavados, and Paco Utray and Zaher Sufi

First International Video Week (Biennale de l'image en mouvement) at the Centre pour l'Image Contemporaine in Saint-Gervais, Geneva

Television

Channel 4 broadcasts 'The Eleventh Hour,' a series of three programs produced by Triple Vision and directed by Terry Flaxton and Penny Dedman, with videos by Georges Barber, Ian Breakwell, the Duvet Brothers, Catherine Elwes, David Hall, Chris Rushton, Gorilla Tapes, Jeremy Welsh, and Graham Young and performances by Kevin Atherton

1986

Exhibitions

'New Video: Japan' exhibition organized by the American Federal Arts and the Museum of Modern Art in New York. Works by Shoichiro Azuma, Masaki Fujihata, Teiji Furuhashi, Mako Idemitsu, Kumiko Kushiyama, Akira Matsumoto, Tetsuo Mizuno, Ko Nakajima, Jun Okazaki and Emi Segawa, Noriyuki Okuda, Shuntaro Tanikawa and Shuji Terayama, and Keigo Yamamoto

Innovation

Opening of the Museo Naciónal Centro de Arte Reina Sofía in Madrid with the exhibition 'Processors,' featuring video installations by Muntadas, Paloma Navares, and Nam June Paik

1987

Artists

Jean-Luc Godard begins the video series *Histoire(s) du cinéma*. The first two parts are shown at the Cannes Film Festival the same year but only broadcast on Canal+ in 1989. A total of six chapters are completed by 1997, plus other video works, *Les enfants jouent à la Russie* and *Deux fois cinquante ans du cinéma français* (1994)

Exhibitions

'L'Epoque, la Mode, la Morale, la Passion' exhibition at the Musée National d'Art Moderne, Centre Georges Pompidou in Paris. Video programming includes works by Robert Ashley and John Sanborn, Dara Birnbaum, Jonathan Borofsky and Gary Glassman, Stefean

Decostere and Chris Dercon, Ed Emshwiller, Jean-Luc Godard and Anne-Marie Miéville, Dan Graham, Peter Greenaway, Gary Hill, Michael Klier, Thierry Kuntzel, Joan Logue, Meredith Monk, Jacques-Louis Nyst, Marcel Odenbach, Tony Oursler, Nam June Paik and Shigeko Kubota, Michael Smith, Bill Viola, William Wegman, and Robert Wilson (May 21–August 17)

First Barcelona Video Biennale, held at the Barcelona Savings Bank, with video installations by Silvia Gubern, Angel Jové, Marie-Jo Lafontaine, Antoni Llena, Mary Lucier, Xavier Olivé, Carles Santos, and Bill Viola

'The British Edge: Video: Rescanning' at the Institute of Contemporary Arts in Boston. Selection by Jeremy Walsh with works by Kevin Atherton, Culture Video, Catherine Elwes, Steve Hawley, Tina Keane, Marion Urch, and Graham Young

Innovation

Creation of the association Muu by a group of artists, critics, and curators in Finland, including Marikki Hakola, Minna Tarkka, and Perttu Rastas. It is founded to foster artistic creation in video, Performance, and installation

'The Elusive Sign: British Avant-Garde Film and Video 1977–1987,' Tate Gallery, London, organized by the Arts Council and the British Council, followed by an international tour. Selection by Michael O'Pray, Tamara Krikorian, and Catherine Elwes, with works by Georges Barber, Ian Bourn, Catherine Elwes, Sera Furneaux, Judith Goddard, David Hall, Mona Hatoum, Steve Hawley, Tamara Krikorian, David Larcher, Jayne Parker, Christopher Rowland, Mark Wilcox, and Graham Young

Creation of the Media Arts Department at the San Francisco Museum of Art

1988
Exhibitions

Video Marathon II at the Pumpehuset in Copenhagen. Presentation of videotapes and installations, notably by Marcel Odenbach and Marie-Jo Lafontaine, and Danish works by King Kong Productions

First Danish Film + Video Workshop Festival, organized by the Danish Film Workshop and held every two years

'Down the Tube,' City Art Gallery, Manchester. Videotapes by Culture Video, Catherine Elwes, Sven Harding, Marty St James, Marion Urch, and Anne Wilson, plus installations by Mineo Aayamaguchi

'Edge '88', international festival of Performance, installations and videos, organized by Rob La Fresnais, is held in various venues in London. Artists include Marina Abramovic and Ulay, Klaus vom Bruch, and installations by Ulrike Rosenbach and Tina Keane

'Genlock,' traveling video exhibition in Britain, organized by Interim Art and LVA, presents videotapes commissioned from Cathy Acker and Atalia Shaw, Kevin Atherton, Neil Bartlett and Stuart Marshall, Isaac Julien, and Julian Sommerville. Also includes a selection of videos by international artists and historical works

'La Imagen Sublime: Video de creación en España 1970–1987,' exhibition at the Museo Naciónal Centro de Arte Reino Sofía in Madrid

'Planes of Memory,' Long Beach Museum of Art, curated by Jacqueline Kain. Retrospective of the first video installations by Peter Campus, Beryl Korot, and Bruce Nauman

'Open Channels III,' curated by Peter Kirby. Program of production funding initiated

in 1985 by the Long Beach Museum. Participants include David Bunn, Paul Kos, Paul McCarthy, Donna Matorin, and Jim Shaw

Television

Beginning of TV2, Denmark. Based on the model of Channel 4 in Great Britain: a television network with limited in-house production and a policy of buying outside programs and broadcasting and distributing videos

Innovation

Creation of Media Art Productions in Cologne

1989
Artists

Chris Marker begins work on the *Zapping Zone* installation (some twenty tapes made between 1985 and 1990). The installation will be assembled in its first version in 1990 for the exhibition 'Passages de l'image' at the Centre Georges Pompidou in Paris. Composed of thirteen video areas and seven computer areas, *Zapping Zone* is an open work that is modified for each new presentation (1992, 1994, 1997, 1998)

Exhibitions

First Muu Media Festival in Kuopio, on the initiative of the Muu group, devoted to video in Finland. In 1991 the festival moves to Helsinki

'Video-Skulptur retrospektiv und aktuell 1963–1989,' exhibition organized by the Kunstverein/DuMont-Kunsthalle in Cologne. Among the forty-five artists represented (sculptures, installations) are Shigeto Kubota, Thierry Kuntzel, Les Levine, Bruce Nauman, Marcel Odenbach, and Nam June Paik. Klaus vom Bruch does a live manipulation of images from a Russian TV program

'The Arts for Television, and Revision' at the Tate Gallery: traveling exhibition of TV artists, initiated by the Stedelijk Museum in Amsterdam

'Video Positive,' traveling exhibition (Tate Gallery in London, Blue Coat Gallery and Williamson Art Gallery in Liverpool) curated by Eddie Berg and Steve Littman. Includes video installations, performances, projections, and talks. The first national video wall is commissioned from Judith Goddard, Steve Littman, Kate Meynell, Steve Partridge, Simon Robertshaw and Mike Jones. Installations commissioned from David Hall, Mineo Aayamaguchi, Zoe Redman, Chris Rowland, Marion Urch, and Jeremy Welsh

First International Biennale-ARTEC '89 is held at the Nagoya City Art and Science Museum in Japan. Artists represented include Ed Emshwiller, Ingo Günther, Catherine Ikam, Takamichi Ito, Piotr Kowalski, Tatsuo Miyajima, Ko Nakajima, Bill Parker, Fabrizio Plessi, Jeffrey Shaw and Dirk Groeneveld, and others (July 7–November 26)

Innovation

Creation of the School of Media Art at the Royal Academy of Fine Arts in Copenhagen on the initiative of Torben Christensen, who became the academy's first Media Art professor in 1994. The members of the Koncern group were the school's first students (I. N. Kjaer, Joachim Koester, Lars Bent Petersen, and Ann-Kristin Lislegaard)

Creation of AV-Arkki, a video production and distribution structure affiliated with the Muu group. Founded by Marikki Hakola, Minna Tarkka, and Perttu Rastas

Creation of the artists group ATV (Alternativ Television) in Germany, by Klaus vom Bruch, Ingo Günther, Marcel Odenbach, and others

1990
Exhibitions

'Passages de l'image,' exhibition curated by Raymond Bellour, Catherine David, and Christine van Assche, at the Centre Georges Pompidou, in Paris. Works by Dennis Adams, Robert Adams, Geneviève Cadieux, Roberta Friedman, Jean-Louis Garnell, Dan Graham, Bill Henson, Gary Hill, Thierry Kuntzel, Suzanne Lafont, Chris Marker, John Massey, Marcel Odenbach, Michael Snow, Bill Viola, Jeff Wall, and Grahame Weinbren. Subsequently travels to the Fundació Caixa de Pensiones, Barcelona; the Wexner Center for the Arts, Columbus, Ohio, and the San Francisco Museum of Modern Art

British Film and Video Biennale at the Institute of Contemporary Arts in London. Traveling program of independent British films and videos curated by Tilda Swinton and organized by the Arts Council and the British Council

'Sign of the Times, A Decade of Video, Film, and Slide-Tape Installations, 1980–1990,' exhibition at the Museum of Modern Art in Oxford, curated by Chrissie Iles in collaboration with the British Council. Includes works by Rose Finn-Kelcey, Judith Goddard, Roberta Graham, David Hall, Susan Hiller, Tina Keane, Tamara Krikorian, Stuart Marshall, Joyne Parker, Holly Warburton, Chris Welsby, Jeremy Welsh, Anthony Wilson, and Cerith Wyn Evans

'The Dazzling Image,' produced by Jane Thorburn for 'The Eleventh Hour' on Channel 4. Features videos and films produced by the Arts Council, the British Film Institute, and Channel 4, including works by Isaac Julien, Sandra Lahire, David Larcher, Cordelia Swann, Cerith Wyn Evans, and Graham Young

Bienal de la imagen en Movimiento '90, exhibition organized by the Museo Naciónal Centro de Arte Reina Sofía in Madrid, curated by José Ramón Pérez Ornia. Presentation of installations by Eugènia Balcells, Gary Hill, Thierry Kuntzel, Barbara Steinman, and Bill Viola, along with a Peter Greenaway retrospective (December 12–24).

'Bay Area Media,' exhibition organized by Robert Riley for the San Francisco Museum of Modern Art. Includes works by Jim Campbell, Bill Fontana, Doug Hall, Lynn Hershman, Paul Kos, Tony Labat, Chip Lord and Mickey McGowan, and Alan Rath

'Image World: Art and Media Culture,' Whitney Museum of American Art, New York. Video installations by Dara Birnbaum, Nancy Burson and David Kramlich, Peter Campus, Carol Ann Klonarides, Bruce Nauman, Nam June Paik, Richard Serra, and Bill Viola

Innovation

Creation of the Kunsthochschule für Medien (KHM) in Cologne. Directed by Siegfried Zielinski from 1994

Television

19/4/90 Television Interventions, broadcast on Channel 4 (produced by Anna Ridley and Jane Rigby), inspired by David Hall's 1971 program *TV Interruptions*. Shorts commissioned from Rose Garrard, Ron Geesin, David Hall, Pictorial Heroes, Steve Littman, Bruce McClean, David Mach, Alistair McLennan, Steve Partridge, and others. Rebroadcast of four works by David Hall from his 1971 program. Presentation of works that will later be exhibited at the Third Eye Centre in Glasgow and the Ikon Gallery in Birmingham

One Minute Television, one-minute films and videos commissioned jointly by the

BBC and the Arts Council, are broadcast on 'The Late Show' on BBC2

1991
Artists

Robert Filliou retrospective at the Centre Georges Pompidou, Paris

Exhibitions

'L'Amour de l'art,' First Lyons Biennale of Contemporary Art. The video section, 'Et si la télévision devenait un art,' curated by Georges Rey, presents various trends in French video: dance video, TV programs, video clips, documentaries, advertisements, and artists tapes

Television

Paper Tiger TV collective produces regular broadcasts on a New York public television station. It uses TV and the news reporting format for critiques of institutions

1992
Artists

Gary Hill retrospective at the Centre Georges Pompidou, Paris. The exhibition, curated by Christine Van Assche, includes seven recent installations (1987–92) and a retrospective of video works

Exhibitions

'Manifeste. 30 ans de création en perspective, 1960–90,' Centre Georges Pompidou, Paris. Video installations by international artists in the museum's collection include Peter Campus, Jean-André Fieschi, Dan Graham, Thierry Kuntzel, Bruce Nauman, Marcel Odenbach, Nam June Paik, Martial Raysse, and Bill Viola. Opening of a permanent space within the museum for viewing videos on demand

'Ateliers 1992,' ARC, Musée d'Art Moderne de la Ville de Paris. The video section features works by Philippe Andrevon, Cuckovic, Bénédicte Espiau, Laure Girardeau, Lydie Jean-Dit-Panel, Franck Magnant, and César Vayssié

'Multimediale 1' at the ZKM in Karlsruhe, Germany

'Documenta 9,' with Dara Birnbaum, Stan Douglas, Gary Hill, Bruce Nauman, Tony Oursler, and Bill Viola in Germany

'Vidéo France '92' at the Institut Français in Florence, Italy, features videos made and produced in France. The French selection is organized by the Centre International de Création Vidéo (CICV) in Montbéliard, a partner in the exhibition. Artists include Alain Bourges, Christian Boustani, Robert Cahen, Dominique Debaralle, Catherine Derosier, Stéphane Gatti, Véro Goyo, Alain Jomier, Sandra Kogut, Jérôme Lefdup, Jean-Louis Le Tacon, Alain Longuet, Yann N'Guyen Minh, Claude Mourieras, Marcel Odenbach, Georges Pasquier and Alain Willaume, Yves de Peretti, Estelle Pianet, Eve Ramboz, Pierre Trividic, Teresa Wennberg, Wonder Products, and Patrick Zanoli

'Trans-Voices,' a public art event organized simultaneously in Paris (American Center) and New York (Whitney Museum/Public Art Fund), includes fourteen videos broadcast by Canal+ in France and MTV in the United States. The French tapes are produced by the CICV in Montbéliard

Innovation

Creation of the 'Revue Virtuelle,' Centre Georges Pompidou, Paris, by Christine van Assche, Jean-Louis Boissier, and Martine Moinot. This virtual 'magazine' addresses all the new technologies (the virtual, computer images, multimedia) from the multiple viewpoints of science, aesthetics, museography, and education. Twelve thematic 'issues' will give rise to public lectures, publications, and exhibitions. A bilingual CD-ROM, *L'Actualité du virtuel/Actualizing the Virtual* (1996), provides a synthesis of these activities

1993
By 1993 all major international exhibitions of contemporary art include video installations
Exhibitions
'Image en scène' video installations at the Palais de Tokyo, Paris, includes installations by Dominik Barbier, Claire Dehove, Eve Rambot, and others

1994
Artists
Joseph Beuys exhibition at the Centre Georges Pompidou, Paris. A program of his films and videos, 'Joseph Beuys, films et vidéos. Je suis un émetteur, je rayonne,' is available for viewing on demand
Exhibitions
'Arte virtual,' Metro Opera, Madrid, sixteen artists from eight countries working in Virtual Reality, interactive video, telepresence, sound sculpture, and robotics. Artists include Mario Canali and Marcello Campione, Sharon Grace, Myron Krueger, and Jeffrey Shaw

1995
Exhibitions
First Biennale of Video art in Santiago, Chile
Third Lyons Biennale of Contemporary Art, curated by Thierry Prat, Thierry Raspail, and Georges Rey, is devoted to moving images. Artists include Vito Acconci, Catherine Beaugrand, Jean-Louis Boissier, Café Electronique, Peter Campus, Emmanuel Carlier, Claude Closky, Cheryl Donegan, Ken Feingold, Paul Garin, Dan Graham, Marie-Ange Guilleminot, Ann Hamilton, Gary Hill, Pierre Huyghe, Fabrice Hybert, Joan Jonas, Jon Kessler, Laurent Mignonneau and Christa Sommerer, Bruce Nauman, Dennis Oppenheim, Orlan, Tony Oursler, Philippe Parreno, Eric Rondepierre, Pierrick Sorin, Mike and Doug Starn, Diana Thater, Bill Viola, and others
'The British Art Show,' Manchester, features video works by Douglas Gordon, Georgina Starr, Mark Wallinger, Jane and Louise Wilson, and films by Tacita Dean, Ceal Floyer, and Steve McQueen
Gwangju Biennial in Korea, September 20–November 20, 6,660 artists from fifty-eight countries. 'Infoart' featuring ninety-four artists, including Bill Viola and Gary Hill
'Señales de Vídeo,' exhibition at the Museo Nacional Centro de Arte Reina Sofía in Madrid, curated by Eugeni Bonet. Features forty works by thirty-four Spanish artists and groups, including Enrique Fontanilles, Grupo 3TT, Javier Montero, Muntadas, Francisco Ruiz de Infante, and Francesc Torres
Sixth International Video Week (*Biennale de l'image en mouvement*) at the Centre pour l'Image Contemporaine in Saint-Gervais, Geneva. Includes Guy Debord Robert Filliou, and Chris Marker, retrospectives and cartes blanches to Saskia Bos, Rudolf Friedling, Johan Grimonprez and Herman Asselbergs, Carol Ann Klonarides, Stéphanie Moisdon Trembley, and Nicolas Trembley
'1995 Video Spaces: Eight Installations' exhibition curated by Barbara London for the Museum of Modern Art, New York. Catalog text by Barbara London; works by Judith Barry and Brad Miskell, Stan Douglas, Teiji Furuhashi, Gary Hill, Chris Marker, Marcel Odenbach, Tony Oursler, and Bill Viola

1996
Exhibitions
'Impermanent,' exhibition at the Kuvataideakatemian Galleria in Helsinki. Twenty-two artists from different countries, including Claire Angelini, Hui Kiang Seng, Jan Kopp, and Pia Lindman, present videos, films, slide shows, sound installations, concerts, poetry, and contemporary dance
'Manifesta 1' in the Netherlands, first European Biennale of Contemporary Art, curated by Rosa Martinez, Victor Misiano, C. Neray, Hans Ulrich Obrist, and Andrew Renton; seventy artists from twenty-five countries
'Hall of Mirrors: Art and Film Since 1945,' Los Angeles Museum of Contemporary Art, curated by Kerry Brougher. Installations and films by John Baldessari, Joseph Beuys, Luis Buñuel, James Coleman, Stan Douglas, Jean-Luc Godard, Douglas Gordon, Dan Graham, Chris Marker, Cindy Sherman, and others
'Being & Time: The Emergence of Video Projection', Albright-Knox Art Gallery, Buffalo, New York. Artists include Willie Doherty, Gary Hill, Diana Thater, and Bill Viola

1997
Exhibitions
Fourth Lyons Biennale of Contemporary Art on the theme of the Other, curated by Harold Szeemann. Artists include Martine Alballéa, Rebecca Bournigault, Chris Burden, Serge Comte, Stan Douglas, Douglas Gordon, Marie-Ange Guillimenot, Gary Hill, Paul McCarthy, Chris Marker, and Richard Serra. In conjunction with the Biennale, an exhibition on the internet, 'Version originale: 27 artistes sur Internet,' curated by Georges Rey, is presented by the Musée d'Art Contemporain in Lyons. Artists include Joël Bartoloméo, Jean-Louis Boissier, Serge Comte, Patrick Corillon, Christiane Geoffroy, Paul-Armand Gette, Hervé Graumann, Marie-Ange Guilleminot and Fabrice Hybert, Pierre Joseph, Matthieu Laurette, Ange Leccia, Philippe Parreno and Pierre Huyghe, Philippe Perrin, Alberto Sorbelli, Jean-Luc Vilmouth, and Bruno Yvonnet
Innovation
Inauguration of the Zentrum für Kunst und Medientechnologie (ZKM) at the Hammenbau in Karlsruhe, Germany
Technology
Sony Corporation introduces first digital camcorder in US, the DHR-1000. This revolutionizes personal video technology

1998
Artists
Bill Viola retrospective at the Whitney Museum of Art, New York. February 12–May 10. Exhibition itinerary includes Los Angeles County Museum of Art, Stedelijk Museum, San Francisco Museum of Modern Art, and the Art Institute of Chicago. Catalog includes 'A Feeling for the Things Themselves' by David Ross; 'Conversation' by Lewis Hyde and Bill Viola; 'Selected Works 1972–96' by Kira Perov and Bill Viola. Catalog of Works; Exhibition History; and Chronology
Exhibitions
Second 'Verbindingen. Jonctions' media art festival organized by Constant vzw with various cultural institutions in Brussels. Includes installations, CD-roms, films, videos, and performances presented through-out Brussels (Palais des Beaux-Arts, Galerie Ravenstein, Kaaitheaterstudios, Beursschouwburg, Moving Art Studio, Filmmuseum)

'Manifesta 2,' the Second European Biennale of Contemporary Art in Luxembourg, curated by Robert Fleck, Maria Lind, and Barbara Vanderlinden

1999
Exhibitions
'Warsaw Lab 7– International Media Art Exhibition', Warsaw, curated by Ryszard W. Kluszczynski. Artists include Jeffrey Shaw and Grahame Weinbren
'Cinéma, Cinéma: Contemporary Art and the Cinematic Experience', Stedelijk Van Abbemuseum Eindhoven, Netherlands. Features work by eleven installation artists, including Eija-Liisa Ahtila, Christoph Draeger, Douglas Gordon, and Pierre Huyghe
'Fast Forward: New Chinese Video Art', Centro de arte contemporanea de Macau. Fourteen artists from China and Taiwan, including Ellen Pau, Zhang Peili, and Chen Shaoxiong

By the end of the 20th-century Video art had been fully incorporated into all major international exhibitions of art. In the early years of the 21st-century notable exhibitions of Video art continued, many of them retrospectives. Other exhibitions incorporating a larger definition of 'digital art' began to be seen

2000
Exhibitions
'RE-PLAY: Beginnings of International Media Art in Austria', Generali Foundation, Vienna, 2000. With international artists from the 1970s and 1980s
'Seoul, media_city, Seoul'. International video and media artists, including Bruce Nauman, Nam June Paik, Tiehai Zho.
'Three Decades of Video Art,' presented by VideoCulture, Detroit, Michigan
'The Other Side of Zero: Video Positive 2000', the final city-wide video festival in Liverpool, Britain

2001
Exhibitions
'Into the Light: The Projected Image in American Art 1964–1977', curated by Chrissie Iles for The Whitney Museum of American Art, New York. Film, videos and slide installations, some not seen in three decades, by nineteen artists, including Vito Acconci, Simone Forti, Dan Graham, Joan Jonas, Bruce Nauman, and Andy Warhol.
'Video Jam', organized by the Palm Beach Institute of Contemporary Art, Florida. Forty-five international artists with single-channel and installation works of digital video. Artists include Adam Ames, Phyllis Baldino, Robert Beck, Skip Blumberg, Seoungho Cho, Les Leveque, Maria Marshall, Kiki Seror, and Pia Wergius
'010101: Art in Technological Times', San Francisco Museum of Modern Art. Video is one among many digital arts represented here by artists including Kevin Appel, Asymptote Architecture, Jeremy Blake, Rodney Graham, Jochem Hendricks, Roxy Paine, Matthew Ritchie, and Yuan Goang-Ming
Innovation
The première of *Atanarjuat (The Fast Runner)*, the first feature-length film to emerge from the aboriginal Inuit Indian community in Canada. Directed by Zacharias Kunik. Shot with a wide-screen digital video betacam and transferred to 35mm for projection

2002
Artists
Aleksander Sokurov makes *The Russian Ark*

using a Sony high-definition digital video camera (Sony, HDW-F900). The ninety-minute film, a period piece shot in The Hermitage Museum, St Petersburg, is one continuous shot (no cuts, no edits, no montage); the first feature film made in this way
Exhibitions
Third Central American Isthmus Visual Arts Biennial, Managua, Nicaragua. Started in 1971 as The Central American Isthmus Painting Biennial. This exhibition recognizes Video art and new media broadly in 2002
Documenta 11, Kassel, Germany, includes numerous digital video and film installations by artists Eija-Liisa Ahtila, Thomas Hirschhorn, Sanja Ivekovič, Joan Jonas, Isaac Julien, Steve McQueen, Shirin Neshat, and Lorna Simpson

2003
Exhibitions
'Video Acts: Single Channel Works from the Collection of Pamela and Richard Kramlich and New Art Trust', P.S. 1 Contemporary Art Center, Museum of Modern Art, Queens, New York. More than 100 performance-based works from the most comprehensive private video collection

The practice of Video art has become inextricably bound with the language of cinema. In coming years, as artists create installations that approach the narrative enormity of cinema, and filmmakers turn increasingly to video technology for feature films, digital video will actually supersede cinema as the filmic medium of the future. Cinema will become an art of video (but not Video art). Artful uses of video technology have already been seen in feature films by renowned cinematic artists, Mike Figgis (*Time Code*, 2001) and Aleksander Sokurov (*The Russian Ark*, 2002).

The task of Video art (as with all of art) will be to challenge the narrative presuppositions and demands of commercial filmmaking, thus creating an alternative Filmic art, digitally based, but conceptually innovative and not commercially driven. The fact that commercial interests will envelope the innovations (as has been the case in the history of Video art) will only enhance the need for artists to keep exploring beyond the boundaries of the marketplace.

List of Illustrations

Measurements are given in centimeters, followed by inches, height before width before depth, unless otherwise stated.

projection, dimensions variable. Installation at the Whitney Museum of American Art, New York. Courtesy of Max Protech Gallery, New York

330, 331, 332, 333, 334, 335 Iñigo Manglano-Ovalle, *Climate*, 2000. Installation view. Courtesy of Max Protech Gallery, New York

336 William Kentridge, *History of the Main Complaint*, 1996. 35mm film transferred to video and laserdisk, 5 minutes, 50 seconds. Courtesy the Artist and Marian Goodman Gallery, New York

337, 338, 339, 340, 341, 342 Iñigo Manglano-Ovalle, *Alltagszeit (In Ordinary Time)* (View 2), 2001. 35mm film loop transferred to DVD. Courtesy of Max Protech Gallery, New York

343, 344 Doug Aitken, *electric earth*, 1999. 8 laserdisk installation, dimensions variable, installation view at Venice Biennale. Courtesy 303 Gallery, New York

345 Eija-Liisa Ahtila, *The House*, 2002. 14 minutes, DVD installation for 3 projections with sound. © Crystal Eye Ltd, Helsinki. Courtesy Klemens Gasser & Tanja Grunert Inc., New York

346 Eija-Liisa Ahtila, *Consolation Service*, 1999. 24 minutes, 35mm film and DVD installation for 2 projections with sound. © Crystal Eye Ltd, Helsinki. Courtesy Klemens Gasser & Tanja Grunert Inc., New York.

347 Eija-Liisa Ahtila, *Me/We; Okay, Gray*, 1993. 3 × approx. 90 seconds, 35mm film and DVD installation for 3 monitors with sound, 3 × approx. 90 seconds. © Crystal Eye Ltd, Helsinki. Courtesy Klemens Gasser & Tanja Grunert Inc., New York

348 Matthew Barney, *Field Dressing (orifill)*, 1989. Video still. Courtesy Barbara Gladstone Gallery, New York

349 Robert Wilson, *Stations*, 1982. Courtesy Electronic Arts Intermix, New York

350 Matthew Barney, *Cremaster 2*, 1999. Production photograph. © 1999 Matthew Barney, Photo Michael James O'Brian, Courtesy Barbara Gladstone Gallery, New York

351 Matthew Barney, *Cremaster 3*, 2002. Production photograph. Courtesy Barbara Gladstone Gallery, New York. Photo Chris Winget. © 2002 Matthew Barney

352, 353, 354 Aleksander Sokurov, *Mother and Son*, 1997. Feature film. © Zero Films

355, 356 Tracey Moffatt, *Night Cries – A Rural Tragedy*, 1989. Video still. Courtesy Matthew Marks Gallery and The Paul Morris Gallery, New York

357, 358, 359, 360 Tracey Moffatt, *Heaven*, 1997. Video, 28 minutes. Courtesy Matthew Marks Gallery and The Paul Morris Gallery, New York

361, 362 Lynn Hershman, *Conceiving Ada*, 1996–97. Courtesy the Artist

363, 364 Lynn Hershman, *Teknolust*, 2002. Hi definition video, starring Tilda Swinton, 83 minutes. Courtesy the Artist

365 Kristin Lucas, *Screening Room*, 1998. Courtesy Electronic Arts Intermix, New York

366, 367, 368 Kristin Lucas, *Cable Xcess*, 1996. Courtesy Electronic Arts Intermix, New York

369, 370 Shirin Neshat, *Passage*, 2001. Production still. Courtesy Barbara Gladstone Gallery, New York. Photo Larry Barns. © 2001 Shirin Neshat

371 Shirin Neshat, *Turbulent*, 1998. Video still. Courtesy Barbara Gladstone Gallery, New York. © 1998 Shirin Neshat

372 Shirin Neshat, *Rapture*, 1999. Production still. Courtesy Barbara Gladstone Gallery, New York. Photo Larry Barns. © 1999 Shirin Neshat

373, 374 Christoph Draeger, *Ode to a Sad Song*, 2001. DVD, 7 minutes. Courtesy the Artist

375 Perry Hoberman, *Cathartic User Interface*, 2000. Mixed media interactive installation, 101.6 × 73.7 × 12.7 (40 × 29 × 5). Dimensions variable. Courtesy Postmasters Gallery, New York

376 Jennifer and Kevin McCoy, *Every Anvil*, 2001. Mixed media sculpture with electronics, 101.6 × 73.7 × 12.7 (40 × 29 × 5). Edition of 3. Courtesy Postmasters Gallery, New York

377, 378, 379, 380, 381, 382 Grahame Weinbren and James Cathcart with Sandra McLean, *Tunnel*, 2000. Architectural interactive cinema installation, commissioned by the City of Dortmund for the vision.ruhr exhibition. Courtesy the Artist

383 Grahame Weinbren, *Sonata*, 1991–93. Interactive cinema installation. Courtesy the Artist

384, 385 Grahame Weinbren, *Sonata*, 1991–93. Interactive cinema installation. Video still. Courtesy the Artist

Acknowledgments

Special thanks to:

Robert Beck, Sabrina Gschwandtner, Galen Joseph-Hunter and Lorrie Zippay from Electronic Arts Intermix
Annette Grant and *The New York Times*
Betsy Baker and *Art in America*
Sylvia Woolf and the Whitney Museum of American Art
Chrissie Iles
Barbara London
Christine van Assche
Rosalind Neely
Nikos Stangos
Pauline Hubner
Sherry and Ralph Hocking
Davidson Gigliotti
Frank Gilette
Vito Acconci
Paul Ryan
Robert and Mary Montgomery
Bill Castellino
Lily

Index

Page numbers in *italic* refer to pages on which illustrations appear.

A

Abe, Shuya 9
Abramovic, Marina 8, 63, 101, 103, 104, 122, 140, 201; *Balkan Baroque* 100, 101; *Delusional* 122; *Freeing the Body* 103; *Performance Anthology* 101
Abstract art 8
Abstract Expressionism 9, 13, 85, 152, 163
Acconci, Vito 8, 9, 11, 30, 61, 63, 69, 72, 76, 97, 169; *Centers* 10; *Command Performance* 76; *Contacts* 97; *Corrections* 76; *Face Off* 30; *Focal Points* 97; *Pryings* 97; *Second Hand* 76; *The Red Tapes* 76; *Theme Song* 30, *31*, 97
Adams, John: *Intellectual Properties* 39
Agostino, Peter d': *DOUBLE YOU (and X, Y, Z)* 70; *TransmissionS* 71
Ahtila, Eija-Liisa 148, 188–91; *Anne, Aki, and God* 190; *Consolation Service* 188, 190, *190*; *Me/We; Okay, Gray* 190, *191*; *The House* 189, 190
Aitken, Doug 9, 178, 184–88; *autumn* 185; *bad animal* 188; *diamond sea* 185; *electric earth* 10, 184, 185, *185*, *186–87*, 188; *eraser* 185, 188; *monsoon* 184, 185; *these restless minds* 188
Alberro, Alexander 86
Almy, Max: *Leaving the 20th Century* 162
Anastasi, William 9, 61
Anderson, Doug 141
Andrade, Sonia 147
André, Marie: *Repetitions* 110
Anger, Kenneth 69; *Inauguration of the Pleasure Dome* 196; *Invocation of My Demon Brother* 196; *Scorpio Rising* 90
Ant Farm 16, 17, 56; *The Eternal Frame* 20, *20*
Antin, Eleanor 147
Antoni, Janine 94
Armitage, Karole 122
Armstead, Kenseth 141
Aron, Ernest 170
Artaud, Antonin 90
Arts Lab 39
Askevold, David 46
Assche, Christine van 16
Atlas, Charles 122; *Blue Studio: Five Segments* 122; *Little Strange* 123; *Mrs Peanut Visits New York* 6, *123*; *The Hanged One* 123
Averty, Jean-Christophe 16; *Les Mariés de la Tour Eiffel* 16; *Ubu Roi* 16
Azari, Fedele 14

B

Bacon, Francis 63
Baird, John Logie 14
Baldessari, John 69, 101, 125; *Folding Hat* 69; *I Am Making Art* 69
Baldino, Phyllis 112; *Color Without Color* 110
Bamgboyé, Oladélé: *Blink* 115; *The Hair or the Man* 114
Barney, Matthew 169, 193–95; *Cremaster series* 169, *193*, 194–95; *Field Dressing (orifill)* 192; *Scabaction* 193
Barry, Robert 61
Bartlett, Scott 52; *OFFON* 52
Baumgarten, Lothar 61
Bechtold, Gottfried 97
Becker, Wolfgang 38
Beckett, Samuel 32, 44, 94, 104, 137, 147, 157
Bell, Alexander Graham 14
Benglis, Lynda 110, 147
Benning, Sadie 112
Berg, Eddie 209
Berto, Juliet 43
Beuys, Joseph 11, 38, 69, 122; *Felt-TV* 38
Big Noise Productions 17
Birnbaum, Dara: *Kiss The Girls: Make them Cry* 26; *Pop-Pop Video* 27; *Technology/Transformation: Wonder Woman* 27, *27*